Classic Car Profiles

Volume 2

First published 1987

© Anthony Bird, Gordon Davies, Peter Hull,
Luigi Fusi, Kenneth Bush, F. Wilson McComb,
James Leech, D.B. Tubbs, Walter Wright,
Ronald Barker, Cyril Posthumas, J.R. Buckley,
Denis Jenkinson, Laurence Pomeroy, Darell
Berthon, Michael Sedgwick, William S. Stone.

A FOULIS Book

Published by:
Haynes Publishing Group
Sparkford, Nr Yeovil, Somerset BA22 7JJ.
England

Haynes Publications Inc.
861 Lawrence Drive, Newbury Park,
California 91320 USA

British Library Cataloguing in publication data
Classic car profile.
    Vol. 2
    1. Automobiles—History
    629.2'222'09   TL15
    ISBN 0-85429-651-4

Library of Congress catalog card number 87-80608

Printed in England by:
J.H. Haynes & Co. Ltd.

Contents

Foreword

I was particularly pleased to hear that G T Foulis & Co had decided to publish a set of volumes comprising the 108 car profiles originally produced by Profile Publications Ltd. When first published many years ago they soon became extremely popular and nowadays are much sought after as rare collector's items.

The subject of each profile was selected for any number of reasons, it could be the fastest or the most flamboyant, the most complicated or the most rare, the most conventional or just because it was a milestone in the history of the motor car.

Each is written by a recognised authority and provides a comprehensive cameo of the history and development and much other detail. There are rare or unique black and white illustrations supported by specially commissioned scale drawings giving end views and side elevations in full colour.

Welcome back to this collection which will provide a wealth of information on such a wide range of memorable motor vehicles.

Kenneth Ball
Ditchling
Sussex

The Model T Ford

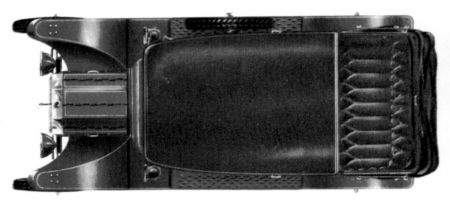

Ford

1915 MODEL T FORD "TOWN CAR" with landau-lette body by the Ford Motor Company.
Owner: George Evan Cook. Esquire, O.B.E.

© GORDON DAVIES

The Model T Ford
by Anthony Bird

Model Ts approaching Cleveland in 1909 Ocean-to-Ocean Race.

(Photo: Ford Motor Co.)

To say of the Model T Ford that it was a remarkably bad car would be tantamount to doubting the judgement of the 15,007,033 satisfied customers who bought the 'Lizzie' during her production life of 19 years in plants and factories in America, Canada and England. Therefore to placate their shades and to turn aside the howls of angry derision which must greet the statement let it be re-phrased and say that Henry Ford, like Carl Benz before him, was an obstinate man whose undeniable ingenuity was tinged with perversity, with the result that his masterpiece was marred by some curiously maladroit features.

As more Model Ts were sold than any other single model (and in relation to its period the figures are even more astonishing than they would be to-day), it had a greater influence than any other man-made object on the American way of life. John Steinbeck wrote, in *Cannery Row**, 'Two generations of Americans knew more about the Ford coil than the clitoris, about the planetary system of gears than the solar system of stars . . . most of the babies of the period were conceived in Model T Fords and not a few were born in them'. Myths and legends have been woven about the Model T which distort the historical perspective occasionally, and many of these originate from the Ford Motor Company. This is not to accuse the Ford Co. of deliberate distortion but, in common with most American motor firms, their view of the early days is parochial and leaves European and English technical progress out of account.

EARLY FORD DESIGNS

The broad outlines of the Ford story are too well known to need dwelling upon. Henry Ford built his first experimental motor quadricycle in 1896; the often-quoted date of 1892 originated with Ford himself but cannot be substantiated. Further experiments followed, but nothing was done commercially until 1901 when Ford resigned his job with the Edison Co. and became Superintendent of the Detroit Automobile Company. After constructing thirty rather uninspired horizontal-engined runabouts this concern collapsed. Henry Ford's next move was to build a sprint car to attract publicity at local track events and so help him to find backers. This policy succeeded and in June 1903 the Ford Motor Company was incorporated with a modest capital of $28,000.

*William Heinemann Ltd., 1945

In conjunction with Tom Cooper, and again strictly for publicity (Ford was not really interested in racing), two more large, but very crude, cars were built for competition work in the short-distance track events then popular in America. These cars, with their unsprung rear axles and exposed mechanism, could not have survived long in the European road races but were mightily effective for their intended purpose. The second of them, the famous 999, is usually described as having an exposed crankshaft, but photographs of the machine (which survives) clearly show a very much exposed camshaft perched in inadequate looking bearings nearly a foot above the cylinder block.

Having got his name before the public Ford now settled down to the task he had chosen; which was to make a sound motor car cheaply enough to sell, not as a rich man's plaything, not, as most cheap cars were then, as an underpowered and inadequate runabout fit only for fine weather use on the few good roads the States possessed, but as an essential tool for the use and pleasure of ordinary people. Plenty of other manufacturers had the same urge, but none held to it as firmly as Ford, and most allowed themselves to be diverted into improving their cars until they were out of reach of the 'man of modest means'.

Ford's first production Model A followed the accepted layout of the typical 'Yankee gas-buggy'; that is, it had a centrally placed, transverse horizontal

The 'go anywhere, do anything' car—c. 1911.

(Photo: Ford Motor Co.

The 'farmer's friend'. (Photo: Ford Motor Co.)

The Ford Stand at Olympia, London, 1912.
(Photo: Radio Times Hulton Picture Library.)

1915 touring car with the new electric headlamps operated from the flywheel magneto. (Photo: Ford Motor Co.)

engine, two-speed epicyclic gear and final drive by central chain to a live axle. Model B was his first four-cylinder car, but it was not very successful, and Models C and F were dressed-up versions of the A. Leaving plenty of gaps in the alphabet, Model K was launched against Henry Ford's wishes to pacify his associates' desire to break into the luxury market. It was wholly unsuccessful both mechanically and financially and its torsional vibration was such that Ford forswore the six-cylinder engine for ever. The little 15 h.p. four-cylinder Model N, a very good car for its period, was also marketed in 1906 and Model T was developed from it by Ford and his assistants during 1907.

ENTER THE MODEL T

With Model T Henry Ford considered he had produced not only the car he most wanted to sell, simple, cheap to make, and light but with ample power—but the car which the public would most want to buy. With the disaster of Model K to reinforce his arguments, and despite the brief appearance of Models R and S (de luxe versions of N) he was able to prevail on his associates and backers to concentrate on Model T, to sell nothing else, and to continue it absolutely unchanged mechanically for so long that it could be sold for less money, but at greater relative profit, to an ever-increasing volume of buyers. It was a gamble, and one which paid off more handsomely than any other in the history of gambling.

It was October 1908 before Model T reached the market, as much preliminary work and planning for big sales had to be done first. The five-seat touring car was sold at $850 in 1909 and $100 dollars more in 1910. Thereafter sales and profits increased and prices fell year by year as Ford had predicted. The one-model policy was set fair to be the most spectacular commercial success of all time, and by 1916 the touring car was selling for $360 and the runabout or two-seater for $345. Production stood at 10,607 units in 1909, 168,220 in 1913 and reached a peak of 2,011,125 in 1923 from which point slow but inexorable decline set in.

Amongst the claims made in the official *Highlights in History of Ford Motor Co.*, are that Ford was the first manufacturer to use wheel instead of tiller steering in 1901, first to mount the engine with its crankshaft in the longitudinal instead of the transverse line of the chassis in 1904 and that the Model T was the first car in the world to have left-hand controls, a monobloc cylinder casting and a detachable cylinder head. It was also said to be the first car in which chrome-vanadium steel was used. None of

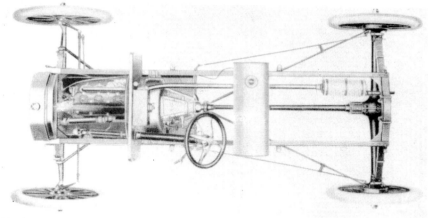

No chassis could be simpler.

(Drawing: Ford Motor Co.)

these things is true, as any student of European and English motor history will know, but there is no doubt that the mechanical specification of the Model T was up to the minute by 1908 standards and that, although the finish may have been a bit rough, the materials were as fine as those used in the most expensive cars.

DESIGN OF THE MODEL T

The Model T had a very simple light chassis, suspension by transverse semi-elliptic leaf springs front and back, and the dimensions were: wheelbase 8 ft. 4 in. and track 4 ft. 8 in. As the total weight of the first tourers (they put on a little as time went on) was less than 13 cwt. and the engine developed 20 h.p. the power-to-weight ratio was better than anything previously offered in the cheap car market.

The frame was very narrow in relation to the track width which was dictated by the absolute necessity, in those days, of making use of the cart ruts on dirt roads. This gave the car a rather spidery appearance, and as the roll centre was high it also induced a characteristic side sway at speed.

In their early advertisements the Ford Co. made much of their use of vanadium steel. This had not, apparently, been in use in the U.S. until Henry Ford

had some pieces from a crashed French racing car analysed and called in an English metallurgist to advise on production and heat treatment. The Model T's chassis members, axles, steering connections and so forth were criticised in England for being too frail for their work. This judgement was wholly erroneous and the Lizzie soon showed herself to be able to take almost unlimited punishment without flinching.

There were weaknesses of course. The chassis was about as rigid as a bed frame but at that time only Lanchester had demonstrated that a rigid, torsionally stiff, frame allied to flexible suspension was a better solution than the usual combination of fairly stiff suspension with a floppy chassis. Ford advertisements claimed that the three-point suspension of the frame on its transverse springs, and the three-point suspension of the power plant in the frame made all the vital parts immune from stresses set up by chassis flexure. This was demonstrably untrue; a broken Ford chassis was almost as seldom seen as a dead donkey, but the frame did rack, and cracked or broken rear engine bearers were an endemic weakness, leading to leaking crankcases and ultimate failure if undetected. A variety of patent cradles and supports to strengthen the engine bearers was sold. The front cross-member also used to sag or crack to the detriment of the radiator.

The engine was a true monobloc structure: that is, not only were the four cylinders with their water jackets cast *en bloc*, but the upper half of the crankcase was also integral with the cylinders. It was a very fine piece of foundry work, and although the crankshaft would look inordinately frail and whippy to the modern eye, the rigidity given to the main bearing supports by the monobloc construction was in the best interest of the shaft and bearing life.

The whole transmission system of epicyclic gear trains with their

The cutaway engine drawing shows the limited oil capacity and explains why the oil-level was supposed to be checked every hundred miles.
(Drawing: Ford Motor Co.)

Engine installation at Highland Park Assembly Plant, Detroit, before the moving assembly line was fully developed.
(Photo: Ford Motor Co.)

The flywheel magneto was the first component to be put together on assembly line principles. (Photo: Ford Motor Co.)

actuating band clutches, the direct drive multi-disc clutch for high gear and the footbrake was built in unit with the engine. This arrangement was almost certainly inspired by the 20 h.p. Lanchester which Henry Ford had for examination according to his own (ghosted) autobiography. The Ford engine and gearbox unit was extraordinarily compact and tidy by the standards of 1908.

At 3¾ in. bore and 4 in. stroke, the L-head side valve engine had a capacity of 2·9 litres, and its output of 20 h.p., or just under 7 h.p. per litre, was about average for the period. The small valves and rather tortuous gas passages and ports restricted breathing, maximum power and rotational speed, probably deliberately, but ensured adequate turbulence and good low speed torque.

This was most necessary as, in common with its predecessors, the Model T was endowed with the two-speed and reverse epicyclic or planetary gear system so common at that time in American usage. Though never openly stated it came to be part of the mythology that planetary change speed gear was a Model T innovation; but the only innovations were that the whole change speed system, and the main clutch and footbrake, were enclosed and ran in oil (previous Ford, and many other American cars had the epicyclic gear drums revolving unenclosed, and their lubrication

consequently was somewhat haphazard): the other new feature was the beautifully simple and logical foot control of the gear change. Admirable though it was, however, the Model T gearbox had the great weakness of all two-speed systems in that the gap between 'low' and 'high' was necessarily very wide. Hence the need for a flexible engine with good low speed torque. A Model T in good fettle could do most of its work in 'high' but once committed to its low speed progress was far from brisk.

The simplicity of the controls was one of the most important factors in Lizzie's enduring and well-deserved popularity. The gear-changing bugbear haunted the motorist of sixty years ago when inflexible engines, heavy flywheels and clutches, and sliding-pinion gearboxes without benefit of synchromesh made a silent change of speed difficult for the expert and virtually impossible, except by chance, for the mechanically ignorant majority, who never could grasp the theory of double declutching and synchronising two cogged wheels rotating at different peripheral speeds before trying to force the one into mesh with the other. In England and Europe it was recognised that the gearbox was a necessary evil and that the more speeds a car had the better its performance could be; therefore the evil was accepted and the motorist put up with 'the clashing and jarring of changing speeds' and 'the side-grubbing of teeth,' as part of the game.

In America, however, the customers' objections to 'shifting' were very strong indeed: hence the popularity of the simple two-speed epicyclic gear systems which could be made so much easier to operate. Three-speed compound epicyclic gears, à la Lanchester, were not much used in the States, many motorists being prepared to accept the limitations of a two-speed system in exchange for ease of operation, but a proprietory three-speed transmission for Model T was one of the many 'bolt-on goodies' offered in the nineteen twenties.

The first 800 Model Ts had a reversing lever, but on the remaining fifteen million gear control was entirely pedal operated as on the English Adams ('PEDALS TO PUSH—THAT'S ALL'); though no doubt the similarity was purely coincidental. The pedal on the extreme left tightened the band brake or clutch on the low speed drum when pushed right forward, thus starting the car from rest, and engaged the direct drive plate clutch for high gear when allowed right back. The half way position left both clutches free, and this position could be held by pulling back the hand brake lever a few notches. After 'neutralising' the transmission the remaining travel of the lever expanded tiny cast iron shoes in wholly inadequate drums on the rear wheels.

The central pedal tightened the band clutch of the reverse gear, which could, of course, only be operated when the other two clutches were held in their neutral state, either by the driver's left foot or by means of the brake lever. As with all epicyclic geared cars, the reverse could be used as an additional brake. The brake pedal itself, on the right, contracted a band brake, exactly similar to the low and reverse clutch bands, on a drum containing the direct drive clutch which necessarily rotated all the time the car was in motion, whether the drive was direct or through one of the gear trains.

There was no foot control of engine speed and two conveniently angled hand levers below the steering wheel looked after throttle opening and spark advance.

The driving technique could be learnt in a few minutes; the hand brake being put on to hold the clutches neutral and the engine being started, the driver took his place, held the neutral position with his left foot whilst releasing the brake; then with the throttle opened a few notches and the left pedal pressed to the end of its travel the car would move off in 'low'. After a few yards the throttle could be eased and the pedal released whereupon, with a characteristic moan from the planet pinions, Lizzie would trundle away happily in 'high'. Changing from 'high' to 'low', when conditions demanded it, needed no alteration of throttle and was simply a question of pressing the pedal down and holding it down firmly enough to make the low speed clutch grip. This could become very tiring if low gear had to be held for any time, and subconscious slackening of the calf or ankle muscles would allow slipping and wearing of the lining material.

LUBRICATION AND ELECTRICAL ARRANGEMENTS

Like everything else on the car the lubricating system was simple to the point of crudity. The engine and gearbox shared a common base chamber and oil supply. The lowest point in the system was the flywheel well and the flywheel was used to pick up the oil, fling it over the gearbox components and into a small funnel-shaped depression near the top of the flywheel housing from which an oil tube carried a constant supply to the timing gear case at the front of the engine. From the timing gears the oil flowed back to the well, and on its journey maintained the level in four depressions in the sump pan which served as troughs for the big end bearings to dip into. There was no direct supply to the main bearings or camshaft which received an adequate sousing from the oil spray flung about by the big ends. It was not a suitable system for a high-efficiency, high-speed engine, but it was perfectly suited to its task.

Oil level was determined by two rather awkwardly placed try-cocks, one for maximum and one for minimum permissible level, and it was a source of wry amusement to Model T owners that the makers' directions said that best results would be obtained by keeping the oil half way between the two cocks. The only snag to the oil circulating arrangement was that on a very steep gradient the oil supply to the front of the engine might be reduced or stop altogether, and so lead to a scored cylinder or damaged big end

Part of the English Assembly Plant at Trafford Park, Manchester, 1914. (Photo: Montagu Motor Museum.)

The 'body drop' at Highland Park 1913.
(Photo: Ford Motor Co.)

The 'body drop' at Highland Park 1923.
(Photo: Ford Motor Co.)

bearing. Also, the oil tube occasionally suffered blockage from bits of fluffy material worn off the clutch and brake linings. There was a built-in safeguard (unintentional perhaps) against the former hazard in that the Model T would often baulk at a really steep hill. This was not from lack of power, but from petrol starvation, as the ten-gallon tank, below the front seat, fed the carburettor by gravity, and unless it was nearly full there was insufficient head to cope with a really stiff gradient. Model T drivers soon learnt the knack of backing up steep hills, thereby avoiding petrol starvation and damaged bearings at the trifling cost of a crick in the neck and a furiously boiling radiator. It must be said, in fairness, that if the petrol supply was adequate a Model T in good fettle could scale 1 in 4 without faltering.

The unpredictable starting of the Model T, particularly in cold weather, soon became a world-wide jest—and one which many may have thought in rather poor taste as they nursed a broken wrist or strained back. Nearly every Lizzie owner had to learn the dodges of pouring boiling water over the induction manifold or the more desperate expedient of heating it with a little bonfire of petrol-soaked rag, of jacking up one back wheel and taking off the hand brake so as to lessen the drag of the oil in the gearbox, of heating the sparking-plugs to cherry red on the kitchen stove and then having to screw them back without losing heat or burning his fingers to the bone.

Many of these difficulties were avoidable and most were attributable to the ignition system, which

'. . . with Amaryllis in the shade . . .' of the photographer's back-drop, 1920.
(Photo: Ford Motor Co.)

functioned perfectly whilst it was properly adjusted but which needed more constant care than it usually received. Basically, it was very old fashioned with a separate trembler coil for each cylinder and with no high tension distributor, but a low tension 'timer' to shunt the primary current to the appropriate coil and plug as required. It was therefore a similar system to that found on many early cars, and one which was generally going out of favour by 1904, with the vital difference that the primary current was derived not from the usual small accumulator, but from a low tension magneto generator built into the flywheel. Provision was made for carrying a small stand-by battery and a two-way switch allowed this to be used for starting; but all ordinary running was done on the magneto and most owners did not bother to keep the battery up to scratch. The magneto therefore had to be relied on for starting and this called for some pretty brisk efforts with the starting handle.

The magneto was, perhaps, inspired by the 20 h.p. Lanchester which Henry Ford investigated. It had sixteen permanent magnets attached to the flywheel itself, and sixteen field coils attached to a suitable stationary ring. Provided graphited oils were not used the Ford magneto was extremely reliable and trouble-free, but the rest of the system had shortcomings. All multi-trembler systems suffered from the defect that inequalities between one coil and the next, and the difficulty of adjusting all the tremblers to buzz at the same rate, led to rough running, loss of power and difficult starting.

The real nigger in the woodpile was the low tension timer which was rather inaccessibly placed on the timing gear case (it was driven from the camshaft), behind

At the British Army Aircraft Trials on Salisbury Plain in 1912.
(Photo: Radio Times Hulton Picture Library)

'Bolt-on-goodies': a 'Speedster' body by Turpin of Brighton on 1920 Model T.
(Photo: Montagu Motor Museum)

12

*A 1916 tourer at Harper's
Kippering Kiln, Galloway.*
(Photo: Montagu Motor
Museum)

the fan where it was difficult to clean and inspect. Unfortunately it really needed very frequent cleaning, and as it was a 'wipe contact' with a roller at the end of the contact arm it also needed sparing but frequent lubrication with very light oil if the roller and contact segments were not to be worn out very quickly. This was a source of much trouble, as the oil would congeal in cold weather, and prevent proper contact at hand cranking speeds; also very few owners were conscientious enough to oil the timer every 200 miles as the Ford Co. advised. Many, indeed, ignored the directions completely and held firmly to the belief that oil must never be used on any electrical mechanism. So in one way and another the inherent weaknesses of the Ford timer were aggravated by the hard life it led, and caused most of the difficult starting and chronic misfiring from which poor Lizzie so often suffered.

After 1915, electric headlamps and horn were fitted as standard equipment, and these derived their power from the Ford flywheel magneto. Consequently switching on the lamps or blowing the horn when the engine was running slowly could starve the coils and set up a fit of the hiccups. After 1919 full-scale dynamo and accumulator lighting and starting equipment was supplied, and many of the starting difficulties were overcome. The 'timer' remained unaltered and was still a weak place in the armour, and many component manufacturers did brisk business in supplying improved varieties of distributor to put on in place of the standard fitting.

Even when the engine fired after an exhausting session at the crank, the Model T owner's troubles were not always over, for Tin Lizzie suffered sadly from the creeps, and every Model T man sooner or later experienced the sensation of having his car gently but inexorably nudging him up against the garage wall. The parking brake was a very poor affair and when the drums were full of grease from the axle tubes (a common trouble) it could not hold the car against the drag of the clutches when the oil was thick. An even worse hazard was not unknown. The engine started best with a fairly generous throttle opening and the resultant vibration could shake the hand brake free if the ratchet and click were worn. As soon as the hand brake was free the machine was, of course, in top gear. Normally when this happened the engine just stalled, but on occasions it might take hold and the car would dart away with the infuriated owner in pursuit. A large chunk of wood to scotch the wheels was to be found in many a Model T.

THE TRANSMISSION

The bevel geared live axle of the Model T, though seldom really silent, was as soundly designed and well executed as those of cars costing three times as much. The propeller shaft was enclosed in a tube which delivered the braking and driving torque reaction to a stout ball-joint at the back of the gearbox, and the single massive universal joint was positively lubricated from the communal oiling system. The pinion shaft and axle shafts ran in roller bearings, and some critics made much of 'cheap Yankee finish' because the journal areas of the shafts were not hardened and ground. The longevity of the Ford axle should have taught them to moderate their gibes, as the bearings were so long, and the wear so slight, that the makers were justified in avoiding the expense, and the risk of distortion, inherent in the heat treat-

*A 1916 tourer at Hastings,
1920.* (Photo: Mr. Joseph
Redhouse)

13

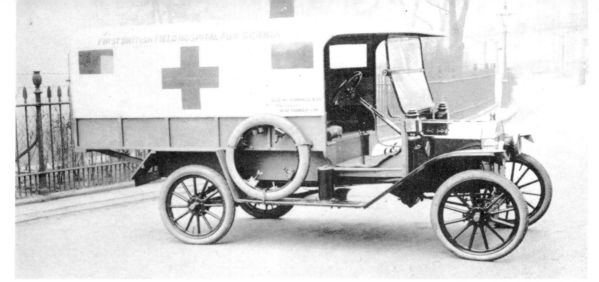

1914-18 War Model T ambulance.

(Photo: Offord & Sons Ltd.)

ment processes of the time.

The only trifling weakness of design was that the side thrust of the crown wheel was not taken by the usual ball or roller thrust race, but by a rather old-fashioned arrangement of a babitted washer sandwiched between two steel collars. These wore rather quickly, particularly if the lubricant was too thick, and some owners replaced them with taper roller thrust bearings. On the whole, though, the axle was as trouble-free as one could wish. It even stood up nobly to the chattering and snatching of the footbrake which reached alarming proportions when the lining of the brake band became glazed. This trouble was only overcome entirely by fitting one of the proprietory brake systems which transferred the foot brake action to a pair of auxiliary contracting shoes on the rear wheel drums. Most owners just put up with the footbrake as it was, and never seemed to come to much harm. Though officially known as the 'emergency brake', the hand brake system was of very little use except for parking on reasonably level ground. The 'One Ton Truck' version of Model T had a lower geared axle with worm and wheel gearing: this, too, gave excellent service.

'The poor arrived in Fords, whose faces they resembled,
They laughed to see the lords, and ladies, all assembled.'
    Beaulieu, 1913. (Photo: Montagu Motor Museum.)

'SHE JUST WENT ON AND ON . . .'

The Model T therefore was a splendid conception endowed with some infuriating habits, and the fifteen million buyers on the whole came to love its pecca-

---

SPECIFICATION: FORD MODEL T, 1908–1927

Chief designers, Joseph Galamb, C. H. Wills under direction of Henry Ford.

Engine Monobloc four-cylinder 3¾ ins bore by 4 ins stroke. Capacity 2.9 litres. Output 20 h.p. L-head side valve layout with single gear-driven camshaft; non-adjustable tappets, detachable cylinder head.

Carburettor Holley or Kingston, single jet. Mixture strength adjustable from dashboard.

Ignition. Low tension flywheel magneto, low tension distributor and a separate trembler coil for each cylinder. Standby battery could be switched in for starting.

Lubrication Splash.

Cooling Vertical multi-tube radiator, thermo-syphon and fan.

Gearbox Epicyclic two-speed and reverse.

Clutches For low speed and reverse, by contracting bands on epicyclic gear drums. For direct drive high gear, by multi-disc clutch.

Transmission Propeller shaft enclosed in torque tube; live axle.

Final drive Passenger cars and light vans, straight-tooth bevel gears. One Ton Truck, overhead worm and wheel.

Brakes Foot, contracting band on periphery of direct-drive clutch. Hand, expanding shoes in rear wheel drums.

Steering Epicyclic reduction gear in boss of steering wheel; drop arm directly attached to end of steering column and transverse drag link.

Electrical system 1909–15: none. 1915–19: Headlamps and horn (8 volt) drawing current from flywheel magneto. 1919–27: full dynamo and accumulator starting and lighting—6 volts.

Dimensions Wheelbase 8 ft 4 in. Track, early models, 4 ft 8 in; later 5ft 0 in.

Wheels Wood-spoked artillery, non-detachable with fixed rims. Detachable rims supplied after 1919, and detachable wheel and hub sets supplied by accessory houses. Wire-spoked bolt-on wheels standardised during last year.

Tyres 30 × 3 ins front, 30 × 3½ ins rear, and variants for straight side and balloon tyres during production life.

Maximum speed claimed by makers, approximately 45 m.p.h. Under easy conditions this could be exceeded quite readily, though the 60 m.p.h. claimed by some owners was not possible with cars in standard form. Best level road cruising speed 28–35 m.p.h.

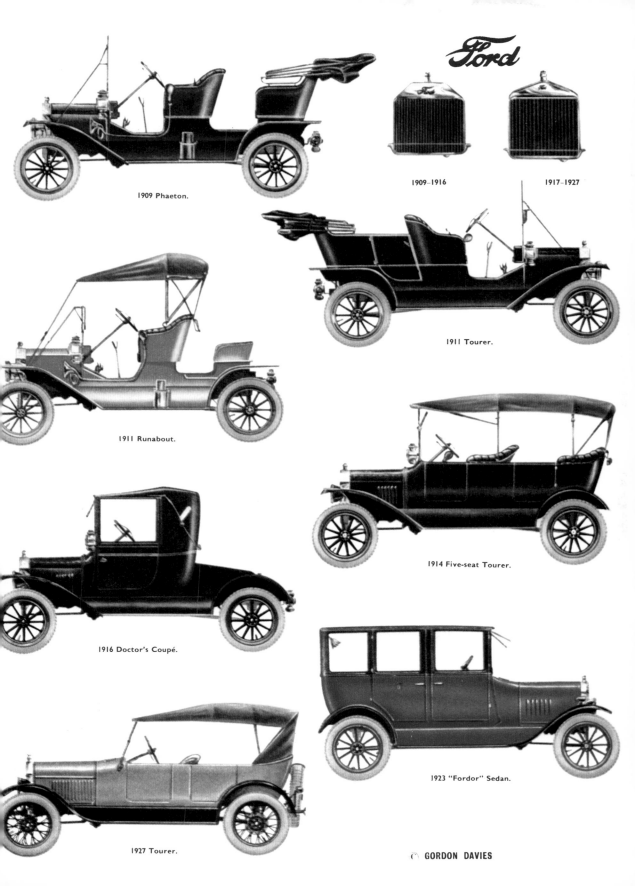

Ford

1909 Phaeton.

1909–1916

1917–1927

1911 Tourer.

1911 Runabout.

1914 Five-seat Tourer.

1916 Doctor's Coupé.

1923 "Fordor" Sedan.

1927 Tourer.

© GORDON DAVIES

dillos because, of all the cars in the world, the Ford was endowed with the strongest and most endearing personality.

Many of its faults could have been eradicated easily, but to have done so would have cut across Henry Ford's concept of mass production and interchangeability. A parallel may be drawn between Model T and the Silver Ghost Rolls-Royce which had a comparable production run, from 1906 to 1925. The Ghost, however, was extensively modified in almost every detail in the light of experience and technical development. It had, for example, three totally different gearboxes and as many rear suspension systems, to say nothing of alterations to pistons, bearings, and compression ratio which almost doubled its developed horsepower.

By contrast, the Parts List for Model T show how astonishingly few mechanical or chassis parts were altered. Underneath Lizzie's changing outward appearance she just went on and on. Her angular brass radiator may have given way to a more rounded one encased in sheet iron in 1916, but it still boiled as vigorously on the slightest provocation. The 1927 Model T may have had a sleek body style, detachable wire wheels in place of the wooden ones, nickel-plated radiator shell and lamp rims, but it was still the old faithful 1908 two-speed 'flivver' with rather sketchy two-wheel brakes and a tendency to wander if pushed up to maximum speed of 45–50 m.p.h.

Lizzie had had her day—but what a memorable **day** it had been.

© Anthony Bird, 1966.

The Type RL Alfa Romeos

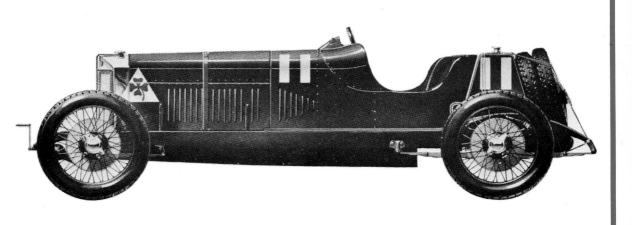

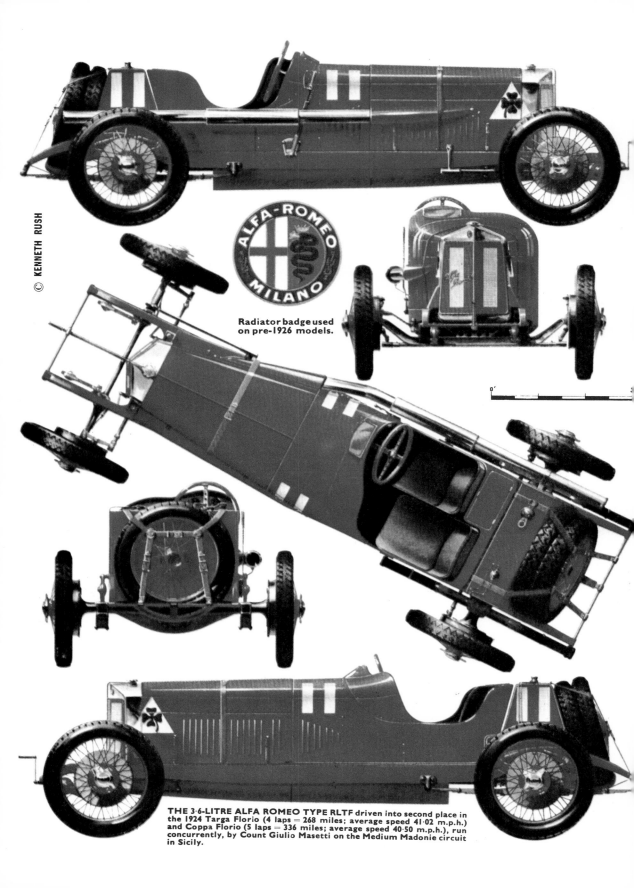

© KENNETH RUSH

Radiator badge used on pre-1926 models.

0´   3

THE 3·6-LITRE ALFA ROMEO TYPE RLTF driven into second place in the 1924 Targa Florio (4 laps = 268 miles; average speed 41·02 m.p.h.) and Coppa Florio (5 laps = 336 miles; average speed 40·50 m.p.h.), run concurrently, by Count Giulio Masetti on the Medium Madonie circuit in Sicily.

The Type RL Alfa Romeos

by Peter Hull and Luigi Fusi

Prototype. One of three experimental RL Cars entered for the 13th Targa Florio race in Sicily on 2nd April, 1922. Driven by Tarabusi, with his mechanic Guatta, it retired on the first lap after hitting a rock which had fallen into the roadway. Sivocci and Campari on the other cars finished in ninth and eleventh places respectively. Note the unusual radiator.

For over forty years two names have been consistently to the fore in the world of motor racing—Alfa Romeo and Ferrari. This is the story of the cars which helped to bring international fame to both Alfa Romeo and to Enzo Ferrari himself in the years following the first World War, the touring, sports and racing Type RL six-cylinder Alfa Romeos.

THE DESIGNER

Talented car designers, like talented architects, frequently do not become as celebrated as the works they produce. Such a designer was Giuseppe Merosi. Although his name was scarcely known even in his native Italy until quite recently, Tito Anselmi, the Italian motoring writer, has said of him 'he deserves a place among the greatest designers in the automotive field the world over'.

Surveyor Cav. Guiseppe Merosi was born in Piacenza on 17th December, 1872. He graduated at the Technical Institute in Piacenza where he actually studied to be a building surveyor, although in later years Enzo Ferrari himself was to describe him as an excellent automotive technician. After doing a year's military service, Merosi founded a cycle factory in his native city, called Ing. Bassi & Merosi. He ran this firm until 1898, when he was employed by Orio & Marchand in Piacenza, who are believed to have made the French Decauville car under licence. They also co-operated with Dufaux of Geneva, who were pioneers of straight-eight car engines and makers of Motosacoche motor cycles. Merosi stayed with Orio & Marchand until the

summer of 1904, and during this time designed several Marchand cars and motor cycles, which went into limited production. One of his motor cycles, ridden by Count Monasterolo of Piacenza, won a race over the 10 km. between Padua and Bovolenta in which Darracq, Itala and Ceirano cars took part.

In 1904 Merosi moved to Turin, where he was employed by the Fiat Car Technical Department, and was one of a team engaged in the design of racing cars. However, he only stayed there a year before going to Messrs Lentz in Milan, for whom he designed a car, but only three examples were built.

In the autumn of 1906 Merosi became Chief of the Car Technical Office of Bianchi in Milan, and stayed with them until October 1909. Eduardo Bianchi's cars had a fine reputation at that time, although they do not seem to have been entered in competitions.

In October 1909 came the start of the most important period of Merosi's life when he was asked to design high performance touring cars for the newly established firm of A.L.F.A. in Milan. These initials stood for the Societa Anonima Lombarda Fabbrica Automobili or Lombardy Car Manufacturing Co. A.L.F.A. had taken over the works of Italiana Darracq, which since 1906 had built French Darracq cars in the Portello district of Milan, but had gone into liquidation.

Before the Great War Merosi designed three touring cars for A.L.F.A., the 2·4-litre 15/20 h.p., the 4·2-litre 20/30 h.p. and the 6-litre 40/60 h.p. All had four-cylinder side-valve engines or push-rod o.h.v. engines, and were sturdy and reliable with a good performance

19

Praised by a potentate. The Aga Khan is here seen trying an RLS sports model on 14th September, 1923. He said that it was one of the most excellent cars he had ever ridden in.

for their day. He also designed a twin overhead camshaft 4½-litre Grand Prix racing car, but the advent of the war prevented this car taking part in the races for which it was intended.

In 1915 the A.L.F.A. works were taken over by the industrialist Nicola Romeo, who was four years younger than Merosi, and who had been in business in Milan as a manufacturer of mining machinery and equipment. Before long, prospering from the manufacture of various munitions of war, Romeo was the head of a huge engineering combine, and during 1917 and 1918 he made Merosi the manager of his railway wagon works, Officine Ferroviarie Meridionali, in Naples.

After the war Nicola Romeo was as keen as any of his old A.L.F.A. employees that the manufacture of motor cars should recommence at Portello once again, and in 1920 ten 15/20s were made and ninety-five 20/30s under the new name of Alfa Romeo. The ES Sport 20/30, made in 1921 and 1922, was particularly successful in Italian competitions. In 1921 a six-cylinder side valve car of 6·6 litres capacity was produced to Merosi's design, but it was not a great success due to its high fuel consumption, and only about 50 were built. In order to get an insight into American production methods, Alfa Romeo acquired a Pierce-Arrow car before bringing out their next model.

It was in 1920 that Merosi started thinking about the design of a car that would be in accordance with the capacity limit for Grand Prix racing in 1921, namely 3 litres. This was the Alfa Romeo that became known as the RL (Romeo series 'L'), from which was derived touring, sports and racing models. The first prototypes were ready by mid-1921 and were tested with great success, but any thoughts of building a Grand Prix version were nullified when the Grand Prix capacity limit for 1922 was reduced to 2 litres.

THE TOURING AND SPORTS CARS

The official introduction of the new model to the general public took place on 13th and 14th October 1921, in the Alfa Romeo showroom at via Dante 18, Milan. In November 1921 a touring chassis was shown on the stand of Salmons & Son, the British

Alfa Romeo concessionaires, at the London Motor Show at the White City. It was not, however, until 1923 that production of the new cars started, a mere half dozen being manufactured in 1922, when entries were made in competitions to test the prototypes.

The official sporting debut of the RL was in the 250

The prerogative of princes. H.R.H. the Prince of Siam (now Thailand) photographed early in 1924 in the yard of the Alfa Romeo works at Portello, Milan, in the back seat of an RLN touring car.

Also suitable for dictators (and their pets). A stark and fierce-looking RLS is appropriately occupied by Benito Mussolini, nursing a lion cub on his knee. Mussolini was an RLSS owner.

The designer takes the wheel. Cav. Giuseppe Merosi driving a sports tourer. The radiator badges on these early cars appear to be attached to the honeycomb.

mile Autumn Grand Prix at Monza, though three prototype cars had also been entered in the Targa Florio race in Sicily back in April, but purely for test purposes. At Monza the driver of the RL was Ugo Sivocci, and he finished second in the up-to-3-litre category, only 11 sec. behind Alfieri Maserati's 2-litre Grand Prix Diatto, which averaged 78 m.p.h., with a fastest lap at 87 m.p.h. Sivocci was fourth in the race overall, being beaten also by an Hispano-Suiza and a Ballot in the over-3-litre category.

When production was started in 1923 it was revealed that there were to be two models, a touring chassis with a six-cylinder 75 × 110 mm., 2,916 c.c., overhead valve engine known as the RL Normale, or RLN, and a sports model with a similar engine of slightly larger capacity, 76 × 110 mm., 2,996 c.c., known as the RL Sport, or RLS. In England the RLN was known as the 21/70 hp. and the RLS as the 22/90 hp. The RLN had a flat radiator, and the RLS a pointed one carrying two Alfa Romeo badges, one on each side of the point. The badge incorporated the viper which formed the coat of arms of the city of Milan.

The chassis of the two cars was entirely conventional with the suspension by means of four semi-elliptic springs, but the RLN had an 11 ft. 3 in. wheelbase whereas the RLS was a foot shorter at 10 ft. 3 in. Big 72 mm. hubs were fitted with Rudge knock-on hub caps, and the back axle was of the fully floating type.

The four-speed gearbox was in unit with the engine, which had an extraordinarily neat and attractive appearance with the use of alloy much in evidence. The gear change could be central or right hand, and an excellent dry multiplate clutch was fitted. The overhead valves were operated by push-rods, and a rather archaic feature of the design was that there was no pressure lubrication to the overhead valve gear. This had to be lubricated by hand by the driver at fairly frequent intervals, a mixture of paraffin and engine oil being recommended for squirting on to felt pads and over the gear generally. In fact, bicycle oil is preferable to the paraffin mixture. Other traditional features on this first production o.h.v. Alfa Romeo engine were the fitting of compression taps, and the fact that the tappets were adjusted at the side

of the engine as on a side-valve, though the clearances were taken between the top of each push-rod and its rocker.

The valves were in line in the cylinder head, which was made of cast iron and was detachable. There were no combustion chamber recesses in the head, the surface of which was completely flat. The 18 mm. sparking plugs were screwed into the offside of the cylinder block. The RLS had slightly bigger ports than the RLN.

The RLN had a single updraught carburettor, whereas the RLS had twin carburettors, either Solex or Zenith. A peculiar difference between the two models was that the RLN had the inlet on the offside and exhaust on the nearside of the engine, and yet these features were reversed on the RLS. There were two forms of induction heating, by hot air from the tappet chamber, and by hot water via a pipe from the radiator. All the inlet manifolding was inside the head instead of being external.

The gudgeon pins in the H-section connecting rods were secured by clamp bolts, and were 20 mm. on the

1923 Targa Florio. The proud crew stands by the winning car, Sivocci with his hand on the steering wheel. The amount of mud on the rear of the car explains the need for the wide front mudguards.

The first international victory. Ugo Sivocci photographed in his 3.1 litre racing car on his way to victory in the 1923 Targa Florio race. The 'quadrifoglio', or four-leaf clover, seen painted on the radiator cowl, has been featured on all works Alfa Romeo racing cars ever since.

RLS but 18 mm. on the RLT. Compression ratio was 5·4 to 1 on the RLN and 5·52 to 1 on the RLS.

The camshaft was set high in the crankcase, although long push-rods were still necessary. The latter were surprisingly heavy, and a spare one would be perfectly suitable for keeping beside the bed for attacking burglars. Not surprisingly the valve gear was rather heavily loaded, leading to possible wear on the cam-followers and camshaft. The RLS had more sporting cams than the RLT, and the camshaft was driven by helical gears, as was the centrifugal water pump driving in tandem with the dynamo on the nearside. The Bosch magneto on the offside was driven by an internally toothed chain. The 50 mm. crankshaft ran in four plain main bearings, and an odd feature of the engine was inspection plates in the crankcase sides such as one sees on large diesel engines in ships.

Both models had wet sump lubrication, with an oil capacity of 1½ gallons.

The output of the RLN engine was 56 b.h.p. at 3,200 r.p.m., and of the RLS 71 b.h.p. at 3,500 r.p.m., the RLN consuming petrol at a rate of about 16–20 m.p.g. and the RLS at 13–16 m.p.g. The maximum speed of the RLN was just under 70 m.p.h., and of the RLS 75 m.p.h. Petrol was brought from the 16-gallon rear tank by air pressure, which was first pumped up by hand by means of a pump fitted to the dashboard, and then was maintained once the engine was running by a mechanical pump.

Early cars had rear wheel brakes only, with the handbrake working a transmission brake, but front wheel brakes were fitted from the 3rd series cars onwards after September, 1923. Front brake actuation was taken through the centre of each king-pin via a chain and sprocket at its base, the linkage from the pedal to the front and rear brakes being by means of long steel strips. Brake pressure was equalised by differential gears on a shaft behind the brake pedal.

Some improvements were made to the 6th and 7th series cars in 1926 and 1927, and it will be noted that series numbers appeared to coincide with the year of manufacture in the 'twenties, as with the Lancia Lambda series numbers. For the improved models there was a change of nomenclature, the RLN becoming the RLT (T for Turismo) and the RLS becoming the RLSS (SS for Super Sport). The RLSS

was now given dry sump lubrication, with an oil tank in the scuttle having a capacity of approximately 3 gallons.

The main difference on the RLT was an increase in the bore to 76 mm. to bring the capacity from 2,916 c.c. to the 2,994 c.c. of the sports models, and this brought with it an increase in output to 61 b.h.p. at 3,200 r.p.m. It also added 3 or 4 m.p.h. to the maximum speed. Compression ratio was lowered slightly to 5 to 1.

The power output on the RLSS was raised by some 12 b.h.p. compared with the RLS, bringing it to 83 b.h.p. at 3,600 r.p.m. This approximated to the output of the contemporary Speed Model 3-litre Bentley engine in standard form. Mussolini, who owned an RLSS, declared that it had a 'magnificent engine', a reminder that another world-famous figure, the Aga Khan, after trying an RLS in September 1923 had described his experience as 'a most interesting and enjoyable journey in one of the most excellent cars I have ever ridden in'. The RLT also differed from the RLN in becoming logical, and having the inlet and

Alfa Romeo hierarchy before the Italian G.P. at Monza, August 1923. In the foreground, left to right, Giorgio Rimini, sales and racing director, Nicola Romeo and Enzo Ferrari. Behind are two directors, and what looks like Giuseppe Merosi, in cap. Sivocci lost his life practising in a P1 Grand Prix Alfa Romeo before the race, and the whole Alfa team was subsequently withdrawn. The P1 was never raced.

The origin of the Ferrari badge. Enzo Ferrari winning the first circuit of Savio race, 17th June, 1923, the Savio being a river near Ravenna. His driving inspired the presentation to him of the shield depicting the prancing black horse on a yellow background, which is the badge carried by all Ferrari cars today.

exhaust passages in the head swapped over to make them on the same sides of the engine as on the RLS and RLSS.

An improvement to the brakes was made on the 7th series cars by enlarging the brake drums, and the RLSS and RLT cars continued to be made until 1927, although by this time Vittorio Jano had taken over from Giuseppe Merosi as Chief Designer for Alfa Romeo, Merosi having moved on in 1926 to work as Chief Designer for Mathis of Strasbourg. Merosi died on 26th March 1956, and the few remaining RL Alfa Romeo cars which are still treasured today are a fitting epitaph to him.

THE RACING CARS

Enzo Ferrari was the leading spirit in the Alfa Romeo racing team in the early 'twenties so far as the organisation of it was concerned, and his fellow drivers included Antonio Ascari, the stout Giuseppe Campari and Ugo Sivocci, the latter trio being known as the Three Musketeers. Strangely enough, both Ferrari and Campari were torn between two ambitions, whether to become racing drivers or opera singers. These works drivers, as well as many amateurs, recorded numerous competition successes with RLS and RLSS

sports cars in Italian events as they were undoubtedly fast cars in their day. Amongst these successes were a class win in the 1923 Gran Premio Turismo at Monza by an RLS (driver Ugo Sivocci), second place by an RLS in the Pozzo Circuit race at Verona in 1924 (driver Enzo Ferrari) and second place to a German N.A.G. in the 24-hour Italian Touring Car Grand Prix at Monza in 1924 by an RLS (drivers Giuseppe Ascari, brother of the famous Antonio, and Attilio Marinoni). An RLSS driven by Massias won its class in the sports car Grand Prix of Provence at Miramas track in France in 1925, but the best performance in an international race by an RLSS was third place in the formule libre 1926 German Grand Prix at Avus by a two-seater RLSS with a 'Gran Premio' body driven by a German Alfa Romeo agent called Willy Cleer. The race was won by Caracciola on a 2-litre straight-eight supercharged Grand Prix Mercedes, whilst second was a 3-litre N.A.G. driven by Christian Riecken.

The swan song of the RLSS in racing so far as works entries were concerned was the first Mille Miglia in 1927 when two cars driven by Count Brilli-Peri and Presenti and Marinoni and Ramponi both retired after leading the race, leaving the ultimate victory to the smaller 2-litre side-valve O.M.s.

A 1924 Targa Florio RL. Manuel de Teffé, Brazilian champion driver at the wheel of one of the team cars, examples of which were raced by private owners in South America in later years.

However, the main successes by RL Alfa Romeos were achieved by special racing cars built in 1923 and 1924 and known as Targa Florio models (see page 2). These cars had much lighter chassis and more powerful engines than the sports models, and were altogether smaller. The wheelbase was reduced to 9 ft. 3 in., and due to the narrowness of the chassis itself, the rear springs were outrigged. The track was fractionally wider than that of the sports cars, and front wheel brakes were featured on all the 1924 cars and some of the 1923 ones.

In 1923 the cars had cowled radiators, and could have spare wheels strapped to a petrol tank behind the two seats, or else a streamlined tail. A feature of the racing cars was the use of balance beams to compensate the brakes in stead of the much heavier differentials on the sports cars.

The 1923 cars had similar four main bearing engines to the sports cars, but with aids to performance such as lightened valve gear and the compression raised to 6 to 1. The engine thus produced 88

RLSS power unit. The exhaust side of the engine, with its integral gearbox. On the far left is the transmission brake drum. Despite dry sump lubrication, the wet sump oil filler of the earlier cars was still retained. A right-hand gear lever was an optional extra at £25, and the extension tunnel for it can be seen blanked off.

b.h.p. at 3,600 r.p.m. Three cars were built with the 2,994 c.c. engine, but a further two cars had a bigger bore of 78 mm., bringing the capacity to 3,154 c.c. and an output raised to 95 b.h.p. at 3,800 r.p.m. These bigger cars had a maximum speed of 98 m.p.h., whilst the smaller-engined cars could do about 90 m.p.h.

Ugo Sivocci gave Alfa Romeo their first international victory in the 1923 Targa Florio driving a 3·1 litre car, whilst Ascari was second in a 3-litre. In addition, that year Ascari won at Cremona with his 3-litre and Count Masetti in a 3-litre won at Mugello and made fastest time in both the Coppa della Consuma (Florence) and Mont Cenis hill-climbs. An historic occasion was when Enzo Ferrari won the first Circuit of Savio race at Ravenna in a 3-litre, and so impressed the parents of Francesco Baracca, the Italian fighter ace of the First World War, that they presented Ferrari with the badge their son carried on his aeroplane when he was shot down and killed in 1918, a shield with a prancing horse on a yellow background. This shield is carried on all Ferrari cars to this day. With the same car Ferrari also won the 1923 Circuit of Polesine at Rovigo.

The 1924 RL racing cars were distinguished externally by a pointed radiator similar to that on the

A late Model RLSS chassis. The 6th and 7th series chassis of 1926 and 1927 had big brake drums. Note the twin carburettors, whilst the oil tank can be seen between the dashboard and the bulkhead.

An RLSS Grand Prix success. Willy Cleer's stripped 22/90 h.p. RLSS Alfa Romeo does its lap of honour after coming third overall in the 1926 German Grand Prix at Avus in 1926, a formule libre race.

sports cars, only smaller, and had two spare wheels strapped to the 150-litre (33 gallon) rear tank. Their push-rod engines were more developed than the 1923 ones, the main difference being the use of a seven instead of a four bearing crankshaft. Three of the cars had 2,994 c.c. engines, and these now produced 90 b.h.p. at 3,600 r.p.m., giving the cars a maximum speed of 93 m.p.h. Two further cars, however, had engines with the bore increased to 80 mm. and the stroke to 120 mm., giving a capacity of 3,620 c.c. These engines had the considerably increased output of 125 b.h.p. at 3,800 r.p.m., which put up the maximum speed of the cars to 112 m.p.h. All the 1924 racing engines had a compression ratio of 6·4 to 1.

Ascari narrowly missed a win in the 1924 Targa Florio when his engine seized only 50 yards from the line when he was in the lead. Willing hands manhandled the car over the line, but victory went to a Mercedes, with Masetti second on the other team 3·6-litre similar to Ascari's car. Also in 1924 Enzo Ferrari scored a victory in the Coppa Acerbo at Pescara in a 3·6-litre.

In 1925 the amateur driver Guido Ginaldi, now an hotel proprietor in Italy, gave a second victory to a 1924 RL racing car in the Coppa Acerbo, in which he finished in front of two Bugattis, and he also drove his car to second place in the Rome G.P. Two third places went to 1924 cars in 1926, at Tripoli (driver Siciliani) and Perugia (driver Presenti).

Pit stop at Mugello, 1923. A wonderfully evocative photograph of a team RL Targa Florio racing car being jacked up during the race on the Mugello Circuit over the Futa Pass near Florence, 10th June, 1923. Count Masetti won on his 3 litre RL racer, and his team mate, Antonio Ascari, finished in third place behind a German Steyr driven by the Italian driver, Count Brilli-Peri.

A privately owned RLSS in Italy today. This 1925 22/90 h.p. car, fitted with a Castagna body, belongs to Marcello Zanotelli of Trento. It is a drophead coupé, but saloon as well as open bodies were fitted to both sports and touring RL chassis. The front brake mechanism operating through the king-pin can clearly be seen.

25

Leader at Rome. Count Gaston Brilli-Peri and Presenti's RLSS at the Rome control in the first Mille Miglia, 1927. They led the race until they retired at Spoleto, on the return leg to the finish at Brescia. Note the numerous lamps and stoneguards, not to mention the bulb horn!

Wunderbar! Cleer, who was a German Alfa Romeo agent, and his mechanic Bonini, enjoy the admiration of the crowd after the 1926 German Grand Prix.

Count Masetti's old 3·6-litre car won its class in the Belgian 24-hour Race at Spa as late as 1932, and RL racing cars performed in later years in South America and England.

THE SURVIVORS

Out of approximately 2,500 RL Alfa Romeos produced between 1922 and 1927 little more than a dozen are known to survive in private hands in the world today. Six of these are in England, four RLSS cars, two 1925 and two 1927, and, amazingly enough, two of the RL racing cars. One of these, belonging to Michael Crowley-Milling, is a 1924 car with a seven-bearing 3-litre engine, originally imported into England by the Alfa Romeo concessionaire, F. W. Stiles, about 1925. The other car, belonging to Christopher Mann, was originally raced at Brooklands by Agostino Lanfranchi in 1925, and appears to be a 1924 RL racing chassis

fitted with a 3-litre four main bearing engine. Both these cars can often be seen racing at Vintage Sports Car Club meetings, and examples of the RLSS cars can frequently be seen attending V.S.C.C. meetings today.

Two RLSS cars are known to be in Manitowoc, Wisconsin, U.S.A., there are two RLSS and an RLT in Australia and an RLN in Johannesburg, South Africa. There is at least one RLT in France. What is thought to be the only RLSS in private hands in Italy is a 1925 drophead coupé belonging to Marcello Zanotelli of Trento. However, Luigi Fusi looks after three RLSS Alfa Romeos in the Alfa Romeo Museum at Arese, one of which has spent most of its life in India. He has also built up examples of 1923 and 1924 Targa Florio cars using original parts.

What is it like to run an RLSS as one's normal transport today? Firstly, one blesses the soundness of Giuseppe Merosi's design, and the good workmanship

Runner-up in the Targa Florio, 27th April, 1924. Count Giulio Masetti on his 3.6 litre Targa Florio RL was second to Werner's Mercedes, after a dramatic incident when Antonio Ascari's similar RL had had engine failure only 50 yards from the finishing line when it was leading the race. French ace Louis Wagner was also in the Alfa team.

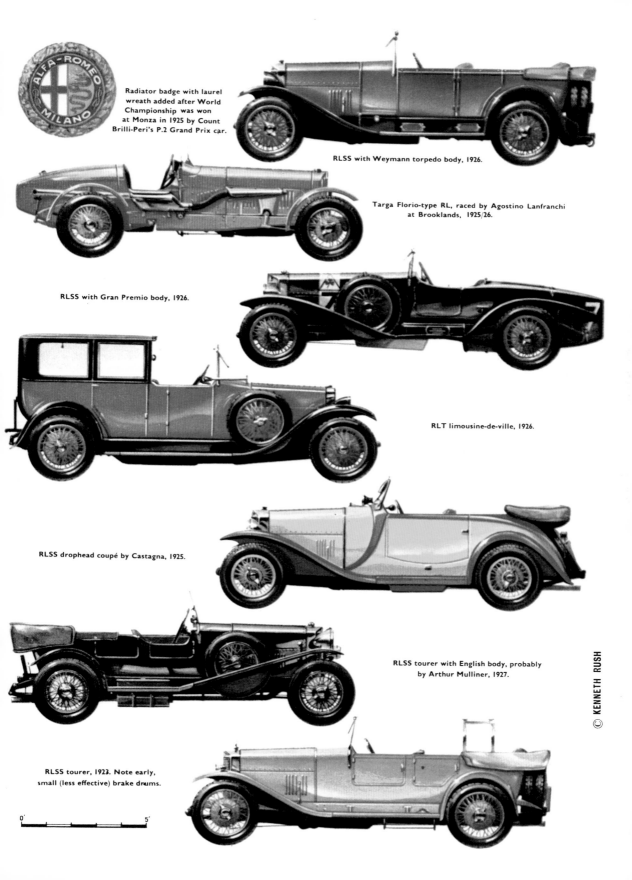

Radiator badge with laurel wreath added after World Championship was won at Monza in 1925 by Count Brilli-Peri's P.2 Grand Prix car.

RLSS with Weymann torpedo body, 1926.

Targa Florio-type RL, raced by Agostino Lanfranchi at Brooklands, 1925/26.

RLSS with Gran Premio body, 1926.

RLT limousine-de-ville, 1926.

RLSS drophead coupé by Castagna, 1925.

RLSS tourer with English body, probably by Arthur Mulliner, 1927.

© KENNETH RUSH

RLSS tourer, 1923. Note early, small (less effective) brake drums.

0'   5'

that went into it, for generally the car is very reliable and free from temperament. As it has a straightforward push-rod engine it is not difficult to service and decarbonise. Spares, of course, are not obtainable 'off the shelf', and thus certain parts may have to be specially made, or adapted.

The steering and roadholding are of an extraordinarily high standard, and the car can be cruised without being stressed at 60–70 m.p.h. Unfortunately certain inclines which a 3-litre Bentley, for instance, could take in third gear at 60 m.p.h., would slow the RLSS down considerably due to its low ratio third gear, on which it has a maximum speed of not much more than 50 m.p.h. This is a frequent drawback with certain Continental cars built more for Alpine than British roads. It is said that cars were available on the English market with higher third gears, which must have transformed their performance.

As for appearance, there are few cars that can compete with the RLSS for good looks, as its pointed radiator carrying the two Alfa Romeo badges is acknowledged to be one of the most handsome ever produced in the vintage era.

*   *   *

Further reading 'Alfa Romeo—A History' by Peter Hull and H. Roy Slater (Cassell & Co. Ltd., 1964); 'Le Vetture Alfa Romeo Dal 1910' by Luigi Fusi (Editrice Adiemme, Milan, in five languages including English).

© Peter Hull and Luigi Fusi. 1966.

(The Publishers gratefully acknowledge Alfa Romeo, S.A., and Cav. Luigi Fusi for supplying the photographs reproduced here).

THE SIX CYLINDER TYPE RL ALFA ROMEOS

	RL Normale 21/70 h.p.	RL Sport 22/90 h.p.	RL Turismo 22/70 h.p.	RL Super Sport 22/90 h.p.	RL Targa Florio 1923	RL Targa Florio 1924
First built	1922	1922	1925	1925	1923	1924
Bore and stroke	75 × 110	76 × 110	76 × 110	76 × 110	76 × 110 / 78 × 110	75 × 110 / 80 × 120
Capacity	2,916	2,994	2,994	2,994	2,994 / 3,154	2,994 / 3,620
B.H.P.	56	71	61	83	88 / 95	90 / 125
(at) R.P.M.	3,200	3,500	3,200	3,600	3,600 / 3,800	3,600 / 3,800
Compression ratio	5·2	5·52	5	5·5	6	6·4
No. of main bearings	4	4	4	4	4	7
Valve operation	Overhead, by push-rods and rockers					
Ignition	High tension magneto					
No. of carburettors	1	2	1	2	2	2
Lubrication	Wet sump, one pressure pump			Dry sump, one pressure and one scavenge pump		
Cooling	Water pump and fan				Water pump, no fan	
Clutch	Dry multi-plate					
Gearbox	4 speeds and reverse, central lever				4 speeds and reverse, right lever	
Suspension	Semi-elliptic springs					
Brakes	Handbrake on transmission, footbrake on all 4 wheels				Handbrake on rear wheels footbrake on all 4 wheels	
Tyres	860 × 160	860 × 160	860 × 160	820 × 120	820 × 120	820 × 120
Fuel tank	16 gall.	16 gall.	16 gall.	16 gall.	22 gall.	33 gall.
Electrical system	12 Volt	12 Volt	12 Volt	12 Volt	—	—
Wheelbase	11 ft. 3 in.	10 ft. 3 in.	11 ft. 3 in.	10 ft. 3 in.	9 ft. 3 in.	9 ft 3 in.
Track	4 ft. 9½ in.	4 ft. 9½ in.	4 ft. 9½ in.	4 ft. 9½ in.	4 ft. 10 in.	4 ft. 10 in.
Weight	36 cwt.	35 cwt.	36 cwt.	32 cwt.	19½ cwt.	20 cwt
Maximum speed	68½ m.p.h.	75 m.p.h.	71 m.p.h.	81 m.p.h.	90 m.p.h. / 98 m.p.h.	93 m.p.h. / 112 m.p.h.
Chassis price	£600	£700	£625	£725	—	—
Cars produced	1,345	537	387	392	3 / 2	3 / 2

The
M.G.
Magnette
K.3

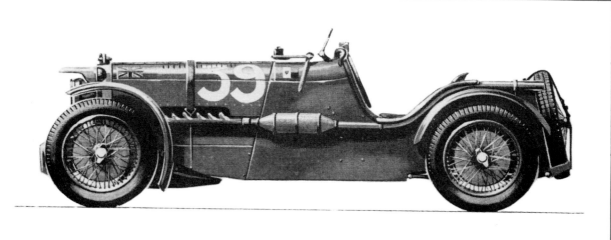

15

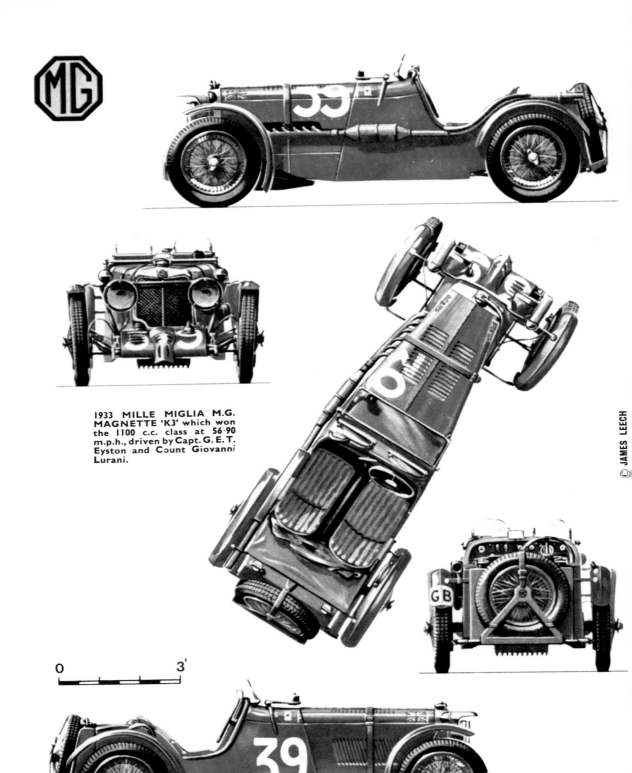

1933 MILLE MIGLIA M.G. MAGNETTE 'K3' which won the 1100 c.c. class at 56·90 m.p.h., driven by Capt. G. E. T. Eyston and Count Giovanni Lurani.

0   3'

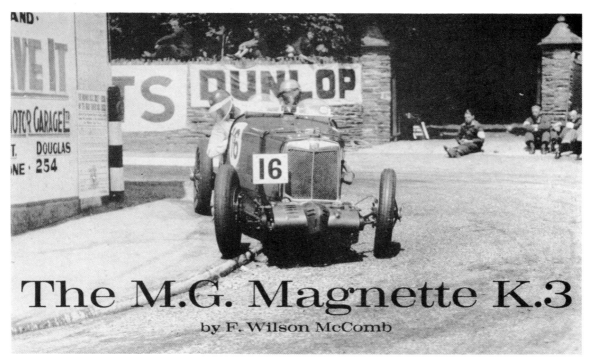

The M.G. Magnette K.3
by F. Wilson McComb

'Hammy' Hamilton cuts it fine when cornering in the 1933 Mannin Beg race. Fortunately the 'K3' was tough enough to stand up to kerb-bouncing. (Photo: Montagu Motor Museum)

At this time, when British-built cars are virtually invincible both in Grand Prix racing and in international rallies, one tends to forget how insignificant a position they held in the early nineteen-thirties. Alfa Romeo, Maserati and Bugatti ruled the roost, and it was taken for granted that the first car past the chequered flag in almost any form of motor race would wear either the blue of France or—more probably—the stirring blood-red of Italy.

The only British machine to make any real impact on motor sport at international level was the M.G., product of a very small company in rural Berkshire. During 1931 and 1932 alone, the successes of the M.G. Midget included outright victory in the Brooklands Double-Twelve, the Irish Grand Prix, the Ulster Tourist Trophy, and the Brooklands 500 Miles Race—not to mention the first 100 m.p.h. and the first 120 m.p.h. in International Class 'H' (750 c.c.), plus a number of significant class successes in Continental races. It was at this stage that the M.G. chief, Cecil Kimber, decided to carry the battle into International Class 'G' (1100 c.c.) with a new six-cylinder model dubbed the 'Magnette'. Following the usual M.G. practice of relating the racing cars closely to the standard production models, Kimber introduced the Magnette range with a saloon known as the 'K1', first seen at Olympia Motor Show in October 1932. This had a 9 ft. 0 in. wheelbase, 4 ft. 0 in. track, and a surprising innovation in the form of a Wilson pre-selector gearbox.

That the racing version was still little more than a pipe-dream is proved by the catalogue of that date. Reference is made to the 'K2' two-seater (which did not come into production until the following February) and the 'K3' racing model, but the latter is shown as a curious long-tailed device with staggered seats and twin head-rests which never, in fact, saw the light of day. Moreover, there is mention of an un-

supercharged 'K3', though no such model was ever built, and different 'K3' prices are quoted on different pages of the same catalogue! Yet in less than six months two 'K3' prototypes were built and tested, a team of three cars also built and tested, and some of the major awards triumphantly carried off in the world's most important long-distance event, the 1,000-mile race held each year in the very Mecca of motor-racing, Italy.

The driving force behind this remarkable achievement was the late Earl Howe, who usually raced a Bugatti but had long cherished the idea of taking part in the Mille Miglia with a British car. He suggested to Sir William Morris, Bart., the man who owned the M.G. Car Company, that if Abingdon built a team of three racing Magnettes, he would personally bear the cost of transporting them to Italy and taking part in the race. Morris, always a practical man where hard cash was concerned, accepted this generous and businesslike offer. Cecil Kimber, far less practical, but a dyed-in-the-wool racing enthusiast, was delighted to be given the go-ahead, and commenced his preparations without a moment's delay.

Two prototypes were hurriedly assembled, the first of them closely resembling the contemporary Midgets except that it was four inches longer in the wheelbase at 7 ft. 6 in., had larger brakes, and was of course fitted with an experimental six-cylinder 1100 c.c. engine with supercharger mounted between the front dumb-irons. I cannot be sure if it used the 3 ft. 6 in. axles of the Midget or the 4 ft. 0 in. Magnette ones, but the generally unbalanced air of the car suggests the latter. Kimber, who took justifiable pride in the appearance of his M.G.s, must have winced when they wheeled this one out of the experimental shop. And few competition cars have been less suited to their first event. This short-chassis fire-eater disposing of some 100 b.h.p., with the most rudimentary of weather

31

protection, a pair of spare wheels strapped on the tail and two minute foglamps flanking the supercharger cowling, was promptly entered for the Monte Carlo Rally!

THE 1933 SEASON

A brave soul named James Wright fought his way through the snow in this car to finish 64th out of 69 survivors, but his subsequent performance revealed more of the Magnette's true potential. In the acceleration and braking test he made equal fastest time with an Essex Terraplane, showed up less well in the braking, and in all took second place behind the rally-winning Hotchkiss of Vasselle. In the Mont des Mules hill-climb which followed, he made comfortably the fastest climb of the day, more than 12 seconds better than the Frazer-Nash which took second place. The Magnette's time constituted a new class record.

Meanwhile the second 'K3' prototype was completed on 4th January 1933, just two weeks before the Monte started. Longer in the wheelbase at 7 ft. 10 $\frac{3}{16}$ in., which curious figure was arrived at accidentally but retained for the entire 'K3' range, this car had better-looking bodywork apart from an ugly sloping front cowling which was banged out of sheet metal at the last possible moment. Since the straight-through exhaust pipe incorporated no silencing device whatsoever, it doubtless sounded as purposeful as it looked when Reg Jackson, head racing mechanic of M.G., drove it down from Abingdon to Newhaven. There he was met by Earl Howe and his personal mechanic,

'Tommy' Thomas, in an Alfa Romeo and a Mercedes. From Dieppe the three cars ran in company through France, stopping at the Bugatti factory to pay their respects. As a Bugatti owner Earl Howe was, of course, known at Molsheim, and the British visitors arrived at a propitious time; they found everything *en fête* because it was the twenty-first birthday of Ettore Bugatti's son, Jean.

Nevertheless, Jackson was somewhat dashed when Le Patron examined the Magnette prototype and firmly announced that the front axle was not strong enough. As John Thornley remarks in his M.G. racing history, *Maintaining the Breed*, 'The great Ettore . . . was not likely to say such a thing for fun'. In any case, Abingdon was not too proud to learn from Molsheim. The great man's opinion was relayed to Abingdon, the M.G. designers reconsidered the axle dimensions, and a batch of stronger ones was ordered at once.

Only one 'K3' owner, Ronnie Horton, refused to have his car fitted with the stronger axle. More than a year later, Ettore Bugatti's doubts were justified when Horton's front axle broke after practice for the 1934 Mannin Beg.

At Milan, Earl Howe met the other team drivers: Count 'Johnny' Lurani, whose status in Italy and knowledge of the language were to prove of great value to the team; Captain George Eyston, already famous for his record-breaking exploits with M.G.s and other cars; the brilliant Sir Henry ('Tim') Birkin, whose tragic death occurred not long after the Mille Miglia; and Bernard Rubin, wealthy industrialist and former member of the Bentley team. Howe's own co-driver, the mercurial Hugh ('Hammy') Hamilton, was unable to get away from his work as a salesman for the London M.G. distributors, University Motors. The drivers made a sort of triumphal tour through

The two leading 'K3's enter the Bologna control during the 1933 Mille Miglia. On the left is the Birkin/Rubin car, on the right that of Lurani and Eyston, the class-winner. (Photo: M.G. Car Co. Ltd.)

Italy, being received not only by the King, but also by Il Duce himself, Benito Mussolini (a much more important person at that time). The team met Enzo Ferrari, and had lunch with Tazio Nuvolari. Captain Eyston, a descendant of Sir Thomas More and a member of one of the oldest Roman Catholic families in England, was also received in audience by the Pope.

But apart from such junketings there was plenty of hard work to do, and in particularly unpleasant weather conditions. Despite rain, sleet, snow and ice, the drivers practised over as much of the course as they could and flogged the unfortunate prototype to the limit. As was the object of the exercise, various weaknesses were discovered and the information passed on to Abingdon. The gearboxes had to be largely redesigned because second gear was too low, and the gearbox oil consumption too high. Not only the road wheels, but the hubs themselves, had to be redesigned. The only component tested insufficiently (because of the weather) was the braking system. When the actual race practice allowed full braking power to be applied six weeks later, all the brakedrums split and new ones had to be sent out from the works.

In all, the long-suffering second prototype spent some five weeks in Italy, returning to Abingdon by mid-February. It was then refurbished to serve as a practice car, and work on the three team cars speeded up still further.

On 11th March at dead of night the four Magnettes left Abingdon *en route* for the Cornish village of Fowey, where they were shipped aboard *S.S. Florentine* together with a cargo of china clay and wet fish. Twelve days later, after a crossing of the Bay so rough that part of the ship's funnel was carried away, the *Florentine* arrived at Genoa with its precious cargo—the faithful practice car and three racing machines—meticulously prepared and capable of 106 m.p.h. at 6,000 r.p.m. on a 4·89:1 final drive, two up and 27½ gallons of fuel in the slab tank. At Brescia, traditional starting-point for the Mille Miglia, the team moved into the Hotel Moderno Gallo and were delighted to find all the hotel equipment emblazoned with the initials 'M.G.'. It seemed like a good omen.

The story of the race itself has often been recorded. It was agreed that Birkin would set the pace in an endeavour to break up the opposition, and this he accomplished magnificently. Over the first 129 miles

Three 'K3's were again entered for the Mille Miglia in 1934, but this time only the Lurani/Penn-Hughes car finished, taking second place in its class. (Photo: M.G. Car Co. Ltd.)

to Bologna he averaged 87·95 m.p.h., overtaking 35 other cars on the way and breaking the class record by 13 minutes. Over the mountains to Florence he maintained his lead. On the run in to Siena, 228·5 miles from Brescia, the leading Magnette slowed, and Birkin had to retire at the control because of a broken valve. But he had achieved his object. The most dangerous opponent of the M.G.s, Tuffanelli's Maserati, had smashed its gearbox on the Futa Pass, and the second Maserati was running slowly, nearly an hour behind schedule.

By Rome, after 365 miles, Eyston and Lurani were comfortably leading the class and had knocked 25 minutes off the 1100 c.c. record, with Howe and Hamilton not far behind. The two British cars were still leading when they clocked into Bologna again on the return leg, with three-quarters of the race completed, though Eyston had to have a new battery because his dynamo had stopped charging.

Both M.G.s were plagued by sparking-plug trouble because the Powerplus superchargers required a lot of lubrication. A plug 'hot' enough to take this without oiling up would burn out on full throttle, and a grade 'cold' enough to stand the heat would oil up on the over-run. It is on record that Eyston and Lurani fitted no less than 157 new sparking plugs in the course of the race. About 100 miles from the finish, Howe and

Nuvolari in action with the 'K3' during the 1933 T.T., which he won at an average speed of 78·65 m.p.h. (Photo: Keystone Press Agency Ltd.)

Hamilton had a puncture. Fifty miles further on, Eyston and Lurani had the same experience. But the two Magnettes were still leading the 1100 c.c. class when they reached the finish, averaging 56·90 and 56·82 m.p.h. respectively despite all the plug-swopping and wheel-changing. Better still, no nominated team had finished intact, but the Magnettes had put up the best performance, so they gained the coveted Team Prize, the Gran Premio Brescia, never before won by a foreign car.

The impact of this success may seem disproportionate nowadays, and yet it *was* a bold and impressive venture to invade the very home of motor racing and carry off this trophy with three brand-new British cars which had never raced before. Few new models have enjoyed such a resounding début.

Back at Abingdon, three more 'K3's had been built by the time the conquering team returned. Two were entered for the International Trophy Race at Brooklands on 6th May, for E. R. Hall and Manby-Colegrave, together with two of the actual Mille Miglia cars—one of them Howe's car, the other Eyston's, to be driven by Mrs Elsie Wisdom; Birkin's machine was presumably still suffering from the damage caused by the broken valve. Of the entire entry only eight cars finished and they were led home by the Hon. Brian Lewis' Alfa Romeo, but Hall finished second, Elsie Wisdom third, and Earl Howe fourth. Manby-Colegrave became deeply involved with a marker barrel, but made up for this lapse in the British Empire Trophy a few weeks later, finishing third at a rousing 106·88 m.p.h. Fourth was Ron Horton with another 'K3' which set up a new Brooklands Outer Circuit lap record at no less than 115·55 m.p.h. during the race. This car had been supplied in chassis form and he had given it the same treatment as his extremely successful Montlhéry Midget, fitting an offset single-seater body which looked extraordinary but proved highly effective.

With so many successes in their first four events, the barometer seemed set fair for the 'K3' Magnettes when six were entered for the Mannin Beg 'round the houses' race in the Isle of Man—but what a nasty shock that event brought for Abingdon! All six Magnettes retired, three of them with rear-axle failure, because the punishing, stop-go nature of the event revealed a hitherto unsuspected weakness in the two-star differential. No time was lost in replacing it by a

On the Brooklands banking during the 1934 International Trophy—Roy Eccles with a 1934 model 'K3', Earl Howe in his Bugatti, and Whitney Straight with his 3-litre Maserati. (Photo: The Light Car)

The second prototype, used as a Mille Miglia 'recce' car in January 1933. Behind are Siena, Earl Howe, Nuvolari, Enzo Ferrari, Count Lurani and Capt. George Eyston. (Photo: M.G. Car Co. Ltd.)

stronger four-star design.

Consolation came in the form of another crushing defeat for the Italians on their own soil. On 15th August, Whitney Straight—then a Cambridge student—took his privately-owned 'K3' to Pescara and trounced a horde of *single-seater* Maseratis in the Coppa Acerbo Junior. This was more than Italian flesh and blood

Three of the 'K3's entered for the 1934 Mannin Beg race. On the right is Eyston's record-breaker, EX.135, with road-racing body. (Photo: M.G. Car Co. Ltd.)

Eyston in EX.135 leads 'Hammy' Hamilton's offset single-seater 'K3' in the 1934 Mannin Beg race. (Photo: Keystone Press Agency Ltd.)

could stand—a protest was lodged, and Straight's engine dismantled to check the dimensions. It merely revealed that the engine was of the correct capacity.

Not so surprising, then, that the greatest Italian of all, Tazio Nuvolari himself, let it be known that he would not be averse to driving a 'K3' Magnette in the

The start of Le Mans, 1934, with the Ford/Baumer 'K3' on the right. It was lying second when put out of the race by a spinning Tracta and the Martin/Eccles 'K3' finished fourth. (Photo: Motor)

The only foreign car ever to win the Italian 1100 c.c. Championship was Raffaele Cecchini's single-seater 'K3', seen here setting up a new record at the Stelvio Hillclimb. (Photo: Fumagalli)

Ulster Tourist Trophy, just three weeks ahead. Fortunately Straight had an entry for the race which he was unable to take up, so Kimber managed to substitute a spare works car for *Il Maestro*. Only three other 'K3's were entered (for Hall, Yallop and Manby-Colegrave) but a total of eight Midgets, because it was reckoned that the T.T. handicap gave the advantage to the smaller-engined cars.

Arriving at the circuit in time for the second practice period (having driven straight from the Belfast docks), Nuvolari climbed into the Magnette, took a good look round, and asked for the driving seat to be raised on wooden blocks. This done, he set sail for his first lap, which proved a heart-stopping experience for his riding mechanic, Alec Hounslow of M.G. John Thornley, the present managing director of M.G.s, has suggested that Nuvolari's method was to start a little over the limit and then ease back from it—on that first practice lap he 'lost' the Magnette completely three times, and in eight laps wore out a full set of tyres. The same principle is followed by some of today's top rally drivers, who consider that they are not really trying if they do not wreck a couple of cars during reconnaissance runs.

In the race itself, the Italian champion's style was much smoother, though still very fast indeed; he broke the 1100 c.c. circuit record seven times, and cut his refuelling so fine that he needed to take on more before doing his *tour d'honneur*. The favoured Midgets were brilliantly led by 'Hammy' Hamilton's 'J4', but his mechanic made a nonsense of one pit-stop, costing a full seven minutes. Hammy regained the lead on handicap, then had to stop for more fuel, and Nuvolari won by a bare 40 seconds. Eddie Hall's 'K3' took fourth place, and Manby-Colegrave finished seventh.

And still the score of successes in that wonderful first season of the 'K3' was not complete. For the Brooklands 500 Miles Race two weeks later, Hall had his Magnette quickly rebodied as a single-seater with a very high final drive ratio, in which form it was capable of *lapping* the Outer Circuit at something like 118 m.p.h. Since the 'K3' proved completely reliable, he was able to drive quite gently to win at 106·53 m.p.h. average for the full distance, while Yallop's more normal 'K3' finished fifth. The following March, Horton maintained 117·03 m.p.h. for one hour in his offset 'K3' to set up a new Class 'G' Outer Circuit record at Brooklands.

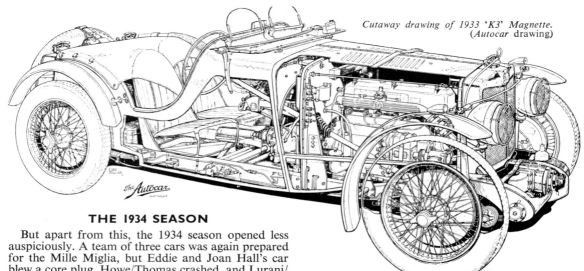

Cutaway drawing of 1933 'K3' Magnette.
(*Autocar* drawing)

THE 1934 SEASON

But apart from this, the 1934 season opened less auspiciously. A team of three cars was again prepared for the Mille Miglia, but Eddie and Joan Hall's car blew a core plug, Howe/Thomas crashed, and Lurani/Penn-Hughes could manage only a class second to Taruffi's Maserati. A fourth 'K3' also ran—one of the old 1933 team cars driven by a German named Fork—and retired with rear axle trouble, but a month later Fork picked up a fifth place in the Avusrennen. Meanwhile the 'K3's suffered another disappointment in the International Trophy at Brooklands, where the handicapper made them pay for their brilliant reputation. Of no less than 13 entered, the highest-placed 'K3' was only eighth.

Most of these cars were the new, 1934 models, with Marshall supercharger, 'N' type cylinder head, improved brake actuation and long-tailed streamlined (though still two-seater) bodywork; the Mille Miglia cars carried slab-tank two-seater bodies, but incorporated the new Roots-type superchargers. The new model's first success came in the Mannin Beg, thus providing a highly satisfactory revenge for their failure at the Isle of Man the previous year. Only eight cars finished, seven of them were M.G.s, and 'K3' Magnettes filled the first *five* places, led home by Norman Black. Tragically and ironically, the Abingdon contingent were unable to enjoy this great success because

one of them, Frankie Tayler, had been killed in an accident to Kaye Don's car before the race. I believe this to be the only recorded fatality in a 'K3'.

No 'K3' had run at Le Mans in 1933, but this omission was now rectified when Ford and Baumer appeared with one and worked right up to second place, only to be forced off the road when a Tracta spun in front of the Magnette. But another 'K3', driven by Charlie Martin and Roy Eccles, finished fourth and won the 2-litre class.

The car that Eyston drove into third place in the Mannin Beg was built of 'K3' components but featured an offset transmission line, and could be fitted with road-racing or a track body as required. Known variously as EX.135, the Magic Magnette or the Humbug (because of the brown-and-cream striped track body), it was destined for a long and honourable career as a record-breaker and eventually formed the basis of the famous Goldie Gardner record car, which achieved more than 200 m.p.h.—still with a 'K3' engine—in 1938. But its first victory came in 1934, when Eyston won the British Empire Trophy at 80·81 m.p.h. Of the 10 finishers, five were 'K3's, and three of them won the team prize.

Two new names now appeared on the scene. One was Raffaele Cecchini, an Italian printer who acquired a 'K3' and neatly converted it to single-seater bodywork. The other was Dick Seaman, then a Cambridge undergraduate, who bought Whitney Straight's old

Bobbie Kohlrausch's mechanic, Artur Baldt, sits in the ex-Howe 1933 Mille Miglia car which was loaned to Kohlrausch for a very successful season of hillclimbs and sprints in Germany. (Photo: M.G. Car Co. Ltd.)

Magnette after competing in various events with an 'F' type Magna. These two entered for the Coppa Acerbo Junior together with 'Hammy' Hamilton, who had just established a new 1100 c.c. record in the Klausen hill-climb with his 'K3', which was fitted with offset single-seater bodywork. Hammy stalled on the starting-line, then, furious with himself, roared through the field in classic Hamilton fashion to win the race, with Cecchini second and Seaman third. Once again the single-seater Maseratis had been humbled in their native land by the heavy, vintage-looking M.G.s—and it is on record that, during that race, Hamilton's 'K3' was clocked at 122·25 m.p.h. through the measured kilometre.

Seaman and Hamilton then travelled in company to Switzerland, where the young undergraduate scored his first victory by winning the Swiss Light Car G. P. As for poor Hammy—brilliant, fearless driver that he was despite chronic lack of funds, and potentially one of the greatest that Britain has ever produced—he met his death in a borrowed 3-litre Maserati during the Swiss Grand Prix itself. Raffaele Cecchini went on to gain class wins in one hill-climb after another, often setting up new class records, and then beat the great Giuseppe Farina's Maserati in the Circuit of Modena to win not only the race, but the 1100 c.c. Championship of Italy. Never before had the Championship been won with a non-Italian car. Seaman also gained a notable success with his 'K3' in September, winning his class and establishing a new sports car record—regardless of capacity—at Mont Ventoux. At the end of the month he finished fifth behind Eyston in the Masaryk G. P. Junior in Czechoslovakia, and in October raised to 72·87 m.p.h. the Brooklands Mountain Circuit record which Straight had established with the same car. Also at Brooklands, 'K3's finished third, fourth, fifth and seventh in the 500 Miles. Other successes were gained by Manby-Colegrave in Ireland, by Thompson in Australia, and by Moritz in Hungary—the latter with the class-winning 1933 Mille Miglia car, which he bought from Fork. Miss Enid Riddell had her 'K3' fitted with large pannier bags to carry feminine fripperies and competed in the all-ladies Paris–Saint Raphael Rally, winning her class and finishing second overall.

A further series of Continental hill-climb successes was achieved in 1934 by a German driver, Bobby Kohlrausch, who had borrowed Earl Howe's old 1933 Mille Miglia 'K3' from Abingdon. He was later to make his name by returning 140·6 m.p.h. with the old Magic Midget 750 c.c. record car.

Driven by Maillard-Brune and Druck, Jacques Menier's 'K3' scored many successes including the 2-litre class at Le Mans 1935. It was still being raced in France in 1947, and is now being restored by an English enthusiast. (Photo: A. Well)

1935 AND AFTER

For various reasons the 'K3' Magnette began to take a back seat in 1935. Most of the M.G. Car Company's attention was focused on a brand-new design, the single-seater 'R' type Midget, with backbone frame and independent suspension all round. By comparison with this, the 'K3' design was old-hat indeed, though its engine remained a brilliant piece of engineering and the 'K3' had by no means scored its last racing success. Again, a dangerous rival had appeared on the scene in the slim, purposeful shape of the single-seater E.R.A. Finally, when Lord Nuffield (as Sir William Morris had now become) sold the M.G. Car Company to Morris Motors in the early summer, it was announced that M.G. racing activities were to cease. Thereafter, the private owners had to fend for themselves without the full resources of the M.G. racing department, which was closed down overnight.

However, on 6th May, at Brooklands—where the new 'R' made its debut in the International Trophy Race—Eddie Hall's 'K3' took third place, while, over in Ireland a week or two later, Manby-Colegrave set up no less than four new lap records in the Bray Round-the-Houses before succumbing to the old bugbear of the 'K3', plug trouble. Robin Jackson won a 50-mile Southport sand race with the very first 'K3' prototype, which still appeared on the circuits from time to time. Jacques Menier, the man who makes that delicious French chocolate, bought a 'K3' and in June entered it for Le Mans, where Maillard-Brune and Druck won the 2-litre class, finishing ninth overall.

Maillard-Brune followed up his Sarthe success by removing the mudguards and finishing second to a Bugatti in the G. P. d'Orleans. This, its ability to compete on equal terms either as a sports or as a racing car at will, was one of the most attractive features of the 'K3'. Third in that same race was a Dutchman, Edmond Hertzberger, in the very last 'K3' to be built (it was exhibited at Olympia in 1934 before being sold). Maillard-Brune went on to finish fourth at Albi, headed by two Bugattis and a Delage, but the Menier Magnette's racing career was far from over, as we shall see.

Even Cecchini managed to extract a further turn of speed from his old single-seater, repeating his class win at Stelvio in 1935, improving on his old record,

The start of the 1934 Coppa Acerbo Junior, in which the 'K3's finished 1–2–3. First home was Hamilton, whose car can be seen stalled on the starting-line. (Photo: Fumagalli)

A 1934 'K3' in chassis form.
(Photo: M.G. Car Co. Ltd.)

and beating the highest-placed Maserati by nearly a minute. Some time later, the Cecchini special turned up in Ireland, and with it Prestwich won the 1937 Cork Grand Prix. Another 'K3' appeared in Czecho-slovakia, of all places, when Zdenek Pohl scored a win in the 1935 Jeneralka Hill-climb. That same car is still being raced today by Zdenek and his brother Jiri, though it now has a Skoda engine; spares for 30-year-old M.G.s are not too easy to find behind the Iron Curtain.

Back in Britain, in the British Empire Trophy Race, Donald Letts came 10th with EX.135—a far cry from Eyston's outright win of the previous year with the same car. The famous Siamese racing driver, Bira, took fifth place in the Nuffield Trophy at Donington with the last 'K3' but one. In a mid-August event at Donington, Reg Parnell came first in Hamilton's old 'K3', with J. H. T. Smith third in Lurani's old 1934 Mille Miglia car. Eddie Hall once again returned fastest time in the Craigantlet Hill-climb, smashing the previous record. And the Marquis de Belleroche, driving Manby-Colegrave's venerable 1933 car, survived the Brooklands 500 Miles to finish fifth.

It is interesting to compare the performances of the Midgets and the Magnettes at this time. The average 'K3' engine could be relied upon to give something over 120 b.h.p. at 6,500 r.p.m., but the four-cylinder units used in the 'Q' and 'R' type Midgets had been subjected to such intensive development that they were capable of 113 b.h.p. at 7,200 r.p.m. with less than three-quarters of the six-cylinder unit's capacity—750 c.c. against 1100 c.c. Moreover, the all-independent 'R' type, once a few teething troubles had been sorted out, displayed better roadholding than the 'cart-sprung' Magnette, and was of course much lighter. Not surprising then, that there was little to

choose between Midget and Magnette towards the end of the 1935 season. At the August Donington meeting, indeed, Briault's 'R' had finished second between the 'K3's of Parnell and Smith.

In an effort to compete with mounting opposition from newer designs, many 'K3' owners in many parts of the world embarked on extensive modification of their cars. Often the result was merely to spoil the whole charm and character of the model, but such aesthetic considerations do not always occur to a man who is bent on winning some silverware.

For a long and full life, few could approach the record of the Menier 'K3' which won the Le Mans 2-litre class on its first outing in 1935. The following year, Maillard-Brune won the 1100 c.c. class and finished second overall (despite persistent ignition trouble) in that other 24-hour French classic, the Bol d'Or. In 1937 he again competed in the Bol d'Or with the same car, though he retired at half-distance. The car then passed to another Frenchman, de Burnay, who succeeded in winning the class and taking second place yet again in the 1938 event. Almost unbelievably, de Burnay reappeared at the Bol d'Or—still with the same 'K3'—in 1939, and covered enough distance to win the 1,100 c.c. class for the third time, though he retired after 21 hours. Heaven alone knows how the old Magnette survived the war, but it turned up in the hands of one Veuillet at the 1945 Bois de Boulogne meeting, taking second place to a 6C Maserati, and scored a similar success at the Bois in 1946. In 1947 Veuillet took it to Rheims, where he finished seventh behind Peter Monkhouse, who was driving a much-modified version of the car in which Frankie Tayler

The twin-lever brakes fitted to the 1934 model 'K3' Magnette.
(Photo: M.G. Car Co. Ltd.)

Another view of the 1934 'K3' chassis showing the pre-selector gearbox. Behind the selector lever is the brake adjuster, and above it the pump for maintaining air pressure in the fuel tank. (Photo: M.G. Car Co. Ltd.)

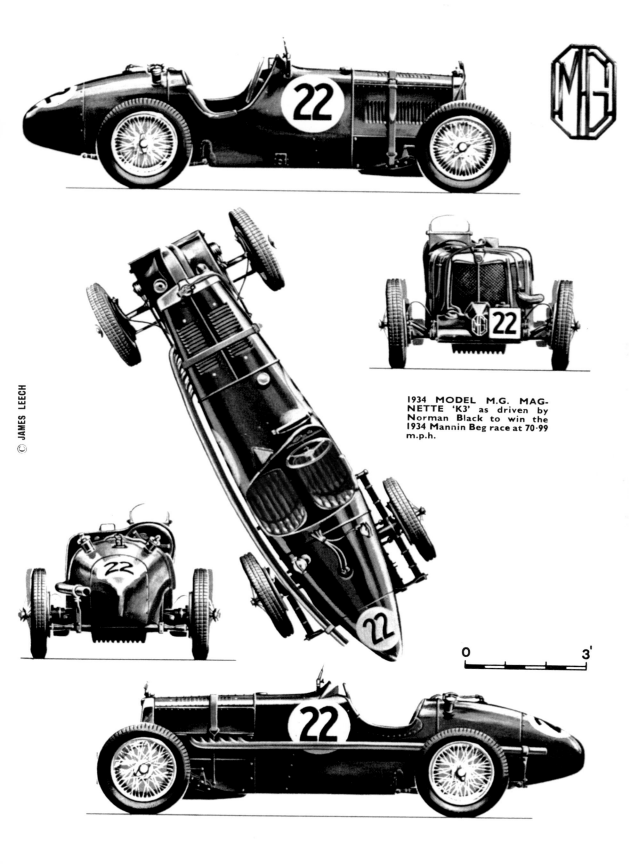

© JAMES LEECH

1934 MODEL M.G. MAG-
NETTE 'K3' as driven by
Norman Black to win the
1934 Mannin Beg race at 70·99
m.p.h.

0   3'

was killed before the 1934 Mannin Beg. The two venerable Magnettes also appeared at the 1947 Lyons meeting, where Monkhouse finished fifth but Veuillet retired.

A few years ago I had a letter from a Frenchman named Bonnafous who wanted to sell an M.G. special. The supercharger was missing, the front axle had been broken and clumsily welded, the body was non-standard and altogether horrible, but the chassis number told me all I wanted to know. So the Menier 'K3' returned to Abingdon after 30 years, and I passed the word around among those who have a weakness for motoring history. The 'K3' is now being lovingly restored to original specification by a young M.G. Car Club member, and will soon be seen on the race-track once more.

In two years the M.G. company built two proto-types and 31 other 'K3's, if one includes the EX. 135 record-breaker. It has been possible to locate and identify 23 at the time of writing, their condition vary-ing from immaculate original specification to a mere rusty chassis frame. The first prototype is in Tokyo, owned by a charming Japanese gentleman who bought it in 1937 and won my heart by telling me, 'When the packed box came to the port Kobe I was absolutely happy highest degree in my life'. The second prototype is in Australia, well cared for by a professional engineer. Sir Henry Birkin's 1933 Mille Miglia car is also in Australia, where it has been restored by an M.G. Car Club member who spared neither effort nor expense to achieve perfection. Hammy Hamilton's car, exten-sively modified by Reg Parnell, is in England, but its engine, alas, is on the wrong side of the Atlantic. The Straight/Seaman car went in 1938 to the U.S.A., where Howe's 1934 Mille Miglia car may also be seen; of its team-mates, one is in Australia and one, much modi-fied, in England. Prince Bira's car is in Australia, Cecchini's appears to be in Ireland, and Charlie Martin's 1934 Le Mans car, completely restored, is exhibited on high days and holidays in California. The 1934 Mannin Beg winner recently turned up in Switzer-land, apparently in perfect condition. As for EX. 135, the gallant old Humbug later rebodied for Lt.-Col. Goldie Gardner, it retired from record-breaking in 1952 and is now carefully maintained at Abingdon.

Over the years, the 'K3' Magnette earned a con-siderable name for itself. Is that reputation dispropor-tionately high? I doubt it. The 'K3' in its heyday stood alone to defend Britain's racing reputation, both at home and abroad. Its victories in its first two years included the Mille Miglia team prize, the Ulster T.T., the Coppa Acerbo Junior (twice), the Mannin Beg, the British Empire Trophy, the Brooklands 500 Miles, the Circuit of Modena, the Swiss Light Car G. P. and the Italian 1,100 c.c. Championship. Those who drove 'K3's included Nuvolari, Birkin, Seaman, Eyston, Gardner, Straight, Hall, Don, Bira, Hamilton, Parnell and Dodson. It holds a secure and well-deserved place in the history of motor racing.

Essentially vintage in concept, the 'K3' looked heavy and old-fashioned beside many of its con-temporaries, but in the words of John Thornley, '. . . it was designed to go fast, keep right way up, and keep on going'. If the essential sports car is (as many believe) epitomised by a mid-'thirties M.G., then surely the 'K3' Magnette is the epitome of the M.G.

© F. Wilson McComb, 1966.

1933 'K3' MAGNETTE SPECIFICATION

Chassis: Open channel side-members, tubular cross-members and cruciform centre bracing. Chassis underslung at rear. Remote lubrication by grouped nipples.

Suspension: Semi-elliptic leaf springs, front and rear, flat under load, taped and cord-bound. Main leaves sliding in phosphor-bronze split trunnions at trailing ends. Hartford duplex friction shock-absorbers, two mounted longitudinally at front, four mounted transversely at rear.

Wheels: Centre-lock Whitworth wire-spoked racing type, $3\frac{1}{2}$ in. rim, 19 in. dia.

Brakes: Elektron shoes, backplates and drums, the latter finned and fitted with cast-iron liners. Brakedrum diameter, 13 in. Mechanical actuation by cased cable from central cross-shaft, with fly-off handbrake operating on all four brakes. Brakes adjustable under way by cockpit wheel. Torque reaction cables to front axle.

Steering: Cam-type box and transverse draglink to axle-mounted slave arm actuating wheels through divided trackrod.

Engine: Six-cylinder 57 × 71 mm. (1,086 c.c.). Four-bearing crankshaft. Gear-type oil pump. Finned elektron sump with float-chamber controlled feed from scuttle-mounted reserve tank. Total capacity, 20 galls + 2 res. Steel connecting-rods, three-ring aluminium pistons. Valves operated through adjust-able rockers by single overhead camshaft, driven by vertical shaft forming dynamo armature. KE.965 valves. Triple valve springs. Opposed ports, six inlet, six exhaust. Compression ratio, 6·2 to 1. Valve timing: Inlet opens 15 deg. b.t.d.c., closes 55 deg. a.b.d.c. Exhaust opens 50 deg. b.b.d.c., closes 20 deg. a.b.d.c.

Transmission: Wilson preselector gearbox with central operating lever (oil capacity, 6 pts.). Top, 1 to 1; Third, 1·36 to 1; Second, 2·0 to 1; First 3·4 to 1; Reverse, 5·07 to 1. Open pro-peller shaft with Hardy-Spicer universal joints. Three-quarter floating rear axle with straight-cut bevel final drive, ratios 5·7, 4·89 or 4·33 to 1 (oil capacity, 2 pts.).

Cooling system: Thermo-syphon with engine-driven pump. Radiator fitted with stoneguard and quick-release filler cap. Capacity of system, $3\frac{3}{8}$ galls.

Exhaust system: Six branches to outside exhaust incorporat-ing regulation Brooklands expansion chamber, tailpipe and fish-tail. Additional internal silencing tube supplied for road use.

Induction and fuel system: $23\frac{1}{2}$-gallon slab tank incorporating 3-gallon reserve, with twin quick-release fillers. Twin electric fuel pumps (one main, one reserve). $1\frac{3}{4}$ in. bore S.U. carburettor mounted on Powerplus No. 9 eccentric-vane type supercharger running at approx. $\frac{3}{4}$ engine speed, driven from crankshaft nose by splined coupling shaft with universal joints. Lubricated at low pressure from cylinder head. Ki-gass starting pump.

Ignition and electrical system: Polar-inductor magneto and 14 mm. sparking plugs. 12-volt dynamo and separate starter. Twin 6-volt batteries in series. Headlamps, sidelamps, dash-lamps, tail-lamps, twin horns and windscreen wiper. All circuits separately wired and fused.

Instruments: 6 in. Jaeger tachometer, oil-pressure gauge, oil and water thermometers, fuel gauge, oil-tank gauge, ammeter, boost gauge and supercharger oil-pressure gauge.

Bodywork: Doorless two-seater conforming to international road-racing regulations, with fold-flat windscreen, twin aero screens, and spare wheel mounted behind slab fuel tank. Bucket seats upholstered in leather. Standard colour, British Racing Green.

Dimensions: Wheelbase, 7 ft. 10 $\frac{7}{16}$ in. Track, 4 ft. 0 in. Weight: chassis, $13\frac{1}{2}$ cwt.; complete car, $18\frac{1}{4}$ cwt. 20·04 m.p.h. per 1,000 r.p.m. with 4·33 to 1 final drive.

Price: Chassis only, £675. Complete car, £795.

1934 SPECIFICATION

As above with the following variations:—

Brakes: Shoes in rolled T-section mild steel. Steel liners. Twin cam-levers and roller cams.

Engine: New cylinder head with improved porting. Standard compression ratio 5·4 to 1, or higher if desired.

Induction and fuel system: $27\frac{1}{2}$-gallon shaped fuel tank form-ing part of bodywork. Hand pump provided to maintain fuel supply by air pressure (so that batteries may be dispensed with). Roots-type Marshall No. 85 supercharger.

Electrical system: External contacts provided for use of slave starter batteries.

Instruments: Fuel supply air pressure gauge added. Fuel gauge and oil-tank gauge omitted.

Bodywork: Narrower streamlined design, still conforming with A.I.A.R.C. regulations. Tapered tail behind fuel tank. No full-width windscreen provided. Spare wheel mounted at side of scuttle.

Dimensions: Weight of complete car, $17\frac{3}{4}$ cwt.

Price: Unchanged.

The Jowett Javelin and Jupiter

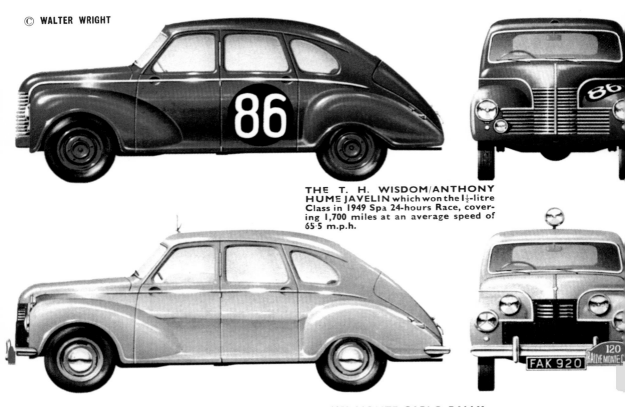

THE T. H. WISDOM/ANTHONY HUME JAVELIN which won the $1\frac{1}{2}$-litre Class in 1949 Spa 24-hours Race, covering 1,700 miles at an average speed of 65.5 m.p.h.

1950 MONTE CARLO RALLY JOWETT JAVELIN TEAM CAR.

1953 STANDARD PRODUCTION JAVELIN.

The Jowett Javelin and Jupiter

by D. B. Tubbs

Another chief designer who was not afraid to drive his cars in competition was Roy Lunn, who came to Jowett from Aston Martin. He is here seen in the Javelin that he shared with Marcel Becquart in the 1951 R.A.C. British Rally. They won the class for closed cars. The car is seen climbing that famous Welsh pass, Bwlch-y-Groes. (Photo: Mr. Charles Dunn)

There is something very J. B. Priestley about the Jowett tale of a staid cloth-capped Yorkshire firm making penny-a-mile motors that suddenly decides in late middle age to go in for export drives and a racing programme. Their fling brings them fun, and some fame, but it takes them out of their class, and the story ends in disaster. One cannot call it failure except in the commercial sense. Jowetts made an enormous number of friends and their designs were always of great technical interest; and when the firm disappeared in 1954 it was one of the oldest in the Industry.

Ben Jowett and his brother Willy, of Idle, near Bradford, designed their first engine in 1900, a 6 h.p. Vee Twin, as a British—indeed Yorkshire—replacement for the 6 h.p. De Dion and 6½ h.p. Aster. They then leaped into unorthodoxy with a straight-three air-cooled engine with o.h.v. and a five-bearing crankshaft. In 1905–06 they announced what they called 'the world's first light car'. This was a neat two-seater designed to give motoring at a penny a mile. Apart from the tiller steering it might well, from its looks, have been made during the 1920s. It weighed only 6 cwt. (a Mini Cooper 'S' weighs 13 cwt.), had a water-cooled side-valve horizontally-opposed twin engine in unit with the three-speed gearbox, central gear-change and a worm-drive back axle. Production started in earnest by 1910 and twin-cylinder Jowetts, now with saloon bodywork and spiral-bevel axle, were still being sold in 1939, making this almost certainly the longest run of any model in history.

By 1936 the 7 h.p. car had been joined by a four-cylinder 10 h.p. (the Jason) which mainly for the sake of tradition and goodwill was also horizontally-opposed. This model was dropped on the outbreak of war, but the twin was made in large quantities as a stationary engine for generators. Jowett also made capstan lathes and aircraft components, so the factory was very well equipped. The brothers Jowett had now retired and the Company was directed by Calcott Reilly.

THE JAVELIN DESIGN

Quite early in the war Calcott Reilly realised that post-war Britain would depend on exports. Plans were laid for an exportable motor-car, and in 1942 Gerald Palmer joined the company from M.G.s, where he had been a draughtsman for six years. It was a shrewd choice. Palmer was a young man with sound engineering training, he was an enthusiast who had built a most interesting 'special', and he had been educated in Southern Rhodesia where life was rugged and roads were very 'colonial'. His brief was a 'universal' car, which must appeal both to home and overseas markets. It had also to be made as far as possible within the Jowett works.

The Jowett company at Idle was far away from the Birmingham/Coventry centres of production and the factories that keep the industry supplied; it was also quite small for a motor manufactory, with only 500–800 people. In these circumstances they could not compete with Morris and Vauxhall on price; Gerald Palmer aimed at the Citroen Twelve price bracket, the front-wheel drive *traction* which had sold for £238 (the 'luxury saloon') in 1939. It was this model he had in mind, not the Lancia Aprilia as people have said; but a would-be 'colonial' model needed more ground-clearance of course, and it was desirable to use a flat-four engine—not only for political and publicity reasons, but also, Palmer realised, because it left more room for inhabitants. The diagram shows how little room a flat four takes up. It is evident that a flat engine and high ground-clearance between them bring some at least of the advantages of front-wheel drive, namely a flat floor and much passenger-space within the wheelbase. The aim was really comfortable riding for four to six people in a small compact car.

It would of course have been possible, with a flat engine, to reduce the height of the sills and use a 'plunging deckline' as Fiat and Peugeot were doing by 1938. Palmer felt that this was ahead of demand; he preferred a tall commanding prow, a higher waistline and what is now called a 'fast' back. The resulting prototype looked like a car that he much admired: the V-12 Lincoln Zephyr. Road tests were to confirm Palmer's choice of lines, for the Javelin, as the new Jowett was called, went fast on the power it had and was quite light on petrol.

The car as first conceived was to be made in and around the factory. Jowett had strong local connections and it was hoped to get castings from a small foundry in Huddersfield. This was the first engine that Palmer had designed. The original plan was for a single-piece cast-iron crankcase with two-bearing crankshaft, and wet cylinder liners, driving to the gearbox of the pre-war Ten. Prototypes also used that model's back axle. This engine ran well but the one-piece iron casting proved noisy and the bearings did not last very long. A light-alloy block was then made, using the same patterns, but this, too, proved too resonant and the block was accordingly split down the middle. This opened the way to die-casting, a technique that still makes news. The Javelin had the first light-alloy (gravity) die-castings in this country. They were ultimately produced by Renfrew Foundries Ltd.

When the prototype was laid down there was no thought of mass production of the body or chassis on press tools. Palmer believed that motorcars should have a frame under them (he still does, along with many other chassis engineers). Jowetts, being a small company, put as much money as possible into the external panels needing dies (compare current Rover 2000). The prototype was designed so that all internal work on the chassis should be done by folding, using simple tools; the frame members, for example, were home-made box longerons, and the roof was clinched over a flange on the cantrail. The curvature on the panels was kept very simple and on the first prototype the four doors were all interchangeable.

The front suspension was by unequal-length wishbones with torsion bars running fore and aft; at the rear a beam axle (now semi-floating, with hypoid bevel gearing) was suspended by transverse torsion bars mounted one above the other, and located laterally by a Panhard rod. Weight was saved by using torsion bars, and the use of simple hexagonal ends instead of splines saved cost and complication. It is significant that hexagon-ended torsion-bars are now used by Chrysler. One of the Javelin prototypes was sold to Chrysler during a U.S. sales tour.

At first it was intended to make two sizes of engine: 1,200 c.c. for the home market and 1,500 c.c. for overseas. The former was dropped; Javelin dimensions became 72·5 by 90 mm bore and stroke, 1,486 c.c. A three-bearing crank had been developed, and the expansion of the light-alloy crankcase had led to the adoption of Zero-lash hydraulic tappets for the pushrod overhead valves. On a compression ratio of 7·2 to 1 (as high as Pool petrol would allow) early production engines were giving 50 b.h.p. at 4,100 r.p.m.

Much testing took place on Yorkshire test hills, including Sutton Bank. This is the second prototype with its designer at the wheel; it will be noted that the four doors are no longer interchangeable (as they had been on the first prototype) but all panels are very flat, for fabrication by simple methods. Bonnet and grille were changed before the car went into production, and at this stage a flat two-piece Vee windscreen was used.
(Photo: Mr. Gerald Palmer)

Designers are sometimes blamed for lack of personal experience with their creations. This was certainly not true of Palmer, who was one of the crew in the Javelin's first Monte Carlo Rally in 1949, shortly before he left the Company. He is standing on the right; on the left are T. C. (Cuth) Harrison and T. C. (Tommy) Wise. They won the 1½-litre class; another Javelin was third. Compare the grille on this car with that of the prototype.
(Photo: Mr. Gerald Palmer)

Between 1942 and May 1947 when the Javelin was unveiled to the public, new men and new money made themselves felt. The prototypes had proved so promising that production plans were changed. The car need no longer be made at home; the lines were not altered, but production methods were. Briggs Bodies obtained the contract to make pressed-steel coachwork for the Javelin along conventional industrial lines, and built a factory at Doncaster for the purpose.

Designed by Gerald Palmer in 1942, the Jowett Javelin worked on the modern principle of 'being quite small outside, but very large inside'. All the shaded area is passenger space. High 'Colonial' ground clearance permits a flat floor, and the compact flat-four engine takes up little room for'ard. A 'commanding' prow was chosen in preference to a falling bonnet à la pre-war Fiat 1100, the general lines of the car being modelled on those of the V-12 Lincoln Zephyr. It will be noted that all passengers are seated within the wheelbase. The back seat ride, especially, was excellent. (Jowett Cars Ltd.)

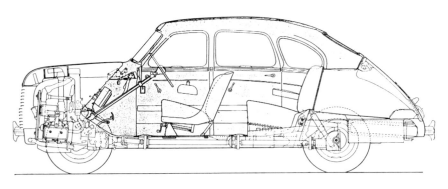

Encouraged by the Monte Carlo results the Jowett Company entered an early production Javelin in the 1949 24 Hours Race at Spa, an event that is every bit as testing as Le Mans. Tommy Wisdom and Tony Hume were the drivers, and this exceedingly normal 1,500 c.c. saloon won the 2-litre Touring Car class after an untroubled run, covering 1,700 miles at an average of 65.5 m.p.h. (Photos: Mr. Louis Klemantaski)

Gestation was slow, bedevilled by wartime and post-war shortages; but the last prototype took part in the 'Motoring Cavalcade' round London in 1946, and during the next couple of years production cars began to emerge. Most of them were exported, for quite a large dealer network had been built up.

THE JAVELIN PERFORMS

In January 1949 the Works entered a car for the Monte Carlo Rally. The crew consisted of T. C. (Tommy) Wise and T. C. (Cuth) Harrison, both well-known Yorkshire trials and rally men, and Gerald Palmer, the car's designer. It is not true that designers never experience their cars. The Javelin won the 1½-litre class and a similar car (R. Smith) was third. Later in the year a Javelin went racing: T. H. Wisdom and Anthony Hume drove a single works car in the Belgian 24-hours race at Spa. They had a trouble-free run, covering 1,700 miles in the time, to win their class at 65·5 m.p.h., the fastest touring car on the circuit.

The motoring papers liked the car very much. *The Motor* (20th July 1949) recorded a top speed of 77·6 m.p.h., 0–50 m.p.h. in 15·3 secs., a standing quarter-mile in 22·7 secs. (almost the same as the 0–60 figure) and 25·6 m.p.g. over a long fast Continental mileage, adding that a tame Javelin on the Staff regularly gave 30 m.p.g. in England. They praised the headroom and legroom, were greatly impressed by the ride ('rode bad *pavé* with complete absence of shock and a remarkable absence of pitch, no doubt [owing to] the large proportion of weight carried between the front wheels'); they called the steering-column gear-change 'a model of its kind', admired the cornering but thought the brakes rather small. They also found the 7·31 third gear rather low.

Other Javelin successes that year included the Austrian Touring Club's Winter Trial (2-litre class; driver: Wohrer), and a hill-climb Rheineck-Walzenhausen (1½-litre class, touring; driver: Vogelsang). The model being now firmly established, Gerald Palmer returned south to M.G./Riley at Abingdon. He is now with Vauxhall.

Palmer's place as chief designer was taken by Roy C. Lunn, who came from Aston Martin and is currently with the Ford Motor Company in America on racing and advanced developments. One of his first tasks was the development of a new front suspension for the Javelin in conjunction with Metalastik Ltd., which was probably the first all-rubber-mounted suspension in production. The designs were also begun for a two-seater sports car based on the Javelin and using the same engine. But before looking at that machine

The inside story of how Professor Robert Eberan von Eberhorst (designer of the 1938-39 3-litre Auto Union G.P. racing cars) came to design the Jupiter is told in the text. Here is Professor Eberan with one of the six prototypes built in the E.R.A. works at Dunstable. (Photo: Mr. Laurence Pomeroy)

it may be interesting to see how the saloon progressed over the years. On 8th April 1953 *The Motor* tested a later Javelin, this time over 2,500 miles in England, Belgium and Germany, and found it a faster and much improved car. The engine now gave 52·5 b.h.p. at 4,500 r.p.m. and top speed was 82·4 m.p.h. with a best run of 84·1; top-gear acceleration above 40 m.p.h. had slowed slightly, but third was now higher (6·7 to 1, 61 m.p.h.) and the standing quarter-mile was now 20·9 sec. The testers (the present writer was one of them) found the engine smoother than before; they said the back-seat ride was better than one got in many chauffeur-driven cars. The overall petrol consumption came out at 29·1 m.p.g., and this included some fast motorway running, e.g. 27 miles of busy Belgium *autoroute* without the speed ever falling below a corrected 75 m.p.h. In spite of terrible frost-rutted roads in Hanover and much high-speed running nothing whatever came loose or gave trouble. It was very impressive for a 1½-litre saloon, but one driver at least came away slightly disappointed. One expects unorthodox design to produce 'personality'—but the Javelin, for all its flat four and torsion bars, seemed oddly anonymous. Perhaps this was no bad thing for an internationally marketed saloon.

THE JUPITER DESIGN

When Lunn took over in 1949 the cry, quite rightly, was still 'export or perish'. Steel was rationed and larger allocations went only to firms who could show their determination to export. M.G. were already selling well in the U.S.A. with their cart-sprung TC Midget, virtually a pre-war design, and had

created an American market for sports cars. Obviously the Jowett ploy was to market a sports car too, thus earning dollars and incidentally getting more steel. A tentative start was made at Idle, under the stimulus of that very keen racing and rally driver, Anthony Hume. But before these plans got very far the programme was suddenly and somewhat catalytically changed, the catalyst being the late Laurence Pomeroy, then technical editor of *The Motor*. It so happened that Pomeroy had a number of friends all interested in the development of a sports car: Leslie Johnson, the racing driver, had just acquired E.R.A. Ltd., Dunstable; Robert Eberan von Eberhorst, designer of the 1939 Auto Union racing cars, was in Italy with Cisitalia and hating it; and George Wansbrough, who had been put in by Lazard Bros. as joint managing director at Idle. The name 'Jupiter' was an alliterative natural, also provided by Pomeroy. Anthony Hume, who had been put in charge of the sports car project, fetched Professor Eberan from the Continent, and E.R.A. Ltd. were charged with producing a Jupiter sports car at Dunstable, using Javelin engine, transmission and suspension units. The bodies were designed by Mr. Korner, of Jowetts.

Professor Eberan got smartly to work, evolving a chassis that was far more sophisticated than anything a mass-producer could have attempted, so that the Jupiter started with a big advantage in road holding, which all road testers commented upon. As will be seen, the car's limitation was the engine, which had been designed many years before, with no thought of racing in mind. The semi-space frame comprised a pair of tubular longerons roughly below the seats, stoutly braced by a St Andrew's cross; a triangulated structure of tubes carried the front i.f.s., and another, more elongated, rose to upper rim height just behind the seats and continued aft in the manner of dumb-irons. Sturdy cross tubes tied it all together. Certain components were specially made, including a rack-and-pinion steering. Technical liaison between Idle and Dunstable does not seem to have been either happy or complete, and, following a change of policy soon after the 1949 Motor Show, when the Jupiter was very well received, development became the responsibility of the factory. Early cars were hardly stiff enough amidships (doors used to stick) and E.R.A. engineers thought that the height and weight of the Jowett bodywork rather spoiled both

The Jupiter chassis designed by Prof. Eberan employed tubes for lightness and strength. This picture clearly shows the main tubes, cruciform bracing and triangulated structure at the rear, where the transverse torsion bars and Panhard rod can also be seen. One front torsion-bar anchorage can be seen behind the front wheel; Note also the divided propeller-shaft and steering-column gear change. Later cars derived extra torsional rigidity from a pressed steel dashboard bulkhead welded to the main longerons. (Photo: Telegraph & Argus, Bradford)

Jupiter development team. Six cars were built at Dunstable under the original E.R.A. contract; subsequent development took place in the Jowett works at Idle, near Bradford. From left to right: Messrs. Horace Grimley, experimental engineer, Roy C. Lunn, chief designer, and Charles Grandfield, chief engineer, with the 1950 Le Mans car. (Photo: Telegraph & Argus, Bradford)

performance and handling which, to quote David Hodkin, technical assistant to Prof. Eberan 'had been developed during the early part of 1950 to very competitive standards for those days'.

Everyone must have worked very hard indeed. Restarting from scratch in May, Eberan and a drawing office which gradually increased in numbers from one to four had their chassis ready in time for a complete car to appear at the Motor Show the same October. The body had a bench seat to take advantage of the steering-column gear-lever inherited from the Javelin and seems in retrospect to have been rather high in the scuttle for a flat-four design, and unnecessarily tapering behind, which made luggage accommodation very small. The glass industry was not yet making curved screens in quantity, so the Jupiter, like the prototype Javelins, had a two-piece vee screen. It also had glass quarter-lights adjoining the screen and winding glass windows, so that with hood up it was more 'convertible' than two-seater.

Most courageously a car was entered for the 1950 Le Mans, with a single bucket seat and an aero screen. After a lot of hard work it was able to weigh-in at 15½ cwt., complete with tankage for 30 gallons. The drivers were Tommy Wisdom and Tommy Wise, who had both wrought valiantly in Javelins the previous year. They not only had a trouble-free run

but set a new 1½-litre record for the race, won their class and averaged 75·84 m.p.h. for the 24 hours. A very fine effort indeed for a new model running in its first race.

Tuning was virtually limited to the modifications listed for the ordinary owner: special gasket and stronger cylinder-head studs raising the compression ratio to 8·5 to 1; stronger inner valve-springs, high-speed distributor, lightened flywheel, racing plugs. A similar car, although this time a fully equipped drop-head and weighing 18½ cwt., was tested by *The Motor* on 22nd November 1950. Speeds on second, third and top were 41, 66 and 86 (with a best run at 88 m.p.h.) standstill to 50 m.p.h. through the gears took 11·7 sec., to 60, 18 sec., to 70, 29·6 sec., and the standing quarter 20·5. Fuel consumption was 25 m.p.g. They praised the top-gear pulling (10–30 in 9·7 sec., 20–40 in 9 sec., 30–50 in 10·7 sec.), the flat cornering and the light steering. 'A minor tendency to over-steer is apparent, but makes itself felt in a mildly progressive manner. . . .' The gear-change was light, quick and easy, although the gears were not very quiet and the body lacked sound-damping; there was not much room for the right foot, because of the way

Class winner. A Jupiter was entered for Le Mans in 1950, a single car running its first race. It won the 1½-litre class, setting a new class record at 75.8 m.p.h. The drivers were T. H. Wisdom (seen here) and T. C. Wise. The body, it will be noted, was practically a standard convertible. (Photo: Mr. Louis Klemantaski)

Some last minute adjustments at Le Mans, 1950. The racing dash is very neat, a steering-column shift unusual on a competition car. Jowetts were one of the first production cars to have a fully opening front. (Photo: Mr. Louis Klemantaski)

Both Javelin and Jupiter had a successful 1951 season in rallies hill-climbs, and races both short and long. Here is the Jupiter of Marcel Becquart and Gordon Wilkins at Le Mans, where Jowett won the 1½-litre class for the second year running. This was the only finisher in the class, other more highly tuned Jupiters having suffered severe engine trouble. (Photo: Mr. Louis Klemantaski)

the wheel arches encroached on the foot space (as in the Javelin) and the hand-brake was not easy to reach. On the whole they quite liked the Jupiter, which was the fastest 1½-litre car they had tested since the war. This car had mechanically adjusted tappets instead of Zero-Lash (because the U.S. patentees could no longer supply), and later machines were to have hydraulic brakes all round instead of Girling Hydro-Mech, the report said.

IN COMPETITION

Competition work continued keenly in 1951. Jowett again won their class in the Monte Carlo Rally, doing well with both models: the Jupiter of W. H. Robinson and R. Ellison was 1st in the 1½-litre class, and equal-best British competitor; Gordon Wilkins and Raymond Baxter were 2nd in another Jupiter, while L. Odell and R. Marshall took 4th place in their Javelin. Thus Jowett won the Manufacturers' Team prize. A Javelin (Sven Servais) won the Swedish Winter Trial, Joachim Nogueira won the Lisbon Rally (Jupiter), and there were some highly promising race results. A Jupiter (Gurzeler) won the Brem-garten sports car race at Berne, and the same driver again made best time at Rheineck-Walzenhausen; and a much lightened Jupiter, called the R-1, again won its class at Le Mans, driven by Marcel Becquart and Gordon Wilkins, being the only car in its class to finish; a companion, more highly tuned car, blew its head gaskets. In the R.A.C. Ulster Tourist Trophy

H. L. Hadley and Tommy Wise took 1st and 2nd places in their class, and it must have been very stimulating to hear that another Jupiter had won the 1½-litre race at Watkins Glen, the most important meeting in the United States, the most important export market. In addition to which, Roy Lunn, the chief designer, co-driving with Marcel Becquart, won the closed car section of the British R.A.C. Rally. The hat-trick was completed the following summer when Becquart and Wilkins again won the 1½-litre class at Le Mans.

Behind this catalogue of victory lay much hard work in getting weight off the cars, stiffening the chassis to improve road-holding, and extracting far higher—and ultimately reliable—power from the engine. The men responsible included Roy Lunn, Charles Grandfield, chief engineer, Horace Grimley, development engineer, and Korner the coachwork man. It is interesting to recall that Horace Grimley had been co-driver with J. J. Hall at Brooklands in 1926 when a Jowett 7 h.p. two-seater, of all unlikely cars, had broken the world's international class record for 12 hours—at 54 m.p.h.

The tremendous technical effort has been described by Mr. C. D. Grandfield, A.M.I.Mech.E., in his paper, 'Development Problems Experienced in Engines of Unorthodox Design', read before the Institution of Mechanical Engineers in 1952. This paper was summarised in *Motor Sport* of March 1953. I am most grateful to Mr Grandfield for lending me his copies of both versions. It is possible unfortunately only to give the barest summary of how the power was increased from 42 b.h.p. on the original 1,500 c.c. prototype to about 68 on the 1952 Le Mans car, which had a 9·25 to 1 c.r. It must be remembered that experiments were greatly hindered during the early post-war years by the British government's obstinacy in refusing to allow high-octane petrols. The company's interest in racing was directly due to the high-speed conditions which they realised would await Javelin and Jupiter cars on modern European motorways. The principal weakness of the engine came from the use of a split crankcase, with long bolts to hold the cylinder-heads down. Prolonged full-throttle work meant blown gaskets and, as power was increased by nearly 50 per cent, broken crankshafts. The position of the sparking-plugs in the Jupiter also caused difficulty, as they were enveloped in spray from the front wheels. This last trouble was cured by using Lucas plug covers evolved for A.J.S. motor cycles.

The original requirement for the Jupiter was 60 b.h.p. at 4,750 r.p.m. on 76–80 octane at 8 to 1 compression ratio. Polishing and streamlining the ports brought this within easy compass, but once 8 to 1 was exceeded crankshaft fatigue set in. The Jupiter in the 1950 R.A.C. T.T. broke its crankshaft. Accordingly the crankcase was stiffened by thicker sections and stiffer webs; the crank itself was modified and so was lubrication. New bearing materials were tried. Much gasket research ended in the cylinder-head gaskets being thrown away and replaced by Wills rings—endless thin steel tubes filled during manufacture with a chemical giving off nitrogen when heated. The rings expanded, filling the joint between head and liner. This settled the head-seal problem and improved water seals were used at the lower end of the liners. Exhaust-valve troubles were solved by making the valves of KE 965, with chromed stems and Stellited tips. There was much experimenting with piston rings; an oil-cooler was fitted.

Jupiters came first and second in their class (1,500 c.c.) in the 1951 R.A.C. Tourist Trophy on the Dundrod circuit in Ulster. H. L. (Bert) Hadley, the pre-war Austin works single-seater driver (no. 45) was first, at 68.71 m.p.h.; second was Tommy Wise. (Photo: Mr. Louis Klemantaski).

The R-1 Jupiter evolved for the 1951 Le Mans was 1½ cwt. lighter than the standard car, and handled much better at speed, thanks to a strong pressed-steel scuttle bulkhead and a similar member behind the seats welded to the chassis longerons. Its frontal area was smaller, giving a top speed just over the 100 m.p.h.; but the c.r. was up to 9·25 and after four hours' running a cylinder-head stud boss cracked, water leaked into the sump and the bearings ran. But it was also an R-1 that was so successful at Watkins Glen.

Three R-1 Jupiters were entered for the 1952 Le Mans. One, driven by Wilkins and Becquart, won its class as we know, but the others (Bert Hadley and Gatsonides) broke their cranks. The final solution shall be given in Mr Grandfield's words: 'This crankshaft business was now one of some real concern. Within the scantlings and without going to exotic materials, we had done what we could and felt that the series III Javelin was pretty safe. Nevertheless, we liaised with the stress experts at De Havillands, particularly Dr. Kerr Wilson, who had had trouble of this nature, but on 5,000 h.p. flat marine engines.

'His investigation was of interest and produced the elliptical web design of shaft . . . ' The elliptical webs and redistributed web thickness provided the answer; the new crank went into production in mid-1953, in what was called the Mark III engine, which powered the Mark III Javelin and later the Jupiters Marks I and IA. The IA had a longer bonnet and a bigger luggage boot, with an outside lid.

Meanwhile some other interesting things were happening at Idle. Production of the Javelin during the early nineteen-fifties was running at about 150 a week. The company were also making about the same number of Bradford vans, which used the famous side-valve horizontally opposed twin that had been developing since 1910.

A NEW RANGE

In 1951 a new range of products was started, based on a common chassis arrangement. This chassis had a wheelbase of 84 in. (9 in. shorter than the Jupiter, 18 in. shorter than the Javelin). The torsion-bar i.f.s. was retained, but the new chassis had semi-elliptics

at the rear. Mr Roy Lunn has kindly written about these vehicles from America: 'A new twin-cylinder engine was developed having an overhead inlet with a side exhaust valve. The same chassis would take the opposed-four and was made in van, pickup, station wagon and car forms. It was also a derivative of this same product line from which I derived the R-4 vehicle with the plastic body. Unfortunately these never did reach the production stage, as the company

Hat trick: Jupiter cars won the 1½-litre class three years in succession at Le Mans. Marcel Becquart looks relatively comfortable at the wheel of the victorious 1952 R1, but Gordin Wilkins is finding the passenger's seat rather a tight fit. They averaged 72.85 m.p.h., finishing 13th over all. (Photo: Mr. Louis Klemantaski)

In 1951 work was started on a new range of products based on a common chassis arrangement. This would take either a new i.o.e. twin or the opposed-four engine and was to have been made in van, station wagon, pick-up and car forms. It also formed the basis of the R4 sports car with plastic body here displayed by Theo Page. Rear springs were semi-elliptic. (Drawing: Mr. Theo Page)

because it was probably gearboxes that brought Jowetts to an end. One sometimes hears 'ruthless Big Business Interests' blamed for the Jowett demise; but the main cause seems to have been a mistaken decision to manufacture the gearbox at Idle, instead of buying it out from Henry Meadows Ltd. There were, literally, teething troubles. Defective gearboxes clogged the assembly and service departments at Idle and caused a fall-off in sales. As a result, the Briggs plant at Doncaster, which had been built specially for Jowett, found undelivered bodies piling up; and before the backlog could be cleared the poor old Jowett company was in trouble. The plant was sold to International Harvester. The Jowett cars had a considerable following and made many friends. The Javelin's ground clearance paid off, as its designer knew it would; and Gerald Palmer, who goes often to Spain, says that Javelins are still to be seen on the Spanish roads in 1966.

No other motor manufacturer can approach Jowett's record of only five models in more than half a century—Twin, Jason 10 h.p., Bradford van, Javelin, Jupiter. What is more, the Southern Jowett Motor Club is the oldest one-make club in the world. It is a shame those new models never appeared.

* * *

In conclusion I should like to thank all those who have helped in compiling these notes, especially the following ex-Jowett people (in alphabetical order): Messrs John Baldwin, C. D. Grandfield, David Hodkin (ex-E.R.A. Ltd.), Roy C. Lunn and Gerald Palmer, together with my friends the late Laurence Pomeroy and Peter Richley, who has lent much valuable material.

© *D. B. Tubbs, 1966.*

was sold out about the time they were announced. . . . We had started designs on an in-line-six overhead cam arrangement as a replacement for the four-cylinder opposed engine, and were planning to maintain a luxury car image with a sporting flavour. . . .'

The R-4 Jupiter evolved by Roy Lunn was a neat little two-seater with laminated plastic body of remarkably clean design; it was rather like the present-day Sprite and Midget to look at, and was to have a four-speed gearbox with overdrive on third and top. It was to weigh only 14 cwt. Some publicity brochures were got out, giving details and speeds on the gears. The latter make interesting reading: on an 8 to 1 c.r. and 4·44 axle ratio the R-4 was to do 27, 44, 70, 82, 100 and 122 m.p.h. on its various gears at 6,000 r.p.m., the peak being given as 5,000 revs. That oval-webbed crank would be coming into its own.

It is appropriate to close on the subject of gears,

Le Mans 1952: Marcel Becquart in profile. This picture shows how the racing R1 cars differed from the original convertibles. Note the slimmer lines, and skimpy wings. A great deal of weight has been shed and the engine developed to withstand higher compression ratios. (Photo: Mr. Louis Klemantaski)

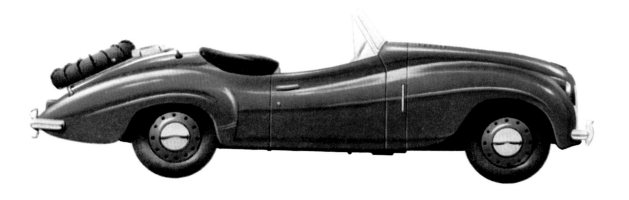

THE 1951 MONTE CARLO RALLY JOWETT JUPITER which won the 1½-litre Class and finished 6th overall. Drivers: W. H. Robinson and R. Ellison.

Designed in 1951, the R4 Jupiter looked well ahead of its time, the lines foreshadowing those of several current two-seaters. With 64 b.h.p. for a kerb weight of 1,568 pounds (14 cwt.) the little car should have performed very well. Unfortunately the Jowett company was wound up before the R4 reached production. (Photo: Mr. Roy Lunn & C. H. Wood (Bradford) Ltd.)

SPECIFICATION: JOWETT JAVELIN
(1949 Model unless otherwise stated)

Engine: Four-cylinder, horizontally-opposed, overhead valves. 72·5 mm. bore, 90 mm. stroke, 1,486 c.c., 50 b.h.p. at 4,100 r.p.m. Compression ratio 7·2 : 1. Diecast aluminium cylinder block (DTD 133B) with wet cast iron liners. Valves pushrod operated from central cast iron, four-throw, three-bearing crankshaft. Cast iron cylinder heads. Twin Zenith carburettors. Sump capacity 9 pints. Coil ignition. Cooling by water pump and fan thermostatically controlled. Capacity 12 pints. Firing order 1, 4, 2, 3.

Transmission: Four-speed gearbox. Steering column control lever. Ratios: 4·87; 7·31; 11·6; 18·9 to 1. 7¼-in. Borg & Beck clutch. Salisbury hypoid rear axle. Divided prop.-shaft with three 'Layrub' universals. Top gear speed per 1,000 r.p.m.— 15·5 m.p.h.

Suspension: Front, independent by unequal length wishbones and longitudinal torsion bars; rear, transverse torsion bars, beam axle. Woodhead Monroe shock absorbers. Pressed steel wheels 16 in. diam., 5·25 × 16 tyres.

Chassis Construction: Integral body and subframe of steel construction.

Dimensions: Wheelbase, 102 in. Track, front, 51 in.; rear, 49 in. Overall height, 60½ in. Overall width, 61 in. Overall length, 168 in. Minimum ground clearance, 7¾ in. Turning circle, 32 ft.

Weight: 1949: 20¾ cwt. *Distribution*: 54/56 front/rear.

1950: 20½ cwt.	,,	,,	,,
1952: 21½ cwt.	,,	,,	,,
1953: 21¼ cwt.	,,	,,	,,

Steering gear: Internal gear and pinion.

Brakes: Hydro-Mech; 1951 Girling hydraulic.

Electrical equipment: 12-volt system with 60 amp-hour battery.

Fuel system: 8 gallons in rear-mounted tank. A.C. mechanical pump.

1952 MODIFICATIONS

Engine: Oil cooler.

Transmission: Indirect gear ratios now 6·6; 10·6; 17·4 to 1.

Suspension: Metalastik joints in i.f.s.

1953 SERIES III MODIFICATIONS

Engine: Mechanical tappets. New oval-web crankshaft.

Performance (1953): 12·5 b.h.p. at 1,000 r.p.m.; 28 b.h.p. at 2,000 r.p.m.; 42 b.h.p. at 3,000 r.p.m.; 51 b.h.p. at 4,000 r.p.m.; Maximum 52·5 b.h.p. at 4,500 r.p.m. Maximum torque 76 lb. ft. at 2,600 r.p.m.

Price (de luxe): 1949: £750 + £209 p.t. = £959.
1950: £735 + £409 p.t. = £1,144.
1952: £810 + £451 p.t. = £1,261.
1953: £775 + £432 p.t. = £1,207.

SPECIFICATION: JOWETT JUPITER
(1952 Model unless otherwise stated)

As for Jowett Javelin with the following differences:
Engine: Compression ratio 7·6 or 8 to 1. Output, 60 b.h.p. at 4,750 r.p.m.

Transmission: Gear ratios: 4·56; 6·30; 9·9; 16·3 to 1. Top gear speed per 1,000 r.p.m.—17 m.p.h. Divided prop. shaft. One 'Layrub' and two Hardy-Spicer universals.

Suspension: Front, independent by unequal length wishbones; rear, two pairs of twin trailing arms and Panhard rod; transverse torsion bars. Pressed steel ventilated disc wheels, 5·50 × 16 tyres.

Chassis Construction: Semi-space frame of tubular welded construction using 3 in. diam. 16 s.w.g. tubes in chrome molybdenum steel for main side members and 18 gauge 2 in. diam. tubes for struts and torsional stiffness members.

Dimensions: Wheelbase, 93 in. Track, front, 52 in.; rear, 50½ in. Overall height, 56 in. Overall width, 62 in. Overall length, 168 in. Minimum ground clearance, 8 in.

Weight: 17 cwt. approx. (1,895 lb). *Distribution* 55/45 front/ rear.

Steering: Rack and pinion.

Brakes: Girling hydraulic.

Fuel Capacity: 10 gallons.

Performance: 13·25 b.h.p. at 1,000 r.p.m.; 30·75 b.h.p. at 2,000 r.p.m.; 48 b.h.p. at 3,000 r.p.m.; 60 b.h.p. at 4,000 r.p.m.; 62·5 at 4,500 r.p.m. Maximum torque 84 lb. ft. at 3,000 r.p.m.

Price: 1950: £850 + £236 p.t. = £1,086.
1952: £975 + £543 p.t. = £1,518.

The handling and cornering powers of the Jupiter were much praised by car critics; they also provided much amusing racing for the private owner. Here W. H. Robinson is seen taking the chicane at a B.A.R.C. meeting at Goodwood on March 22, 1952. (Photo: Mr. Guy Griffiths)

The 40/50 Napier

NAPIER

1921 40/50 H.P. NAPIER (with later modifications) with Saloon body by Maythorn & Son Ltd., based on the car on exhibition in the Land Transport Section of the Science Museum, London. (*Above* and *centre left.*)

1920 40/50 H.P. NAPIER with Coupé Cabriolet body by the Cunard Motor & Carriage Co. Ltd. Owner: Murray G. Beecroft, Esquire. (Previous owners: Ronald Barker, Esquire, and Philip Hingley, Esquire). (*Centre right and below*).

The 40/50 Napier

by Ronald Barker

Almost from the very start, in 1919, there was little or no more hope for the 40/50 h.p. Napier than for the 'thin red line' of the Light Brigade, so surely were the odds loaded against its commercial success. For one thing, Montague Napier himself is said to have decided before this model was even put into production that he would not continue manufacturing cars for more than a very few years following World War I, pinning his faith in the aero engine industry as his company's most logical field for future activity. If there had been any chance that he might be persuaded to modify this view, it was damned by a succession of setbacks that sealed the 40/50's doom long before the 187th and last had been sold in 1924.

Of these the few that are generally known to have survived could be counted on the fingers of one hand, whereas Rolls-Royces of the period could almost be said to proliferate; and the percentage of Bentleys, for instance, that still remain in use after a total production run of little over a decade is almost unbelievably high. Was this Napier, then, a poor car? If not, why were almost all of them pulverized under the scrap merchants' hammers and torches before the Vintage movement could save them?

This car was designed to compete directly with the Rolls-Royce Silver Ghost as one of the world's super cars, and like the 40 h.p. Lanchester, Leyland Eight, vee-12 Super Fiat and others, it fell short of the mark in overall excellence while bettering the Derby product in certain respects.

If the Napier had had the advanced braking system and more up-to-date steering and roadholding qualities of, say, the Hispano-Suiza of the period, coupled with the Rolls-Royce's mechanical refinement in transmission and that car's superior elegance, it could well have succeeded in its aims. But even then probably it would have failed through early production difficulties and, one guesses, lack of a parallel sales impetus behind it and service facilities to support it. As it was, the Napier's engine design was streets ahead of that of the current Rolls-Royce, and the same unit could have been developed to maintain this ascendency over the later overhead valve Phantom I Rolls-Royce introduced in 1925; but in most other respects it was decidedly inferior to the R-R. The chassis design in general showed little advance over Napier's pre-World War I products and did not match the advanced thinking incorporated in its power unit.

THE DESIGNER

The car as a whole was credited to A. J. Rowledge, who had been responsible for the astonishing Lion aero engine completed just too late to take an active part in the Great War yet still sufficiently potent (in supercharged form) for the late John Cobb to use it in the Railton Mobil Special when taking the World Land Speed Record for the last time in 1947—reaching over 400 m.p.h. in one direction.

Certainly the Rowledge imprint is etched deeply in the 40/50 engine, but if he was also concerned with this car's transmission and chassis design, then clearly he was there out of his depth. It seems more likely that he passed on this responsibility to a less competent subordinate, or that he knew no better than to follow 1914 concepts rather than break new ground. Moreover, the wealthy buyer was not concerned with the merits of a compact power unit,

1919 Cunard-bodied three-quartered cabriolet.

55

1921 Cunard aluminum-decked tourer with concealed hood.

which allowed the bonnet to be considerably shorter than those of other luxury cars of the period. He liked to have a long bonnet stretching before him as an outward and visible indication of his opulence. Another factor contributing to the car's failure may have been Napier's acquisition of the Cunard Motor and Carriage Co., who thus almost monopolised the 40/50's coachwork design and construction, whereas the Rolls-Royce policy of patronising a wide number of coachbuilders obviously made for freedom and variety of design.

Napier had pursued an utterly different course to Rolls-Royce before the Great War, with products ranging from a humble 10 h.p. twin-cylinder to a vast 90 h.p. 14½-litre six. When production ceased in 1914 the range comprised 4-cylinder cars of 15, 16 and 20 h.p., and two sixes—the 30/35 and 45 h.p. The latter's engine, incidentally, had the same bore and stroke (4 × 5 in.) as the later 40/50, but was a big side-valve on entirely conventional lines.

When the war ended Montague Napier was in poor health and living, like Henry Royce, in France.

Sedan by Cunard at the 1921 London Motor Show. The interior was panelled in Chinese lacquer. Note the 'Rapson Unpuncturable Pneumatic Tyres' and the rear part of the body carried separately on C-springs.

H. T. Vane was Chairman of the Board. Although it was stated that A. J. Rowledge had designed the 40/50 in 1918, it seems probable that the engine at least must have been on the drawing-board before then.

Six prototypes of the T75 (type number of the basic 40/50) were built, and by July 1919 work on these had reached the stage where the board had sufficient confidence in the project to authorize 500 production cars to be put in hand—of which only about 38 per cent were ever completed. Meanwhile Napiers first gave the Cunard Motor and Carriage Company a helping hand financially, and later

A wire-wheeled tourer built for the King of Siam in 1921, on the Colonial chassis which provided extra ground clearance.

Limousine-landaulet with division by Cunard, supplied to the Lord Mayor of Cardiff in 1921. Note the oil as well as electric sidelamps.

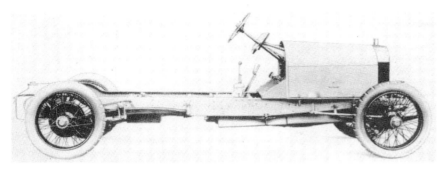

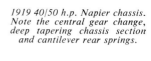

1919 40/50 h.p. Napier chassis. Note the central gear change, deep tapering chassis section and cantilever rear springs.

bought a controlling interest.

In October 1919 *The Autocar* published its first full (and fulsome) description of the new car, when the chassis price was given as £1,750, and the following month there were no less than four exhibits on the company's stand at the Olympia Motor Show—a bare chassis, limousine, sporting phaeton and cabriolet. Then the setbacks started, with labour troubles at the Acton factory that so delayed the production schedule that chassis did not start passing to the coachbuilders until June of 1920, according to one source. Next the coachbuilders' working hours were reduced, followed by a strike at Cunard, and so it went on. From March 1920 Cunard were compelled to impose a 15 per cent increase on the prices of all their bodies. According to Lord Montagu's book *Lost Causes of Motoring*, the final figures for completed chassis when production ceased at the end of 1924 were:

T.75 (standard)	120
T.77 (colonial)	17
T.79 (long wheelbase)	45
T.80 (short wheelbase)	5

Obviously appreciating the technical strength of the latest Napier aero and car engines, Rolls-Royce enticed Rowledge to Derby, where he remained until his retirement in 1945, I suspect most closely concerned with that company's aeronautical projects.

PERFORMANCE AND HANDLING

Meanwhile the motoring journals ran several tests of the 40/50 in which the car's engine performance, tractability, extraordinary mechanical refinement and quietness drew the highest praise. *The Motor*, on 22 August 1922, praised '*its almost amazing top-gear performance. For all practical purposes this latest production of a very famous concern is a top-gear car... The exhaust of the Napier is noiseless, and its engine absolutely cannot be heard if the car is anywhere near other traffic. With top gear engaged one can get away as smoothly and as swiftly from a standstill as the most fastidious would require . . . the car glides forward as though pulled by an elastic band . . . We should, in fact, put top-gear hill-climbing at the head of the long list*'. The testers found it took famous Fish Hill out of Broadway in top with great ease.

The Autocar ran it up to Newlands Corner from the Guildford-Leatherhead road, then to Pitch Hill beyond Shere; but finally, in a narrow lane near Cranleigh '*we actually found something which called for momentary use of third*'.

During 1921 there was a colourful interchange in *The Autocar*'s correspondence columns between the tyre manufacturer Lionel Rapson and S. F. Edge, who had received a golden handshake from Napiers nearly 10 years earlier. Rapson considered the Napier a far better car than the Rolls-Royce, whereas Edge now sided with Rolls-Royce; he thought the Napier had a very fine engine indeed, but considered it '*a long way ahead of the general arrangement of the chassis*'. I would think this a sound judgement rather than sour grapes.

Cunard tourer with individual front and rear hoods.

As the speedometer dial ran out of figures beyond 60 m.p.h., and the manufacturers quoted this as the maximum to which the car was geared, the motoring journals did not admit to exceeding this speed. However, my own 1920 cabriolet could send the needle way beyond this point to around 70, although this was clearly well over the peak of the power curve. *The Motor*'s test quoted 16 m.p.g. when averaging 30 m.p.h. on English roads with a full load, whereas *The Autocar* gave a range of 13-16 m.p.g., which agrees with my experience and seems very reasonable in relation to engine capacity and the car's all-up weight.

Although the Napier was, nevertheless, much lighter than an equivalent Silver Ghost, its steering was just as heavy at low speeds through being so high-geared. The transmission foot-brake, operating of course on the rear wheels only, was immensely powerful for a light pedal pressure while it lasted, but suffered from rapid fade and slow recovery. Linings almost a half inch thick could not carry the heat away, and an undertray projecting right back beneath the gearbox shielded them from any cooling draught. At low speeds this brake tended to roughness and would sometimes set up a rear axle patter that increased one's stopping distance. The handbrake was practically useless as a stopper.

Regarding suspension, Napier were obviously not prepared to sacrifice stability to comfort, so the car handles much better than one might have expected without giving quite such a soft ride as its luxury rating suggested. So, all in all, it is always to Rowledge's beautiful engine that one's thoughts turn when the 40/50 Napier crops up in conversation.

Towards the end of 1918 advertisements were claiming that: '*The post-war model will surpass any yet produced*', and the engine was said to have 50 per cent more power for 200 lb less weight than the equivalent pre-war product.

While the Company was justified to some extent in stating that the 40/50 unit owed much in its design to the Lion aero engine—in particular, its low weight, compactness and the use of an overhead camshaft—the detail similarities were not numerous. The 450 h.p. Lion had three banks of four cylinders in the form of a broad arrow, with an angle of 60 deg. between the vertical one and each of its neighbours. The cylinders were individual steel forgings, but each bank had a common light alloy head. There were two inlet and two exhaust valves in each combustion chamber, with separate camshafts for inlet and exhaust in each bank —six in all.

THE 40/50 ENGINE

For the 40/50 the six cylinders were formed in a single light alloy casting embracing also the upper half of the crankcase, with shrunk-in cylinder liners of cast iron. The detachable cylinder head, also of

A 1919 coupé stands beside a 1922 landaulet. Both bodies are by Cunard.

light alloy, had screwed-in valve seats of non-cor-rosive steel, and bronze inserts for the sparking-plugs. In fact, Montague Napier may well have pioneered the monobloc light alloy cylinder block casting with shrunk-in iron liners, having used this arrangement for his racing engines during 1901–5. There were two valves to each combustion chamber, operated by a single, central camshaft with tappets in the form of rocking levers (Napier Swinging Tappets) interposed between the cams and the tops of the vertical valve stems at each side.

Valve clearances were adjusted by set-screws in the tappet ends, locked by clamp bolts. The upper end of the valve stem was threaded, a locknut on this securing the upper valve spring carrier, which ex-tended down to form a cap over the valve guide and so restrict the quantity of oil that could reach the combustion chamber by that route.

Lubrication of the valve gear was very thorough. The main oil feed ran up to the front camshaft bearing, where it was divided between four outlets—one into the hollow camshaft which lubricated its own 7 bearings, one to each of the two rocker shafts, and one to spray over the upper worm and wheel that drove it. The tappets were formed with a trough in the middle to contain a roller follower in contact with the cam, the trough being lubricated through a drilling in the tappet. An extra cam on the shaft actuated a small plunger air pump mounted on top of the light alloy valve cover, to pressurize the rear fuel tank. A hand pump on the dash supplied the initial pressure after the tank had been opened for re-fuelling, or when the car had been standing for some hours.

An interesting refinement was a camshaft brake or damper. This took the form of a disc rubbing against the forward face of the bronze wormwheel, with adjustable spring-loading. No doubt it contributed to a valve gear almost inaudible at any speed from idling to full revs. In fact, the only separately identi-fiable noise at tickover was the *click-click* of the ignition contact points closing in the magneto and coil distributor.

Although each inlet valve was supplied through a separate port, the manifold was cast integral with the head, on the off-side; on the opposite side the exhaust ports were served by a six-branch casting swept up to clear the horizontal sparking-plugs. There were no external pipes for the cooling system, the pump feeding water to front of the cylinder block and a single outlet at the front of the head returning it to the radiator.

Napier were certainly among the first to fit a bellows-type thermostat in the cooling system to by-pass the radiator until the engine was warmed. It was carried in an aluminium housing cast integral with the water pump body. A very ordinary-looking pressed steel fan with four blades was driven by a Whittle belt from a pulley on the front of the crank-shaft.

There were threaded inserts in the holes in the head through which the holding-down studs passed; and the very long sleeve nuts, which ran down through deep drillings from the top surface of the head to reach them, pressed against these inserts. Light alloy pistons each had three narrow compression rings above the gudgeon pin and one wide oil-control ring just below it, the long skirt beneath this having

An open-fronted limousine used by the Crown Prince of Sweden, who is standing beside the car, 1923.

Napier's managing director, H. T. Vane, with a balloon-tyred coupé by Cunard, 1924.

lightening holes. Tubular connecting-rods were direct-metalled at the big-ends and their caps secured by two bolts. The gudgeon pins were locked in the piston bosses by set-screws.

A fully machined crankshaft, which lacked counterweights or a vibration damper, ran in seven substantial bearings with separate white-metalled bronze shells. All the main and big-end journals were counter-bored to a large diameter to reduce weight, numbers 2, 4 and 6 mains having oil-retaining end caps since they carried the feed to the big-ends. In addition to a filter gauze below the filler cap, there were strainers on both input and output sides of the oil pump. A dial-and-pointer gauge on the off-side of the crankcase indicated the sump level.

Externally the engine was very pleasing aesthetically, its aluminium unburnished except for the water plates; curiously enough, it did not usually bear the name of its manufacturer.

Some years ago the late H. C. Tryon told me an intriguing story about one of the early development problems with this engine and how it was overcome. Tryon began as a works test driver for Napiers in the early years, became one of their star competition drivers (with one particularly brilliant season at Brooklands) and thereafter played a big part in the engineering development of the cars and aero engines. He stayed with the company after car production had ceased, to carry a large share of responsibility for the aviation designs.

When the first 40/50 prototype was put on the road, it was plagued by a distressing roughness when pulling hard at very low revs, which it was designed to do. Tryon suspected that this was a thumping from the rear main bearing, accentuated by 'diaphragming' of the crankcase, which lacked the necessary rigidity in that area due to the casting being too thin locally. By that time too many crankcases had already been cast to scrap them all if this could be avoided. Tryon's colleagues held little hope for a remedy he proposed trying, and were astonished when it did the trick. It was simply to fit a special piston with a concave crown in number 6 cylinder, to reduce the compression ratio and lighten the load on the rear main.

Confirming the truth of this, a few years ago an Australian owner visiting this country, who had just overhauled his 40/50's engine, asked me for advice; it had a bad low-speed roughness, and a repeat strip had failed to show any cause for this. Were all the pistons identical, I asked him? Certainly! So I suggested that he should have a new piston cast with concave crown for number 6. In the spare parts list included in the instruction book there is only one part number for a piston—but maybe the book was printed before the fault or the remedy were discovered

'*Under normal circumstances the start should be made in second gear*': advised this instruction book, with every justification for the engine's low-speed torque was remarkable, the gear change rather tricky, and the clutch as sweet as could be as well as exceptionally light to operate. In fact, it was usually perfectly practical to set off in third or even top on the level.

TRANSMISSION AND STEERING

The clutch was a dry, single-plate design with the friction linings riveted to the driving members, and a 5-finger release mechanism. Instead of the conventional intermediate shaft between clutch and separate gearbox, the Napier had a lattice girder casting, light

Clover-leaf 3-seat cabriolet by Cunard, 1921.

A 1924 40/50 h.p. Napier Sedanca-de-Ville.

and rigid, to unite two leather-and-steel laminated flexible couplings. To assist gear engagement with the car at rest and to speed upward changes a clutch stop was provided, in this case a small Ferodo-lined shoe which pressed against a drum cast round the gearbox input spider.

The 4-speed gearbox was a robust, straightforward design, with shafts unusually short and rigid for the day carried on substantial roller bearings. It had a central gate change with short lever movements. Bolted around the universal joint spider splined to the output shaft was a wide, cast iron drum for the

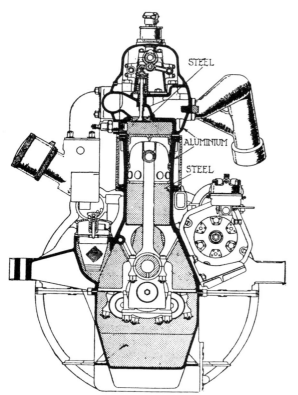

locomotive-type transmission brake; this was absent on the last few cars made, which had 4-wheel brakes.

Napier publicity made much of an anti-rolling device, built into the forward anchorage of the torque tube encasing the propeller shaft. The tube end was supported in a substantial iron casing slung from a frame cross-member by two ball-jointed links. Secured to the torque tube was a centre-piece with two 'ears' in contact with strong helical springs carried in the casing; these resisted torsional movement of the tube within the casing. Since the two links were free to swing sideways as well as fore-and-aft, the car's body was very well insulated from movements of the rear axle assembly, and the usual rear-wheel steering effects of a torque tube axle combined with cantilever springs were reduced as well. It was both clever and effective.

The front universal joint for the propeller shaft was a normal Hooke type, with steel pins in steel bushes, while the rear one was a block-and-trunnion type to allow telescopic movement. Final drive was by spiral bevel. For the handbrake there were Ferodo-lined expanding shoes within ribbed iron drums at the back wheels, very narrow and of diminutive diameter. The linings were attached to the shoes by T-head bolts instead of rivets, and for some reason there were no backplates.

A very high-geared worm-and quadrant steering mechanism was used, the steering swivels had ball thrust bearings, and the road springs were completely enclosed in leather gaiters with screw-cup lubricators. The Napier frame had tapered side members with a deep centre-section and five cross-members; for the Colonial model, with increased ground clearance, there were special side members and suspension parts.

THE NAPIER-S.U. CARBURETTOR

Of special interest was the single, water-jacketed Napier-S.U. carburettor. Although the first S.U. constant vacuum carburettor was built around 1903,

Engine cross-section, 1919. Note fingers between camshaft and valves, flat-topped drilled pistons, tubular connecting rods, sloping Napier-S.U. carburettor with metal dashpot piston, horizontal sparking plugs and camshaft-driven air pump above the valve cover for fuel system.

61

Exhaust side of the 40/50 h.p. Napier engine. Note the enclosed vertical shaft for the overhead camshaft drive, aluminium cylinder block and head. (Photo: Montagu Motor Museum)

The Napier-S.U. constant vacuum carburettor incorporates an independent starting-slow running device (on the left in this view). Five heavy leads run to the two-stage self-starter, which has a pre-engaged pinion. (Photo: Montagu Motor Museum)

it was left to Napier to develop the metal dashpot piston that superseded the old leather bellows. They also incorporated an auxiliary carburettor in the main instrument for starting and slow-running—a scheme that was reintroduced in recent years. This had a fixed jet, a strangler for cold starts and a tiny throttle butterfly; it drew air from beneath the valve cover where warmth would be retained for hours after the engine had stopped.

The engine relied completely on this pilot carburettor for idling, its speed being set by a lever on the steering-wheel boss. Another lever adjusted the mixture strength passing through the main carburettor by raising or lowering the jet in relation to the needle, in the usual way. Another pipe of small diameter connected the dashpot to the valve chamber, to feed it with what the handbook described as *'oil-bearing air'*.

H. C. Tryon told me that the carburettor was developed entirely on the test-bed, and that once the correct jets and needle had been established, no individual tuning was ever necessary. The only fault in operation was that fuel surge in the float chamber weakened the mixture when the car was driven very fast round left-hand bends, which could be overcome by lowering the jet for a moment with the mixture lever.

All the car's electrics were by C.A.V., with both battery and magneto ignition to independent sparking-plugs. Dynamo and magneto were driven in series by an auxiliary drive on the near-side, the coil ignition distributor by skew gears from the dynamo spindle. The following passage from the Instruction Book is enlightening: *The battery ignition is controlled by an automatic switch designed to switch off the current (by*

Rear axle with anti-roll device on forward end of torque tube.

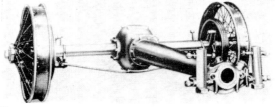

SPECIFICATION OF NAPIER 40/50 H.P.

ENGINE

6 cylinders in-line. Bore and stroke 102 × 127 mm. (4 in. × 5 in.), 6,177 c.c., R.A.C. rating 38·4 h.p. Power output, 82 b.h.p. at 2,000 r.p.m. Light alloy cylinder block with shrunk-in steel liners, and detachable light alloy head, single overhead camshaft driven by vertical shaft with worm-and-wheel gears from front of seven-bearing crankshaft. Tubular connecting-rods, aluminium alloy pistons with cast-in steel expansion control rings.
Carburettor: Napier-S.U. constant vacuum dual carburettor, with built-in auxiliary carburettor for starting and slow running. Sloping dashpot with metal piston, water-jacketed throttle body. Inlet manifold cast in head.
Ignition: Twin ignition by C.A.V. coil and magneto to sparking-plugs set horizontally in opposing sides of combustion chambers. Firing order 1–4–2–6–3–5.
Ignition and Valve Timing: Maximum advance battery ignition, 37 deg; magneto ignition, 30 deg. Valve clearances, ·002–·003 in. Inlet opens 5·5 deg a.t.d.c., closes 38 deg a.b.d.c.; exhaust opens 45 deg b.b.d.c., closes 2 deg a.t.d.c.
Lubrication: Detachable wet sump, full pressure system with rotary gear pump and external filter, 2·5–25 p.s.i. running pressure.
Cooling: Water: pump, fan and thermostat.

TRANSMISSION

Clutch: Dry single-plate with friction material riveted to pressure plate and detachable flywheel backplate. Clutch stop operating on ring around flexible leather coupling on gearbox input shaft.
Gearbox: Separate four-speed and reverse, central change, all roller bearings. Ratios: Top 3·33, 3rd 4·48, 2nd 6·00, 1st 11·80. Alternative final drive, 3·75 to 1.
Final drive: Enclosed propeller shaft in torque tube to spiral bevel drive axle.

CHASSIS

Brakes: Footbrake operating contracting fabric-lined shoes on drum behind gearbox. Handbrake operating fabric-lined expanding shoes in rear wheel drums. Late models 4-wheel brakes.
Suspension: Front, semi-elliptic leaf springs in leather gaiters. Rear, cantilever springs in leather gaiters, anti-roll device incorporated in forward anchorage of torque tube.
Wheels and tyres: Rudge-Whitworth centre-lock wire wheels, 895 × 135 beaded edge tyres. Pressures: Front, 55–60 p.s.i.; Rear, 65–70 p.s.i.
Steering: Worm and quadrant.

DIMENSIONS

Wheelbase 11 ft. 5 in. or 12 ft. Track 4 ft. 8 in. Length (chassis) 15 ft. Width 5 ft. Weight (chassis) 25 cwt.

MAXIMUM SPEEDS *(manufacturer's figures)*

3·33 final drive: top 60 m.p.h., 3rd 45, 2nd 33, 1st 18. 3·75 final drive: top 54, 3rd 40, 2nd 30, 1st 16.

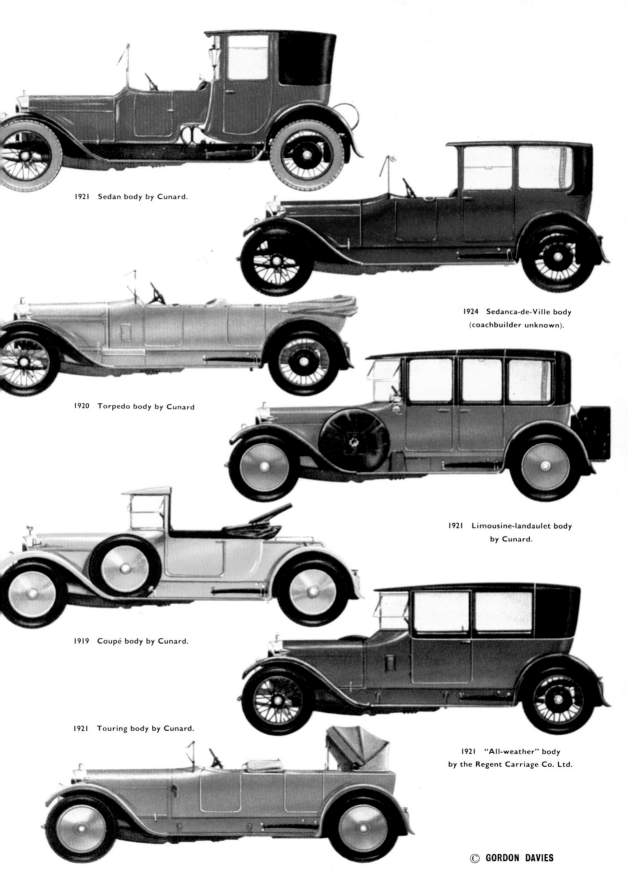

1921   Sedan body by Cunard.

1924   Sedanca-de-Ville body
(coachbuilder unknown).

1920   Torpedo body by Cunard

1921   Limousine-landaulet body
by Cunard.

1919   Coupé body by Cunard.

1921   Touring body by Cunard.

1921   "All-weather" body
by the Regent Carriage Co. Ltd.

© GORDON DAVIES

40/50 prototype? This picture, published in The Autocar *in August, 1918, probably shows a 30/35 Napier. It is, however, apparently outwardly identical to the 40/50 which did not make its début until the following year.*

the expansion of a hot wire) if the ignition is left 'on' when the engine is left standing. The two ignition systems were timed slightly out of phase, but controlled, of course, by a common lever on the steering-wheel. Maximum advance for the battery ignition was 37 deg. and for the magneto 30 deg. To operate the electric self-starter there was a two-pressure button set in the floorboard behind the driver's left heel. The first pressure pre-engaged the starter pinion with the flywheel ring, and the second set the motor turning.

*　　　　*　　　　*

While the 40/50 is not specially remembered for any epic journey or feat of endurance, its reliability and mechanical efficiency were established in the autumn of 1921 when an open touring car was put through a reasonably strenuous Alpine Trial under official R.A.C. observation. The total journey covered 2,118 miles London to London, and the party was absent for 20 days—but three of those were Sundays when it did not turn a wheel.

Most of the major Alpine passes open in those days were traversed, including such familiar ones as the Stelvio, Simplon, Mont Cenis and Pordoi. The report does not state how long these climbs took, and obviously nothing was hurried since the overall fuel consumption was to be kept as modest as possible. However, we are told that during the ascent of the Stelvio the Napier had to be reversed on 25 of the 44 hairpins, and on a further 10 during its descent the other side.

During the entire run there were 'no involuntary stops beyond those caused by five accidental stops of the engine'. Absolutely nothing was done to the car other than to fulfil the servicing and lubrication requirements as laid down in the handbook; since this involved 35 operations every 500 miles, plus a few extra ones at other intervals that would have amounted to 148 during this mileage, one wonders whether this is how much of the three Sundays was spent!

On its return the Napier was taken to Brooklands for a speed test, and before this the radiator was topped up for the first time since the car had left London. It took just over 4 pints. At the same time the oil sump was also topped up for the first time, taking one gallon. Over a half-mile on the circuit the 40/50 was timed at 72·38 m.p.h., despite the fact that this example was fitted with the low-ratio (3·75 to 1) final drive. Overall fuel consumption for the trip worked out at a very remarkable 18·7 m.p.g. and the average speed (not including stops) was 20·7 m.p.h. Other relevant statistics worth quoting include the total running weight of 46½ cwt, and the compression ratio of 4·267—an interesting figure is not quoted in any other source of information about the car.

© *Ronald Barker, 1966.*

All photographs not *acknowledged are reproduced by courtesy of* Autocar.

The 1926-27 1½-Litre Delage

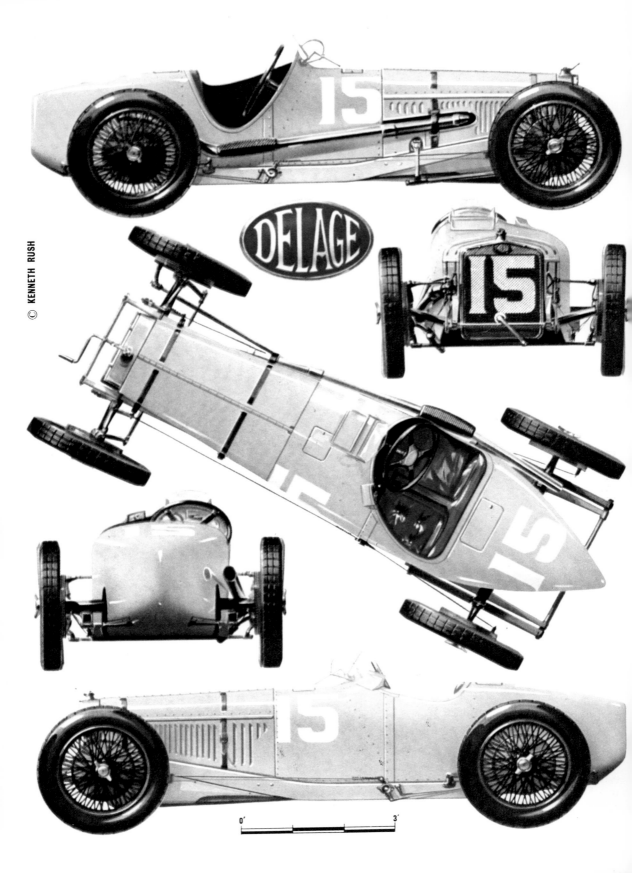

© KENNETH RUSH

DELAGE

0'   3'

The 1926-27 1½-Litre Delage

by Cyril Posthumus

First in Spain. Robert Benoist smiles as he receives the chequered flag in the Spanish G.P. at San Sebastian. (Photo: Fotocar, San Sebastian)

(See facing page): THE 1½-LITRE GRAND PRIX DELAGE driven into second place by Edmond Bourlier and Robert Senéchal in the 1926 Grand Prix of Europe (484 miles; won by Jules Goux, Bugatti, at 70·53 m.p.h.) at San Sebastian, Spain.

Amidst the infinite and fascinating variety of racing cars produced during the past seventy years, some stand out from the ruck as veritable milestones along the hard, unending road to perfection. One such was the 1926–27 1½-litre straight-eight Delage, the French car which won every major race it contested in 1927, carrying Robert Benoist to an unassailable European Championship, and with which the British driver Richard Seaman defeated all the modern voiturettes in four major International races during 1936.

It was the last and, in many eyes, the greatest of racing designs emanating from the Delage factory at Courbevoie-sur-Seine, whose founder, Louis Delage, believed implicitly in the value of racing. Delage laurels included the 1908 G.P. des Voiturettes, 1911 Light Car G.P. at Boulogne, 1913 G.P. de France, 1914 Indianapolis 500 Miles race, and the 1925 French and Spanish G.P.s, but the straight-eight 1500 was to surpass all these feats. When he had money, the flamboyant Louis Delage spent it freely. His Château du Pecq at St Germain was one of his more famous indulgences, but the 1926–27 G.P. Delage was another on which no expense was spared, and which has perpetuated his name in the automobile world.

A REMARKABLE ENGINE

The 1926–27 Delage's *forte* was its engine. After much experience in developing the Planchon-designed 2-litre V12 Delage of 1923–25, Ingénieur Albert Lory, who came from Salmson with Robert Benoist, plumped for the simpler straight-eight layout when designing a new Delage for the 1,500 c.c. G.P. Formula of 1926–27. This required a minimum weight limit of 600 kg., two seats (though one was unoccupied) and

a minimum body width of 80 cm. (31½ in.), the weight being raised in 1927 to 700 kg., and the second seat no longer being required.

Lory's engine had an iron cylinder block with fixed cylinder head on an alloy crankcase, twin overhead camshafts operating sixteen valves, a bore and stroke of 55·8 × 76·0 mm. (1,488 c.c.), twin Roots-type superchargers, and a one-piece counterbalanced crankshaft running in ten big roller races. The lavish indulgence in roller and ball races was eloquent of Lory's determined fight against friction. In all, no less than 62 were used in this remarkable engine! The big ends, camshafts, and the train of 21 timing and auxiliary gears driving oil pumps, water pump, magneto and camshafts all ran in roller or ball races. The two finned superchargers, mounted centrally alongside the engine on the nearside, were driven from the driving train by one internal shaft on the left, and the magneto by another shaft on the right, both running in ball races.

Lubrication was on the dry sump system, with the main bearings fed by direct jets and the big ends by centrifugal force. Generous water passaging to ensure maximum cooling at vital points was provided, the overall result being that this engine turned at over 8,000 r.p.m., a prodigious crankshaft speed at that time. The revolution counter read to 9,000 r.p.m., the instrument being marked green from 6,000 to 7,500 r.p.m., orange from 7,500 to 8,000 r.p.m., and red from 8,000 to 9,000 r.p.m. An unprecedented piston speed of 4,000 ft. per minute was attained, and the power output was over 165 b.h.p. in 1926. This figure was attained on a petrol-alcohol-benzole-ether fuel, with the twin blowers compressing at only

Début. The three straight-eight 1½-litre Delages lined up at the pits at San Sebastian for their first race, the 1926 Grand Prix of Europe.

$7\frac{1}{2}$ lb. per sq. in. That it could stand considerably higher internal pressures was proved ten years later when Giulio Ramponi, testing Seaman's engine on the brake with 12 lb. p.s.i. supercharging, inadvertently

No. 15 in trouble at San Sebastian. Benoist, overcome by the pitiless heat, has gone for medical attention, while volunteer reserve driver Senéchal prepares to take over.

let it exceed 9,000 r.p.m. for several minutes without mishap.

The engine drove through a multi-plate clutch and a five-speed gearbox in which 4th was direct and 5th speed an overdrive, intended to reduce stresses at sustained high speeds. The gearbox also drove a mechanical brake servo. An open propeller shaft transmitted the power to the bevel final drive on the rear axle.

THE CHASSIS

With that remarkable (but heavy) engine, Lory's genius was largely expended. His chassis was unduly slender and whippy, thereby impairing roadholding. It is generally but incorrectly believed that the engine of the 1,500 c.c. Delage in its earliest (1926) form was offset in the frame with the objects (a) of exploiting the 'no-mechanics' rule introduced the previous year, and (b) of finding more room for the driver. Credit for doing this must go, in fact, to the Delage's rival, the 8-cylinder 1½-litre Talbot-Darracq, which had its engine *desaxé* from its inception. The Delage engine and transmission were central, as confirmed by the starting-handle hole in the radiator. None the less, the driver was seated lower than the propeller shaft on his left, with little room to spare, and the exhaust system was uncomfortably close to the scuttle and pedals. Just how uncomfortably was soon to be revealed.

The radiator, broad, squarish and similar to the 1925 G.P. type, was mounted vertically, but very low and well ahead of the front axle. Suspension followed the conventions of the day in being semi-elliptic with short, hard leaf springs and Hartford friction shock absorbers. Streamlining was helped by a full length undertray and flush fuel filler caps. Finish was in pale blue, with darker wheels. It has been estimated that building the team of four for the 1926 season

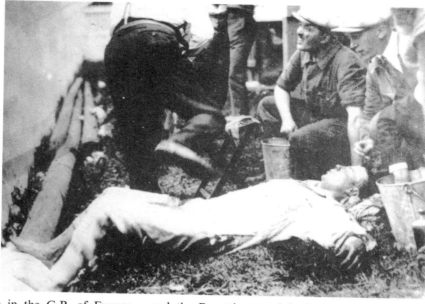

cost Automobiles Delage something like £36,000. Nor was it their final expenditure.

TRAVELLING OVENS

The unreadiness of the new Delages contributed to the fiasco of the 1926 French G.P. at Miramas on 27th June. Their withdrawal, together with that of the Talbot team, left three Bugattis to dispute a farcical race. But four weeks later the cars from Courbevoie were at San Sebastian, in Spain, to face the seasoned Bugatti team in the G.P. of Europe. Freak equatorial weather added to the drama, for temperatures of 110 deg. F. laid appalling stress on a serious Delage defect—that exhaust pipe lurking so snugly on the offside of the body was turning the drivers' cockpits into veritable furnaces and their pedals red hot.

That the new cars were very fast was established from the start, but after ten laps or so their hard-won lead disappeared as the Delage drivers pulled in one by one for relief from stifling heat and fumes. Holes were cut in the scuttles and cowls to coax extra air in, and second drivers took over. Morel collapsed with sunburn and burnt feet and went to hospital, Benoist and reserve driver Wagner needed medical treatment, and Bourlier lay inert behind the pits, while the cars stood silent in the scorching sun and the Bugattis moved farther and farther ahead. Then the elements relented, a cooling wind sprang up, the team revived and Robert Senéchal, a last-minute volunteer relief, shared one car with Bourlier to snatch second place from the Bugattis. The other Delages placed fourth and sixth, while Wagner set the fastest lap.

Having cost Delage the year's most important race, that unanticipated design defect very nearly cost him the next one. This was the British G.P. at Brooklands held on a hot August day, and Lory's devilish exhaust pipes again cooked the drivers so that they stopped periodically to douse their scorching feet in bowls of water. 'One could actually hear their boots hissing as they went into the water' wrote Major H. O. D. Segrave, a member of the rival Talbot team, afterwards. The exhaust set fire to the bodywork of

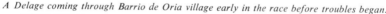

A Delage coming through Barrio de Oria village early in the race before troubles began.

Delage comes to Britain. Benoist taking one of the sand-bank artificial corners at Brooklands during practice for the first British Grand Prix, held in August 1926. (Photo: Radio Times Hulton Picture Library)

Wagner's car and he had to retire it, later relieving Senéchal to share victory in an exhausting race, pursued by a Bugatti and another Delage.

No Delages ran in the 1926 Italian G.P. Instead they were sent back to Courbevoie for drastic rebuilding. Lory redesigned the engine to bring the exhaust valves and that troublesome exhaust system to the nearside. Next, varying Talbot's example, he offset the entire engine-transmission-final drive line

The Benoist/Dubonnet Delage which placed third in the British G.P., showing the extra louvres cut in the scuttle and the compulsory Brooklands silencer.

four inches to the left, thus gaining more cockpit room but squeezing the twin blowers out of their place on the nearside of the engine. Instead Lory produced a long single blower of identical capacity, mounted it high ahead of the engine and drove it from the timing gear train. To accommodate the repositioned starting handle the radiator had to be remodelled, so while he was about it Lory designed a handsome new one, taking another leaf from Talbot's book by inclining it and improving the streamlining.

FIVE VICTORIES–AND A SMALL SETBACK

In this improved form, and with that superb engine now delivering a full 170 b.h.p., the Delage team and their No. 1 driver Benoist proved unassailable in 1927. They kicked off early in the season with a damp but easy victory in the G.P. de l'Ouverture at Montlhéry, Benoist driving a car with a modified 1926 radiator as the new ones were not ready yet. After this preliminary canter, the team turned out in full strength for the French G.P., also at Montlhéry, where Benoist, Bourlier and Morel outpaced the trouble-fraught Talbots to score a 1–2–3 victory. In the Spanish G.P. at San Sebastian, Benoist met tougher opposition from the audacious Italian Emilio Materassi in a factory-entered Bugatti, which was faster than the Delages through the turns but slower along the straights. The result was a tremen-

The winning Delage of Wagner/Senéchal follows Segrave's Talbot and Eyston's Aston Martin during the British G.P. (Photo: Radio Times Hulton Picture Library)

Revised: the Delage in its all-conquering 1927 form, with engine moved 4 in. from centre, the exhaust system transferred to the near-side and new radiator fitted. (Photo: Motor)

First in France. Benoist winning the 1927 French G.P. at Montlhéry, where Delages placed first, second and third. (Photo: *Autocar*)

dous duel which ended only when Materassi overdid things at Bascardo's Corner and crashed into a wall when leading with nine laps to go. The Delage, close behind, rushed into the blinding dust, missed the Bugatti by inches, and spun, Benoist in his confusion restarting the reverse way of the course! Resuming the proper direction, he went on to win, with Bourlier's Delage third behind Conelli's Bugatti.

Three weeks later occurred the only set-back to total Delage supremacy that season, in the minor G.P. de la Baule, a 62-mile beach race for unlimited capacity racing cars. Driving the only 1,500 c.c. Delage entered, Edmond Bourlier led until half-distance, then spun and stalled. Oiled plugs delayed his restart and he was caught by G. E. T. Eyston's 2·3-litre Bugatti.

Undeterred, in fact with insolent confidence, Delage sent only one car, driven by Benoist, to the G.P. of Europe at Monza, Italy, to face O.M., Miller and Duesenberg, but no Talbots or Bugattis. In pouring rain, Benoist just ran away with the race, finishing 22 minutes ahead of an O.M., with a Miller third. The full team then came to Brooklands for the second British G.P., scoring another devastating 1-2-3 success, well in front of the rival Bugattis.

Louis Delage was present to watch their triumph, which clinched the European Championship for Robert Benoist. The winning car proudly appeared on the Delage stand at the Olympia Motor Show a few days later.

TO FURTHER GLORY

On the crest of the wave, but with hard economic times looming, Louis Delage decided to sell his beautiful watch-like cars at the end of 1927. Malcolm Campbell acquired one, winning the Junior G.P. and the 200 Miles Race at Brooklands, and the Boulogne G.P., all in 1928. The following year Louis Chiron took a Delage minus its front brakes to Indianapolis, U.S.A., placing seventh in the famous 500 Miles Race against the specialised American track machines. W. B. Scott acquired the Campbell car for a successful spell of racing and class record-breaking at Brooklands, while Earl Howe acquired two Delages and won 1,500 c.c. class races at Dieppe in 1931, Avus in 1932 and Nurburgring in 1933. His was also the first 1½-litre car to finish in the Grand Prix class Acerbo Cup race in Italy in 1932, but shortly afterwards this car was written off against a tree during the Monza G.P. Howe raced his other Delage until

First in Italy. Benoist yet again, his lone Delage in the centre of the front row, between the American Cooper Special and an O.M.

First in Britain. Delage's second British G.P. victory was a 1-2-3 clean sweep; Benoist the inevitable winner looks bemused, Senéchal with the bouquet looks happy; technicians check on the engine.

A cockpit view of the car, showing gearchange and brake levers, and the finned brake servo drum on the gearbox.

1935, placing third that year in the Albi and Berne races.

REJUVENATION

It was at that Berne race of 1935 that the idea of acquiring Earl Howe's Delage was first put to Dick Seaman by his head mechanic Giulio Ramponi and team manager Tony Birch. After initial resistance on the grounds that it was too old, Seaman agreed to buy the car plus another engine and many spares. That winter the Delage underwent a course of rejuvenation eloquent of the advances made in racing design and metallurgy in ten years.

Weight reduction was a prior aim, for which Ramponi prescribed new duralumin wheels saving 7 lb. per wheel, a new radiator saving 20 lb., a new combined fuel tank and tail, 95 lb. lighter than the old, and a change in gearbox from the heavy ENV epicyclic fitted by Earl Howe to a 5-speed Delage gearbox 70 lb. lighter, as used in the 1925 V12 G.P. cars. Lockheed hydraulic brakes replaced the old mechanically-operated type, higher compression Hepworth and Grandage pistons were fitted, the blower pressure increased to 12 lb. p.s.i. and the valve timing meticulously checked and modified by Ramponi.

Brake-tested by Laystall, the engine now gave over 185 b.h.p. which, combined with Seaman's skill, placed it on a par with the more modern E.R.A. and Maserati 1500s. New, outrigged front springs and a rebuilt front axle, and the packing of the dumbirons with hard wood to resist chassis twist were other modifications. The whole car was painted a sinister black, with silver wheels, then taken by Seaman to Nurburgring, Germany, for a fortnight's testing before its debut in racing.

The black Delage's first meeting was at Donington Park in May, 1936, where it ran in two short races and won both. Then Seaman began serious work with the R.A.C. 1½-litre race at Douglas, I.o.M., which the Delage won non-stop, defeating nine modern E.R.A.s. Car and driver then went abroad, briefly leading the Eifelrennen at Nurburg before leaving the road, winning their heat at Picardie but crashing in the final (Seaman was unwell), then winning the

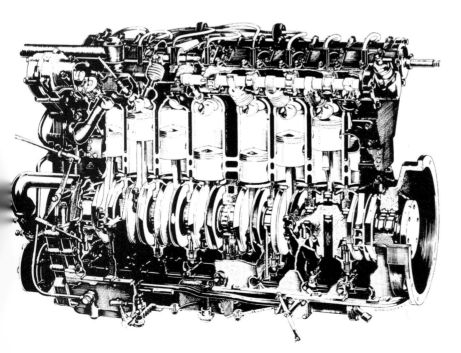

The remarkable 1½-litre eight-cylinder Delage engine; a cutaway drawing by Robert Cresswell. (Drawing: Motor copyright)

Earl Howe is chased by Bira's more modern E.R.A. at Dieppe, 1935. (Photo: Motor)

Specification

1½ litres capacity, supercharged. Designer, Albert Lory, assisted by M. Gauthier.

ENGINE: 8 cylinders, 55·8 mm. bore, 76·0 mm. stroke (1,488 c.c.); cast iron block and integral head, alloy crankcase.
Camshafts: Twin overhead, gear-driven. *Valves:* Two per cylinder at 50 deg. *Ignition:* Single Bosch magneto, shaft and gear-driven; one 18 mm. sparking plug per cylinder. *Carburettors* 1926: Two Zenith. 1927: Single Cozette-horizontal. *Supercharging* 1926: twin Roots-type on n/s of engine, 110 mm. rotors. 1927: Single Roots-type, 220 mm. rotors, in front of engine. Boost 7½ lb. p.s.i. *Pistons:* Light alloy, compression ratio 6·5 to 1. *Crankshaft:* One-piece counterbalanced; roller main bearings, split roller big ends. *Lubrication:* Dry sump, triple pumps. *Power output* (1927): 170 b.h.p. at 8,000 r.p.m.
TRANSMISSION: Multi-plate clutch; five-speed gearbox (4th, direct, 5th overdrive) in unit with engine; open propellor shaft, bevel final drive.
CHASSIS: Steel, channel section. *Suspension:* Semi-elliptic leaf springs front and rear; Hartford friction shock absorbers. *Brakes:* Mechanically-operated internal expanding on all four wheels, 14 in. diameter × 1½ in. wide drums, assisted by friction servo on gearbox. *Wheelbase:* 8 ft. 2½ in. *Track:* 4 ft. 5 in. front and rear. *Maximum height:* 35 in. *Steering:* Worm type. *Wheels:* Rudge-Whitworth quick-release wire. *Tyres:* 765 × 120 Michelin or 30 in. × 4·75 in. Dunlop.
WEIGHT Unladen, 1926: 14·76 cwt. 1927: 15·8 cwt.
MAXIMUM SPEED 1927 form on 5·2 to 1 direct 4th gear: approx. 128 m.p.h.

Capt. (later Sir) Malcolm Campbell winning the 1928 Boulogne G.P. (Photo: Motor)

Pescara and Berne 1,500 c.c. races. After that, with no time for detail maintenance, the Delage was returned to Britain for the 200 Miles Race at Donington, in which Seaman won both the 1,500 c.c. class and the race outright, defeating many larger cars.

Sadly, while Seaman was re-enacting the Delage invincibility of ten years earlier, private tragedy had

Richard Seaman in the rebuilt ex-Earl Howe Delage chases Earl Howe himself, now in an E.R.A., in the 1936 R.A.C. International race at Douglas, I.o.M. Seaman won non-stop. (Photo: Motor)

Fourth on the trot. Seaman and the black Delage after winning the 200 Miles Race at Donington Park; chief mechanic Giulio Ramponi takes a look at the engine. (Photo: Motor)

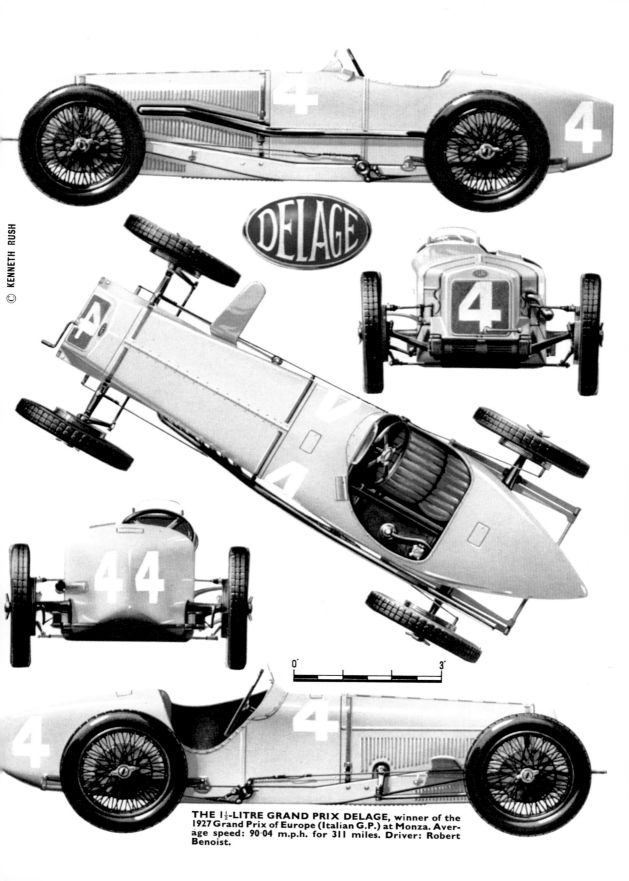

DELAGE

THE 1½-LITRE GRAND PRIX DELAGE, winner of the 1927 Grand Prix of Europe (Italian G.P.) at Monza. Average speed: 90·04 m.p.h. for 311 miles. Driver: Robert Benoist.

assailed Louis Delage. His company failed and was absorbed by the Delahaye concern, who paid Delage a small monthly pension and bade him keep away. He sold his possessions one by one and died, virtually destitute, in 1947.

When Dick Seaman joined the Mercedes-Benz Grand Prix team in 1937, his famous black Delage was purchased, together with the ex-Scott car, and all available spares, by Prince Chula of Siam for his cousin B. Bira to drive. Alas, in striving to modernise the design with independent front suspension and a new frame designed by Lory, the princes broke its winning spell. They abandoned it for their E.R.A.s, but during the war Reg Parnell acquired the car plus many parts, reassembling the Seaman car with its old chassis, and producing two 'spare parts' Delages from the rest, using the two frames built for Chula.

All three were raced in the early post-war period of racing, but R. R. C. ('Rob') Walker retrieved the Seaman car from the circuits for a major rebuild, restoring it to as near 1936 condition as possible, using a spare engine and gearbox and a new body. Only one G.P. Delage survives in its original 1927 form, in the United States, this being the car brought to Indianapolis by Chiron in 1929. Although inaccurately finished and wearing modern tread tyres, it stands as a cherished memorial to an unforgettable racing car.

© *Cyril Posthumns, 1966.*

List of Race Victories

1926 British G.P., Brooklands (L. Wagner/R. Senéchal)
1927 G.P. de l'Ouverture, Montlhéry (R. Benoist); French G.P. Montlhéry (R. Benoist); Spanish G.P., San Sebastian (R. Benoist); European G.P. Monza (R. Benoist); British G.P., Brooklands (R. Benoist)
1928 Junior G.P., Brooklands (M. Campbell); 200 Miles Race, Brooklands (M. Campbell); Boulogne G.P. (M. Campbell)
1931 Dieppe voiturette race (Earl Howe)
1932 Avus 1,500 c.c. G.P. Germany (Earl Howe)
1933 Eifelrennen 1,500 c.c. race, Germany (Earl Howe)
1936 R.A.C. Light Car Race, Douglas, I.o.M. (R. J. B. Seaman); Coppa Acerbo 1,500 c.c. race, Italy (R. J. B. Seaman); Prix de Berne, Switzerland (R. J. B. Seaman); 200 Miles Road Race, Donington Park (R. J. B. Seaman)

One of the 'spare parts' Delages assembled by Reg Parnell after the war. This one, with i.f.s. devised for Bira, and a slim and elegant new body, is being driven by Roy Parnell at Shelsley Walsh, 1946. (Photo: *Motor*)

The 4.5-Litre, S-Type Invicta

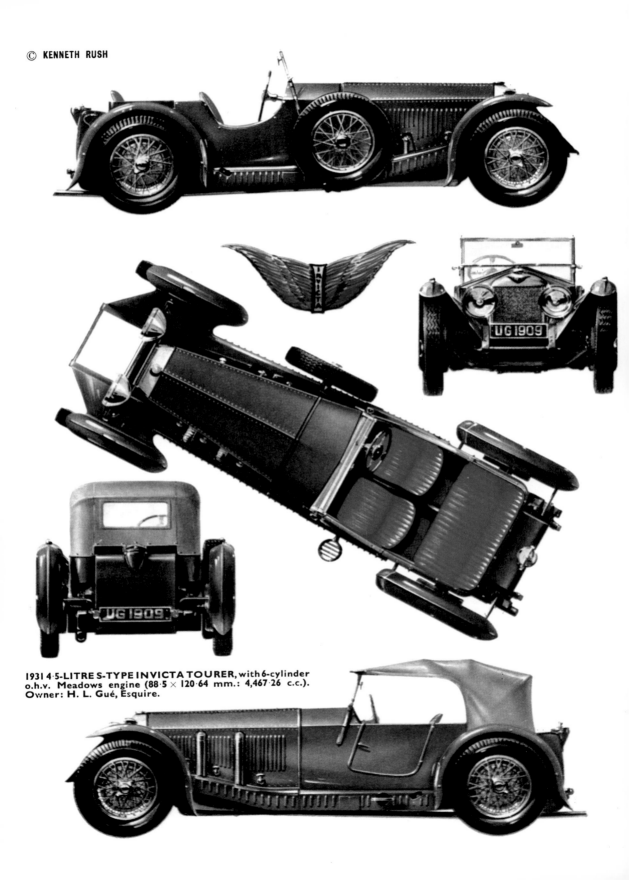

© KENNETH RUSH

1931 4·5-LITRE S-TYPE INVICTA TOURER, with 6-cylinder o.h.v. Meadows engine (88·5 × 120·64 mm.: 4,467·26 c.c.). Owner: H. L. Gué, Esquire.

The 4·5-Litre, S-Type Invicta

by J. R. Buckley

Miss Violet Cordery and G. Fields entering the Paddock at Brooklands, 1931. (Photo: Montagu Motor Museum)

The origins of the Invicta Company go back to the year 1924. Like the Bentley Company it remained in existence for only twelve years, and again like that company actively produced motor-cars for only ten of those twelve years; some seven cars being assembled from spares by the company's service depot in Flood Street, Chelsea, between 1934 and 1936, after works production had ceased.

Both the Invicta and the Bentley were designed by men with a personal background of competition motoring and both were produced to a standard—the best—with price as only a secondary consideration. It is probable that this factor contributed largely to the failure of both firms to weather the storms of the financial depression of the early and mid-1930s.

Captain Noel Macklin, later Sir Noel Macklin, was a great admirer of the steam car, and at varying times owned both Doble and Stanley steamers. It is not surprising therefore that the extreme flexibility and very high power-to-weight ratio inherent in the good steamer were pre-eminent characteristics of every Invicta Macklin produced, with the exception only of the 1½-litre cars made late in the firm's life.

Associated with Macklin in the Invicta Company were Oliver Lyle, already well known in the world of sugar, W. G. Watson helping on the design side, and the Earl Fitzwilliam, who earlier had been responsible for the Sheffield Simplex cars, which had unsuccessfully challenged Rolls-Royce and Napier in the large luxury car market. The factory started life in a very modest way in the 3-car garage of Macklin's country home at Cobham in Surrey, and here the first three Invictas—2½-litre cars with Coventry Climax 6-cylinder engines—were produced in 1924.

The cars were reasonably successful, but failed to reach the high standard which Macklin had set. Fortunately at this time, Macklin met Henry Meadows of Fallings Park, Wolverhampton, an established manufacturer of fine I.C. engines, and the next Invicta and all Invictas thereafter—again, the 1½-litre

excepted—were powered by Meadows engines.

For 1925 the cars were still of 2½-litres capacity, but now recognisable as the forbears of later cars, but the overall design was completely reviewed for the year 1926 when the new 3-litre Invicta appeared. It was produced in both L.C. and S.C. chassis forms which stood, not as one might imagine for 'long' and 'short' chassis, but for *large* and *small* chassis versions.

This 3-litre Invicta in two short years made the new firm's reputation and continued in production until 1929. As a result of the car's outstanding success, very largely in long-distance observed reliability trials, the Invicta Company was awarded the coveted Dewar Trophy in 1926 and again in 1929.

The first 4½-litre car was seen at the London Motor Show of 1928—then held at Olympia—to be followed in 1929 by the most expensive Invicta ever produced, the 4·5-litre type N.L.C. The instruments, finish, controls and fittings of this car were modelled on, and made to, Rolls-Royce standards. The chassis of the type N.L.C. at £1,050 (the Invicta Company never built bodies on their cars) cost only £50 less than that of the contemporary 20/25 h.p. Rolls-Royce, at a time when Rolls-Royce were considering the marketing of a lower-priced car to meet the markets of the prevailing difficult times.

For the N.L.C. car the chassis was completely redesigned. It was much stiffer, with side members both deeper and heavier in section, and the track was increased from 4 ft. 4 in. to 4 ft. 8 in.; floor line was lower, springs lengthened, and a much heavier front axle fitted.

It was an expensive car launched at precisely the wrong moment. The same year the Stock Markets of America crumbled into ruin, and the repercussions were felt all over Europe. People thought hard before buying a new car which in saloon form cost £1,800.

Late in 1929 and complementing the N.L.C. in the firm's catalogue and its later successor, the 'High' chassis type A—which was in effect the N.L.C. shorn

79

The bare bones of the matter: 1931 S-type chassis (above) inlet side; (below) exhaust side.

of its luxury equipment—was the entirely new sports chassis, the type S. Its subsequent scarcity value of to-day was assured in that only 77 of these cars in all were made.

Better known at the time and since as the low chassis Invicta (though occasionally as the M.P.H. model) and frequently and incorrectly as the 100 M.P.H. Invicta, it attracted immediate attention by virtue of its unusual and very attractive appearance and fine finish. It was probably the best-looking sports car in the vintage tradition ever to be produced in England. I can think of no contemporary unsupercharged motor-car of similar capacity, made here, which could outperform it—and very few built elsewhere. It looked exactly what it was: a comfortable, very rapid and desirable fast-touring motor-car.

The name of the '100-M.P.H. Invicta' was bestowed upon the car erroneously because, in a day when cars which could do a genuine 100 m.p.h. could almost be counted on the fingers of a man's hand, the makers never claimed this maximum speed for it. As produced in 1929 and 1930 there is no doubt at all that the standard production S-type had a maximum speed not far short of this very elusive figure. It was however relatively easy to tune an Invicta to give this maximum speed, without impairing the power and flexibility in the lower and middle speed ranges, which was always the car's greatest attraction.

Raymond Mays, writing of the two Invictas he owned in the early 1930s, says that they gave him some of the most exhilarating motoring he ever had, with their ability 'to crest most main-road hills at nearly the century.'

The only thing the S-type Invicta had in common with earlier cars and those which complemented it in the firm's catalogue, was the 4·5-litre Meadows engine; that engine was used for all 4·5-litre models, the 'N.L.C.' the 'A' and the 'S-type' cars.

The chassis was an entirely new design and it is said that it was inspired by that of the fantastically successful racing 1·5-litre Grand Prix Delage of a year or so earlier.

Fabricated from nickel chrome steel, it was swept upwards in front over the axle, the radiator sitting down neatly inside the chassis side-members. From immediately above the front axle it sloped steeply downwards to a point below the engine bulkhead, and here reached its maximum sectional depth; for the next 3 ft. 6 in. of its length—the space usually devoted to the passengers—the chassis frame ran parallel to the ground, and thereafter was carried down below the back axle and up again, to support a 20-gallon fuel tank at the rear. It was braced at the front, and again immediately in front of the radiator and at the rear, by heavy section tubular steel cross-members, and elsewhere by deep, channel-steel sections. Front

Then! G. Fields and Dudley Froy and the "works" Invicta, 1931 Double-Twelve at Brooklands. (Photo: Montagu Motor Museum)

springs were carried under the frame, and those at the rear were outboard of the chassis side-members. All were housed in gunmetal trunnions. Behind the rear engine mountings was an extremely robust cast aluminium bulkhead, on which was mounted a 2-gallon reserve petrol tank, and a reserve oil tank feeding directly to the engine's sump. Cast alloy brackets from the bulkhead carried an instrument panel fabricated from sheet brass.

Headlamp brackets, front wing stays, shock-absorber mountings, engine bearers, the petrol tank brackets and 6-inch diameter filler cap were all, like the suspension mountings, gunmetal castings, though the engine, sump, gearbox casing and bell housing in the S-type were cast in aluminium; this was one way in which the cost of the S-type Invicta was kept down to a reasonable level. The other was in the use of standard Smiths instruments. In the earlier N.L.C. chassis cars, the crankcase, gearbox, bell-housing and sump castings had been in Electron, and instruments by A.T. Ltd.

The radiator—lower and more square than that of the N.L.C. and A-type cars—was of nickel with a matrix, and the oblong Invicta badge was replaced by a winged badge in blue, green and gold enamel.

Transmission was by a single plate clutch and 4-speed sliding pinion gearbox (also a product of Henry Meadows Ltd.), in unit with the engine. This box, in conjunction with a final drive ratio of 3·6 to 1, gave overall gear ratios of 3·6, 4·9, 7 and 10·4 to 1. Reverse gear ratio was 12 to 1. Rather surprisingly alternative ratios were neither available at the time the car was introduced nor were they found to be desirable at any time later throughout the production life of the car, though for one or two special events 'works' cars used a 2·9 to 1 rear axle. An open propeller shaft with oil-proof ring-type universal joints, similar to that used in the Phantom Rolls, took the drive to a massive semi-floating hypoid rear axle.

Brakes on all four wheels were rod controlled and operated through Perrot-type shafts in 14 inch steel drums fitted with cast alloy cooling fins, and mounted on heavy cast aluminium anchor plates.

The electrical system and the 10-inch lamps were by Rotax.

The power unit had a bore and stroke of 88·5 mm. × 120·64 mm., capacity being 4·467-litres (or 272·5 cubic in.) R.A.C. horse power rating was 29·124 and developed power, when the cars were introduced, was given as 115 b.h.p. There can be little doubt that this was a most conservative estimate, since the same engine, in marine form, operating with single ignition and one carburettor only, and with a modest 6-to-1 compression ratio, was rated by the Admiralty for boat service at 100 b.h.p. *continuous* rating at 2,800 r.p.m.

Two 40 mm. S.U.-type H.V.5 horizontal carburettors having bronze barrels and float chambers supplied the mixture, and ignition was dual firing 12 plugs. A Scintilla magneto fed six plugs on the inlet side of the engine, and a Scintilla coil and distributor supplied six on the exhaust side. The whole system was synchronised, and there was an over-riding manual control by means of ratchet lever mounted on the steering wheel boss.

"Drill Order—Summer": Colonel J. R. Buckley's 1930 coupé.

GO 9765

Now! The Tourist Trophy car, once owned by G. Field, still winning races 34 years later with its present owner, J. Earle Marsh.

Dual swept exhaust manifolds with twin exhaust pipes covered by chromed flexible conduits led the exhaust gasses to a silencer mounted alongside and below the engine.

The clutch was fitted with an adjustable clutch stop and all three pedals could be adjusted for reach over a 5-inch sector. Cooling was by pump and fan, with cast aluminium water transfer ports fitted externally between cylinder block and head. However, since the water capacity is around five gallons and the pump is very efficient, the car may be run without the fan in operation in England apart from rare hot summer weather.

The maximum speed of the car when introduced was in excess of 90 m.p.h., and 78 m.p.h. was available—if needed—in the high ratio 3rd gear at 3,200 r.p.m. the then safe maximum engine speed.

The performance was improved upon before production ceased in 1934, by which time the engine limit had been raised to 3,600, and brake horse power output to a stated 140 b.h.p., when the S-type was able to justify the name the public had given it: the 100 M.P.H. Invicta.

In much the same way as the Speed Model 3-litre Bentley was almost invariably known as 'the Red-label' Bentley, so also the Invicta type-S came to be known as the 100 M.P.H. Invicta, though the firms neither sponsored nor approved these type names.

Engines subsequently modified to Sanction III standards, i.e. utilising improvements designed by W. O. Bentley and H. Weslake for use on the Meadows engine in the Lagonda L.G. 45-type car of 1936, have a permissible safe crankshaft speed of 4,000 r.p.m. and, with compression ratios of 7·5 to 1, give maximum speeds of over 100 m.p.h. and 80 m.p.h. in 3rd gear, with acceleration of an even more startling order than was standard in the early cars.

It must be stressed however that the S-type Invicta was primarily a very fast but comfortable high speed touring car, and though it met with moderate success in racing in the hands of private owners in the early 1930s, its greatest appeal lies in its ability to cover big mileages at high average speeds with no strain, either to driver or to the machinery.

In fact the charmingly effortless manner in which the car will cross Europe, up hill and down, with the speedometer needle steady at 60 m.p.h.—traffic permitting—and the revolution counter showing a modest 2,000 r.p.m., is the real secret of the car's appeal. Motoring in this way, quite high average speeds can be maintained, and there is still a large untapped reserve of power and speed available should the need arise.

Like most low-speed engines there is a very large amount of torque available in the lower and middle speed ranges. The Invicta can be throttled down to 6 to 8 m.p.h. in top gear—despite its 3·6 to 1 ratio—and will then accelerate rapidly and without fuss, still in top gear, when the accelerator is depressed. The acceleration figures given by the contemporary Motoring Press (see page 12) speak for themselves on this subject.

Once launched, Macklin made little effort to prove the car on racing circuits. From the beginning to the

Skegness sand races: Raymond Mays leads a 36/220 Mercedes-Benz round the pylons. (Photo: Montagu Motor Museum)

end of the firm's history it was company policy to prove all Invictas in long-distance trials of various types. A 3-litre car having been driven completely round the world only two years earlier, under R.A.C. observation, with no failure beyond a half-shaft in the axle, it was not considered necessary to prove the S-type by subjecting it to further trials of this type.

Instead the company concentrated on entering the cars in the most difficult long-distance trials in the motoring calendar, and notable successes were achieved. Shortly after its introduction the car was entered in the Austrian Alpine Trials of 1930, one of the most searching of all trials. It won the Alpine Cup, and made fastest time in the Arlberg Hill Climb. It took the Alpine Cup also in the Hungarian Alpine Trial the same year, and the Glacier Cup in the International Alpine Trials and—as a side line—again made fastest time in the Gallibier Hill Climbs.

The following year, starting from Stavanger, it won the Monte Carlo Rally outright and the Mont-des-Mules hill climb following the Rally. This, despite the fact that in Norway, early in the Rally the car slid off the road on ice, cut a telegraph pole in two and had to be driven almost the whole route with a twisted chassis and both axles out of line. In 1932 starting from Umea, in Sweden—almost on the Arctic circle—it gained 2nd place in the Monte Carlo Rally, but repeated its success in the Mont-des-Mules climb. But face was saved in the International Alpine Trials that year. Three S-types were entered, three Glacier Cups were won, each car securing maximum points and a record time for the Stelvio Pass hill climb.

Later in 1932 the S-type took the International Sports Car Record for Shelsley Walsh hill climb and, by way of variety, the Mountain Circuit lap record at Brooklands track for unsupercharged cars and gained 2nd and 4th places in the Mountain Championship at Brooklands track.

It is an interesting speculation to compare motoring competition then and its present-day counterpart, with cars which bear not a great deal of resemblance to the ones one buys.

The Invicta which Donald Healey drove in the 1932 and 1933 Monte Carlo Rallies, and with which he won

Last-minute preparation: Raymond Mays with the white Invicta. (Photo: Montagu Motor Museum)

Winter sunshine: Donald Healey's car after winning the 1931 Monte Carlo Rally. (Photo: Autocar)

the Mont-des-Mules hill climbs, had already covered over 50,000 miles before starting in 1932. It was used as daily transport, it won its class in the Brighton Speed trials in 1933 and obtained 2nd place in the R.A.C. rally the same year.

The actual cars which raced at Brooklands, in the Tourist Trophy races and elsewhere, are still winning

Morgan's Invicta about to be overtaken by Kaye Don in a Type 51 supercharged Bugatti, Brooklands, 1933. (Photo: Radio Times Hulton Picture Library)

G. Fields in the T.T. car at Brooklands. (Photo: H. L. Gué)

club races at Silverstone, Goodwood and Oulton Park to-day, thirty five years later.

This enviable performance was not therefore obtained at the expense of durability or reliability. The Invictas are about as indestructible in normal use as a car can be. Well over thirty years after most were built, 48 of the 77 cars are known to survive (there may be more), and most are in excellent order.

The actual car which eclipsed the lap record set up by Sir Henry Birkin in the 4·5-litre supercharged Bentley in the Tourist Trophy Race in Ireland, by lapping the 13¾-mile Ards circuit at 77·69 m.p.h. in 1933, is in impeccable order and could probably repeat its earlier performance. The two cars with which Donald Healey competed in the Monte Carlo Rally in 1931 from Stavanger, in 1932 from Umea and in 1933 from Tallinn, in Esthonia, are in daily use today despite astronomical mileages.

The very admirable 4·5-litre cars were not the only cars the company produced, though today when one hears Invicta motor-cars being discussed it is invariably of the 4½-litre cars that one thinks and usually the S-type machines.

There were several models of the 1·5-litre cars made. The early ones, in contra-distinction to the 4½s, being substantially underpowered. As a wit once described them 'a good car marred by an impotent engine.' Powered by a six-cylinder 1·5-litre engine developing 45 b.h.p. it was necessary to utilise a 6-to-1 final drive ratio to obtain any sort of performance at all, and the engine was temperamental.

To overcome the trouble the unit was supercharged with a Powerplus supercharger coupled direct to the crankshaft. This enabled the final drive ratio to be increased to 5-to-1 and thereafter bearing life was rather uncertain.

A very nice 1·5-litre car, with twin overhead camshafts and a capacity of either 1·5 or 1·66-litres supercharged, and fitted with a Wilson gearbox and lightened chassis, was evolved in 1933 but it never got beyond the prototype stage of development.

Personality: G. E. Milligen's immaculate 2/4-seater. (Photo: Jeremy Mason)

Lewes Speed Trials: Donald Monro in the S-type Invicta 'Red Gauntlet'. (Photo: Montagu Motor Museum)

Concentration: Lord Ebury, Prescott, 1954. (Photo: T. C. March)

Confidence: R. M. Blomfield's Invicta at Prescott, 1946. (Photo: Guy Griffiths)

Combat: A. Price 'round the bend' at Prescott in S.139. (Photo: Louis Klemantaski)

The final development of the type-S, the 5-litre double overhead camshaft Invicta, the type S.S., gave promise of being one of the outstanding motor-cars of its time.

The chassis was a refinement of that of the type-S fitted with light alloy Lockhead hydraulic brakes of 16 inches in diameter and with all the springs carried outboard of the chassis frame. Engine was 93 mm. bore × 120 mm. stroke, capacity being 4890·9 c.c., with two exhaust and one inlet valve per cylinder. Transmission refinements included a 5-speed Wilson-type pre-selector gearbox and designed speed was 130 m.p.h. Catalogued chassis price was a modest £1,875 and included a kit of tools and spare wheel.

It is believed that two of these chassis were completed, but if they were ever sold to the public, the most diligent search has failed to trace them. Contemporary Press reports linked the name of Humphrey

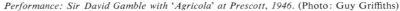

Performance: Sir David Gamble with 'Agricola' at Prescott, 1946. (Photo: Guy Griffiths)

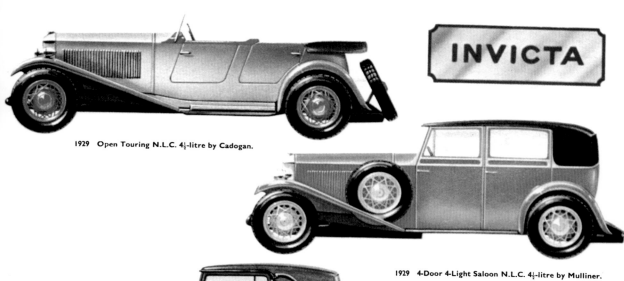

INVICTA

1929   Open Touring N.L.C. 4½-litre by Cadogan.

1929   4-Door 4-Light Saloon N.L.C. 4½-litre by Mulliner.

1933   S-type Fixed Head Coupé.

1930   S-type Drophead Coupé by Freestone & Webb.

1935   S-type Drophead Coupé by Grose.

1930   S-type Drophead Coupé by Corsica.

1931   S-type Fixed Head Coupé.

© KENNETH RUSH

Pilot's View: the cockpit of Hedley Gué's S-type. (Photo: H. L. Gué)

Cook with a team of three of these cars for use in the Le Mans Race, and Reid Railton was consultant designer with Macklin and Watson.

If only the Depression had not come along just then—but the history of the world has been changed by that small word—IF!

Years later, W. G. Watson did use a Meadows twin overhead camshaft engine in his post-war Invicta Black Prince, though of only 3-litres capacity, and Henry Meadows produced another twin overhead camshaft engine with 8-cylinders-in-line for use in the early Jensen.

© J. R. Buckley, 1966.

Power: John Shutler breaks the Vintage record at Prescott. (Photo: Richmond Pike)

SPECIFICATION INVICTA 4·5-LITRE TYPE-S.

Engine. 6-cylinder O.H.V. push-rod operated. Two valves per cylinder in detachable cast iron head. Separate detachable block on light alloy crankcase. Bore and stroke 88·5 × 120·64 mm. Capacity 4467·26 c.c.s or 3·464 in. × 4·75 in. capacity 272·5 cu. in. 4 main bearings, aluminium pistons on H-section steel connecting rods. High pressure forced feed lubrication to mains, big ends, rocker and timing gears.
Ignition. Dual by magneto and independent coil and distributor firing 12 plugs. (18 mm.)
Carburation. Dual by twin S.U. 40 mm. type H.V.5 instruments.
Clutch. Single dry plate.

Gearbox. 4-speed and reverse sliding pinion.
overall ratios;—3·6; 4·9; 7 and 10·4 to 1.
reverse gear;—12 to 1.

Suspension. ½-elliptic springs front and rear. Shock absorbers, hydraulic front and rear with André Hartford friction dampers in over-riding control.

Frame. Nickel chrome steel channel frame underslung in rear.
Wheelbase. 9 ft. 10 in.
Track. 4 ft. 8 in.
Wheels. Rudge Whitworth 72-spoke centre-lock wire wheels with 19 in. × 6·00 tyres.

Acceleration Figures. (Press Road Tests.)
Top gear. 10-30 m.p.h. 6·5 secs. 10-50 m.p.h. 12·5 secs. 10-60 m.p.h. 15·0 secs. 10-70 m.p.h. 19·0 secs. 10-80 m.p.h. 23·5 secs. 10-90 m.p.h. 32·5 secs.

Chassis Data.
Valve clearance: (both ·004 in. (hot).
Magneto Points: ·015 in.
Distributor: ·012 in.
Firing order: 1. 4. 2. 6. 3. 5.
Carburettors: S.U. 40 mm. H.V.5.
Oil Pressure: 25/30 lb. hot. (Standard sump).
Optimum temperature: 75 to 80 degrees centigrade.
Plug settings: Mag. ·025. Coil ·030.
Timing: Valves. inlet opens 10 deg. b.t.d.c. inlet closes 50 deg. a.b.d.c. Exhaust opens 60 deg. b.b.d.c. exhaust closes 15 deg. a.t.d.c. (1 tooth on flywheel=3·103 degrees).
Timing: Ignition. 42 deg. b.t.d.c.—fully advanced.
Tracking: front wheels. ¼-inch toe-in at wheel centre height.

The Le Mans Replica Frazer Nash

TMX 545

THE LE MANS REPLICA FRAZER NASH which was driven into 3rd place in the 1949 24 Hour Grand Prix d'Endurance at Le Mans by N. Culpan and H. J. Aldington. Average speed 78·5 m.p.h. for 1884·8 miles.

The Le Mans Replica Frazer Nash

by Denis Jenkinson

The Scuderia Ambrosiana Frazer Nash is seen finishing in 8th place in the 1951 Mille Miglia. In view of the night motoring in this race two extra headlights were fitted, and a full-width screen was used to protect the co-driver as well as the driver.

(Photo: A.F.N. Ltd.)

During the 1920s and 1930s the name Frazer Nash was always associated with sports cars that were hand-built and very functional, with a rakish and 'sports car' appearance, so it was no surprise when Frazer Nash production restarted after the war with a modern car with a similar outward appearance. Just before the war the Aldington brothers, who own the firm of Frazer Nash, were importing B.M.W. cars and having great success with the 2-litre sports model, the immortal Type 328. This car was well ahead of its contemporaries so it was logical for Frazer Nash to use this design as the basis for their post-war models. The Frazer Nash–B.M.W. tie-up went deeper than that, for Colonel H. J. Aldington visited Munich when the war ended and arranged for many of the design details to be taken over by the newly-formed Bristol Car Division of the Bristol Aeroplane Company, and in particular the 6-cylinder, 2-litre engine with its ingenious in-clined overhead valve layout operated by a single camshaft in the cylinder block and pushrods and rockers. This was the famous 328 engine and it became the mainstay of the Bristol and Frazer Nash models, together with a Borg Warner-built 4-speed gearbox.

Having assisted the Bristol firm with the launching of their series of saloon cars, which were in effect logical developments of 1939 B.M.W. cars, H. J. Aldington set about launching the post-war Frazer Nash, and to assist in this he brought Dr Fiedler, the B.M.W. chief designer, back from Germany. As an experiment a Frazer Nash was built with an all-enveloping two-seater body in a style begun by B.M.W. in 1939/40, but it was soon decided that the post-war car should carry on the traditions of the old chain-driven Frazer Nash cars and be a stark and racy-looking two-seater that could be used as an ordinary road car or as a competition car.

Plans for this new model were announced in May 1946, but it was not until the beginning of 1948 that the first car was viewed by the Press. Later that year the Frazer Nash stand at the Earls Court Motor Show displayed a very stark but functional two-seater with tiny mudguards, no doors and a tiny perspex aero screen, and it looked all ready to go racing. It was called the 'High Speed' model, or Competition two-seater, and the makers had every intention that customers should use it for racing as well as a road-going sports car. One of the earliest sales was to Czecho-slovakia, to Zdanek Treybal, while at home E. J. Newton was one of the earliest customers. With racing getting under way again there was plenty of interest in this new Frazer Nash model and, as it was a develop-ment of the successful 328 B.M.W., its true worth could easily be evaluated. The Bristol firm supplied the engine to Frazer Nash specification as regards power output, which was 120 b.h.p. at 5,500 r.p.m., together with the four-speed gearbox and these were mounted in a tubular chassis. Independent front sus-pension was similar to the 328 B.M.W., with lower

In full road trim the Le Mans Replica Frazer Nash was a very practical car and could be used in the toughest of continental rallies. The car illustrated is XMX 4, owned by Lt.-Col. H. P. O'Hara-Moore, who is seen talking to Alex von Falkenhausen of B.M.W., after winning the Rallye Soleil-Cannes in 1952. The low-mounted spot lights were 'extras'. (Photo: A. Traverso)

wishbones and a transverse leaf spring, but the rear suspension was a development of touring B.M.W.s, having a one-piece axle sprung on longitudinal torsion bars and located by a large A-bracket whose apex was pivotted on top of the differential housing, with its base pivotted on the chassis side members. Hydraulic brakes with two-leading shoes at the front were used, and B.M.W.-type centre-lock disc wheels driving through four locating pins were fitted. This new model cost £2,250 plus the double purchase tax imposed by the Government in those days, bringing the total to £3,501 10s. 0d.

In early 1949 the finalised version of this 'High Speed' model was exhibited at the Geneva Motor Show, where it created great interest. The car (TMX 543) was borrowed from John Newton, carefully covered with masking tape at any vulnerable point, and driven out to Geneva by W. H. Aldington, with his wife as passenger. On arrival it was cleaned and polished by the Swiss Frazer Nash importer and appeared on the Show Stand as if it had been delivered in a sealed crate. The Aldingtons always made a strong point of the fact that their cars were usuable road cars first and foremost, and secondly racing cars or Motor Show cars. Some years later at Earls Court I remember seeing a Frazer Nash on the Show stand that had not only been driven there but still had petrol in the tank, and at the end of the Show, while other firms were traditionally sounding the horns of their exhibits, the Frazer Nash staff started the engine of their car and the horn blowing was accompanied by

the glorious crackle of a highly-tuned Bristol engine!

The Aldingtons always believed in racing their products to convince people of the worth of their cars, and in the spring of 1948 H. J. Aldington lent a car to Count 'Johnny' Lurani, whose Scuderia Ambrosiana entered it for the Tour of Sicily with Dorino Serafini as driver and Rudi Heller as co-driver.

The 'High Speed' model Frazer Nash as it made its first appearance at the Earls Court Motor Show in 1948. The low-mounted headlights were later replaced by ones mounted higher, and tubular shock-absorbers were added to the front suspension. (Photo: Motor)

The finalized version of the 'High Speed' model as it appeared at Geneva in 1949. TMX 543 is seen on the shores of Lac Leman after W. H. Aldington had driven it out to Switzerland and it had been 'cleaned up' ready for exhibition. (Photo: A.F.N. Ltd.)

Lurani and H. J. were also taking part in the event with a Bristol saloon, so Bristol and Frazer Nash were among the first British makes to fly the flag in post-war continental races. Serafini led the whole race for more than half distance and then skidded into a kerb and bent the steering, which caused his retirement, but the car had shown its capabilities in rugged mountain racing. Following this, three cars set off from England to take part in the Mille Miglia, but Dickie Stoop had a rather lurid accident with one of them on the way down through France, so only two started the race. Once again Serafini and Heller drove for Lurani, and the other car was driven by Tenbosch and Monkhouse. The opposition was much stronger in this race and neither Frazer Nash figured in the running.

In mid-season the Le Mans 24-hour race took place and this was to prove a turning point in the life of the post-war Frazer Nash. An ex-racing motor-cyclist, Norman Culpan, decided to have a go at car racing, and bought a brand new 'High Speed' model and entered it for Le Mans, with H. J. Aldington as his co-driver, and with the staff of A.F.N. Ltd. to help him with the pit-work. Culpan had looked at the model

at the 1948 Motor Show, without asking any questions of the stand staff, and next day phoned W. H. Aldington and placed an order, having been more than satisfied with what he had seen. His first attempt at motor racing was more than successful for the car, TMX 545, ran splendidly and he and H. J. finished 3rd in the 24 Hour Grand Prix d'Endurance at Le Mans. Because of this success the name of the model was changed from 'High Speed' or 'Competition 2-Seater' to 'Le Mans Replica', and the post-war fame of Frazer Nash cars was properly under way. The Le Mans Replica model was well and truly established; many owners were now racing them, as well as using them for normal road motoring. At the International Trophy meeting at Silverstone in August, Culpan finished 3rd, behind two XK 120 Jaguars, while Treybal was 5th and Newton 7th, and the sight of the very business-like-looking Le Mans Replicas in Production Sports Car races was to become part of the British motor racing scene. With increased production the price was reduced to £1,750 plus tax, equalling £2,723 14s. 6d.

During 1950 the success of the Le Mans Replica as

This chassis view shows the large diameter tubing used for the immensely strong frame and also the Bristol/Frazer Nash gearbox built by Borg Warner. Alongside the right-hand frame tube can be seen one of the torsion bars of the rear suspension passing through the cross-member to its front anchorage point. (Photo: Motor)

This rear view of the chassis shows the simple but effective rear suspension, the axle located by an A-bracket on top of the differential housing, while short links connect the axle ends to longitudinal torsion bars. The Girling rod operated brake mechanism is from the hand-brake. (Photo: Motor)

Left: The robustness of the chassis can be seen in this three-quarter front view, showing the mounting of the telescopic shock-absorbers, the oil cooler in front of the water radiator, and the three-carburettor Bristol engine. (Photo: A.F.N. Ltd.)

Below: In this three-quarter rear view of the chassis it can be appreciated that the rear suspension did not call for any overhanging weight, while the mounting of the engine well back from the front axle gave a low polar-moment of inertia, a desirable feature for good road-holding. (Photo: A.F.N. Ltd.)

a thoroughly race-worthy production sports car gained great impetus and they invariably won the 2-litre class, being beaten only by larger-engined cars such as Jaguars. 'Johnny' Lurani's Scuderia Ambrosiana bought a car for Franco Cortese to drive in Italian events, and in the Tour of Sicily he lay second until a split fuel tank put him out of the race. In the Mille Miglia he finished 6th and was 2nd in the 2-litre category against strong Ferrari and Maserati opposition. At home Culpan was still racing his car, finishing 3rd in the Manx Cup race in the Isle of Man, while Bob Gerard was 3rd overall in the Tourist Trophy at Dundrod and won the 2-litre class with HBC 1. At Silverstone the Le Mans Replicas were 3rd, 4th and 5th behind two 'works' Ferraris, and at Shelsley Walsh they were 1st, 2nd and 3rd in the overall sports car class. Racing was proving the Le Mans Replica and, though the basic design did not need changing, the cars were being developed as production went along, and the Bristol firm were continually improving the engines in co-operation with Frazer Nash. A.F.N. Ltd. did not run a 'works' car themselves, preferring to let their customers do the racing, but naturally gave every help and advice to those competing. As the car had been built primarily as a road-going sports car and had cut its teeth in the Tour of Sicily it was tough and rugged, so it was not a great problem for a private-owner who was racing to maintain the car himself. There was no call for A.F.N. Ltd. to run a 'customer racing service' tuning and maintaining cars.

With each success more and more people took an interest in the Le Mans Replica model, even though Frazer Nash were offering other models with all-enveloping bodywork and a more luxurious finish, and in 1951 the Le Mans Replica reached a peak in competitions. Lurani bought a new car for Cortese to drive and he won the 2-litre class against 10 Ferraris in the Tour of Sicily, being 4th overall, and was 8th in the Mille Miglia and 2nd in his class. The Le Mans Replica was proving to be successful in all manner of competitions, from mountain racing to aerodrome racing, as well as in sprints, hill-climbs, and rallies. It was a true all-round sports car in the best meaning of the words, and was maintaining the name of Frazer Nash at the same high level as the old chain-gang cars. During 1951 one car achieved a feat that few sports cars have equalled: it took part in and completed the 24 Hour Le Mans race and then took part in and completed the Alpine Rally. In 1932 H. J. Aldington

had completed the Alpine Rally in a chain-gang T.T. Replica and then finished in the Tourist Trophy race on the Ards circuit, and the 1951 feat was even better. The car was WHX 225 and at Le Mans Eric Winterbottom and John Marshall finished 14th, while in the Alpine Rally Winterbottom and Duff won their class, gained a Coupe des Alpes going through the whole mountain rally without a single mark lost, and missed best overall performance by a fraction of a second on one of the special tests.

The Le Mans Replicas were being sold in many parts of the world, in Sweden, Italy, Portugal, the United States of America and, of course, in increasing numbers in Great Britain. At Silverstone eight of them took part in the Production Sports car race, Tony Crook winning the 2-litre class, and his time was only beaten by two XK 120 Jaguars running in the large car class. Numerous drivers tried to persuade the factory to run a 'works' car in races, but the Aldingtons preferred to let their customers do the racing, especially while they were being so successful about it. In some cases they arranged for a well-known driver to borrow a customer's car, such as when Stirling Moss drove Sid Greene's car, WMC 181, in the British Empire Trophy in the Isle of Man. He won the race, with Gerard in second place. During this season T.A.S.O. Mathieson, Roy Salvadori, Donald Pitt and numerous others kept the Le Mans Replica Frazer Nash well to the fore in all manner of racing events. In Sicily the Targa-Florio was revived on the Little Madonie mountain circuit and Cortese drove Lurani's car once more. Earlier in the season he had won the Enna Grand Prix in the mountains of Sicily with this car, so he was a great favourite with the Sicilians, and he

The 1949 Le Mans race gave the Frazer Nash its name, and the lone entry which finished third is seen during a pit stop with N. R. Culpan handing over to H. J. Aldington. Above the pit the lap counter shows the car having completed 122 laps to the 126 laps of the leading Ferrari, number 22.

(Photo: Louis Klemantaski)

H. J. Aldington is seen here at speed in Culpan's Frazer Nash in the 1949 Le Mans 24 Hour race, during which the car was kept down to 5,000 r.p.m. in top gear, which gave a speed 110 m.p.h. on a 3·7 to 1 axle ratio.

(Photo: Louis Klemantaski)

Many hands help with the refuelling of the Le Mans Replica Frazer Nash in the 1951 Targa Florio, driven by Franco Cortese, seen exclaiming to his pit attendant. Note the perspex aeroscreen used for this race, and the Scuderia Ambrosiana badge on the side of the scuttle. (Photo: A.F.N. Ltd.)

gave them more reason for admiration for the little Frazer Nash when he won the Targa Florio outright, a distance of 576 kilometres of mountain roads which took just over 7½ hours to complete. At the time I was at the Italian Motor-cycle Grand Prix meeting at Monza and 'Johnny' Lurani was an F.I.M. official. I well remember the excitement with which he came rushing up to tell me that 'his' car had just won the Targa Florio. He was almost off the ground with excitement and I recall that I completely overlooked the fact that it was a British car that had won, for I was competing in a rather serious Grand Prix meeting!

In England, Tony Crook made fastest sports car time at the Shelsley Walsh hill climb, and to round off a splendid season for the Le Mans Replicas Crook went to Montlhéry with his car PPG 1 and broke the International Class E record for 200 miles at a speed just in excess of 120 m.p.h., putting 123·5 miles into the first hour. He was running on normal pump

petrol, on an 8·5 to 1 compression ratio and pulling a 3·2 to 1 rear axle ratio, thus proving conclusively that the Frazer Nash was no specially-prepared freak car, but a most useable sports car which also was very fast and reliable. It is interesting that Crook's performance at Montlhéry ties up with other known measured speeds of the Le Mans Replica, for during the Targa Florio Cortese was timed at 121 m.p.h., while at Dundrod during the Tourist Trophy Donald Pitt was timed at 123 m.p.h. On acceleration the Le Mans Replica was equally impressive, for I personally won a ¼-mile sprint meeting with one in 16·1 seconds.

Without doubt, 1951 saw the Le Mans Replica Frazer Nash at the highest point in its history and holding a very enviable position in the motor sporting world, but this was not the end of its career for 1952 started off with yet more success. A car was sold to Stuart Donaldson, an American, who entered it for the Sebring 12 Hours to be driven by Harry Grey and Larry Kulok. Virtually from new the car was taken out, raced and won, Kulok and Grey beating all the opposition to win the 12 Hours Sebring race outright. Class wins were always expected of the Frazer Nashes, but it was often proving that it could take on all-comers, irrespective of engine size. Donaldson was delighted with his purchase and wrote to A.F.N. Ltd., telling them with some pride of the victory and that his drivers reported a trouble-free 12 Hours during which they continually reached 5,200 r.p.m. in top gear, and at one point in the night it reached 5,500 r.p.m. They had obviously not cruised round waiting for the opposition to retire, but had driven the car hard, as it was meant to be driven.

The Le Mans Replica had been in production for nearly four years and, though the engine had undergone many improvements and power increases, the basic car had been changed very little. There had been no need for change as it was capable of tackling most of the opposition in almost any sort of competition, but during 1952 a revised version of the Le Mans Replica was introduced, known as the Mark II. The general conception of the car was the same, but attention was given to weight saving, lower frontal area and improved road holding, for by now there were numer-

The victorious Frazer Nash is seen approaching the finishing line at the end of the 1951 Targa Florio. In view of the Sicilian heat Cortese removed the metal grille from the radiator aperture, and used a low windscreen. (Photo: Fotografia Randazzo)

The privately entered car of R. F. Peacock and G. Ruddock is seen taking the Mulsanne corner during the 1952 Le Mans race in which it finished 10th. (Photo: *Autocar*)

Bob Gerard driving his Le Mans Replica Frazer Nash in the British Empire Trophy race in the Isle of Man in 1951 when he finished 2nd to Stirling Moss. This car had a slightly modified radiator grille with parallel sides instead of the more usual tapering type. (Photo: Guy Griffiths)

ous 'specials' and small-production cars like Cooper and Connaught, which were showing signs of challenging the supremacy of the Le Mans Replica. The Mark II model had a more powerful engine, with an extractor exhaust system finishing just in front of the offside rear wheel, a lighter and lower body, smaller mudguards and lighter pressed-steel wheels that bolted on to the hubs, in place of the heavier B.M.W.-type centre lock wheels and hubs. In developing the Mark II model the factory began to compete with a development car of their own, employing Ken Wharton as the driver, while Tony Crook also competed with his own Mark II. This new model was well able to deal with most of the opposition, especially in the more rugged type of road race, and Wharton finished a strong 2nd to a C-type Jaguar in the Jersey Road Race. He was equally successful on aerodrome circuits, such as Boreham, and Crook was 3rd in the 'round-the-houses' 2-litre race at Monte Carlo. Bob Gerard and David Clarke finished 4th in the Goodwood 9 Hours race, behind much larger-engined Aston Martins and Ferraris, proving that the earlier Le Mans Replicas were still to be reckoned with where endurance counted. Other owners were still racing and rallying their Mark I cars with success, but the Aldingtons

were not too happy about the advent of the Mark II as it had been built more as a pure racing car than an all-round sports car for road use as well as for racing. This alteration in policy had been forced on them by a change that came about in British motor racing. The light 'aerodrome racer' was beginning to make itself felt, and the need for a road-going racing car was non-existent. Most racing was taking place on smooth aerodromes, cars were taken to meetings in transporters, and road equipment was becoming something that merely had to satisfy the scrutineers that it complied with the regulations. It was the coming of the lightweight 'aerodrome racers' that sounded the death knell for the Le Mans Replicas, for Frazer Nash had to move with the times and drop some of the ruggedness of the earlier cars. The Mark II cars managed to hold their own during 1952, but in 1953 the writing was on the wall.

Frazer Nash had not concentrated solely on the Le Mans Replica model, and were selling touring versions with full-width two- and three-seater bodywork, while they also branched out into fixed head coupés. These models gradually took over from the old, original, stark two-seaters. The last Mark II was sold in 1953, and altogether some sixty cars were built in

Tony Crook is seen in action at Silverstone in 1950 with his early 'High Speed' model, with the low-mounted headlamps. Crook was to become a prolific user of Frazer Nash cars, graduating to a Mark II model. (Photo: Guy Griffiths)

Stirling Moss driving Sid Greene's Le Mans Replica Frazer Nash is seen winning the British Empire Trophy in 1951. The absence of an off-side headlamp was allowed by the regulations. (Photo: Guy Griffiths)

A Le Mans Replica Frazer Nash on its home ground. The Winter-bottom/Marshall car is seen negotiating the Esses on the Sarthe circuit during the 1951 Le Mans 24 Hour race.
(Photo: London & County Press (Knightsbridge) Ltd.)

the Le Mans Replica series; even today many of the Mark I cars are still giving good service and being used in Club events.

The factory continued to race their development Mark II model, though it was modified and rebuilt out of all recognition, and Ken Wharton stayed as the 'works' driver. During development of the factory Mark II a de Dion rear axle layout was evolved and some earlier Le Mans Replica models were modified to this layout. Its last appearance was in the ill-fated Tourist Trophy race at Dundrod in 1955, where it was involved in a multiple crash and was written-off, Wharton luckily escaping without serious injury. The Bristol company had been running their own racing team since 1953, and the close co-operation that Frazer Nash had with them over engine development was having to be shared with them, as well as with firms like Cooper and Lister so, after the Tourist

Trophy disaster, the Aldingtons withdrew from racing and the glorious reign of the stark, racy-looking Le Mans Replica Frazer Nash came to an end. It is true to say that it represented one of the last, if not *the* last, of the old-school sports cars in the vintage tradition of stark simplicity.

© *Denis Jenkinson, 1966.*

SPECIFICATION: LE MANS REPLICA FRAZER NASH

ENGINE: Six cylinders in-line, cast iron block and crank-case, light alloy cylinder head. 66 × 96 mm., bore and stroke, 1,971 c.c. capacity. Inclined overhead valves, inlet valves operated by pushrods and rockers from camshaft in cylinder block, exhaust valves operated by pushrods, rockers, transverse pushrods and further rockers. Inlet ports vertical in between rocker shafts, central 10 mm. sparking plugs. Three downdraught Solex carburettors. Four-bearing crankshaft, lead-bronze (steel backed) strip-type bearings, water cooling with pump circulation and pressure delivery to cylinder head. Pressure oil lubrication with external radiator, integral oil feed through alloy connecting rods to gudgeon pins. External exhaust system.
TRANSMISSION: Single dry-plate clutch, four-speed and reverse gearbox, top—3·54, third—4·57, second—6·46, first—10·33, reverse—10·23. Syncromesh on 2nd, 3rd and top ratios. Open 2-jointed short propeller shaft, spiral bevel final drive (alternative ratios available).
CHASSIS: Ladder construction of large-diameter steel tubes.
SUSPENSION: Front: independent by top transverse leaf spring, lower wishbones and telescopic hydraulic shock absorbers. Rear: rigid axle mounted on longitudinal torsion bars, located by A-bracket pivotted to chassis at its feet and ball location at apex on differential housing.
STEERING: Rack and pinion.
BRAKES: Hydraulic brakes operating on all four wheels from foot brake, with two leading shoes in front brakes. Light alloy drums with iron liners and air scoops for cooling. Handbrake by mechanical linkage to rear drums.
FUEL SYSTEM: Alloy fuel tank of 20 gallons capacity with reserve supply of 2 gallons. Fuel feed by mechanical pump driven from camshaft.
WHEELS: Drilled disc wheels, four pin drive, centre lock eared hub caps, 5·25 × 16 inch tyres.

Equally at home in mountains, the same car is seen during the 1951 Alpine Rally, as run at Le Mans with the addition of a full-width screen and a luggage grid on the tail. Winterbottom/Duff won the 2-litre class and a covetted Alpine Cup. (Photo: Autosport)

Above and below, left: The Mark II Le Mans Frazer Nash as raced by the factory during the 1952 season. Driver: Ken Wharton.

The 1948 "High Speed" model.

Frazer Nash radiator badge.

F. R. Gerard's 1950 car. Note revised radiator grille with parallel sides.

Sid Greene's car, with which Stirling Moss won the 1951 British Empire Trophy race, had an all-metal tail, unlike the 1949 Le Mans car (see page 2).

A very typical scene during the heyday of the Le Mans Replica Frazer Nash. In this gaggle of cars approaching the first corner on the Isle of Man circuit are seven Le Mans models, which have already outpaced larger-engined Allard cars. (Photo: Guy Griffiths)

MAJOR RACE RESULTS ACHIEVED BY LE MANS REPLICA FRAZER NASH CARS

Year	Race	Place	Driver
1949	Le Mans 24 Hour race	3rd	H. J. Aldington/ N. Culpan
1950	Mille Miglia	6th	F. Cortese
	Manx Cup, Isle of Man	3rd	N. Culpan
	Tourist Trophy—Dundrod	3rd	F. R. Gerard
	Silverstone Production car race	3rd	E. J. Newton
1951	Tour of Sicily	4th	F. Cortese
	Mille Miglia	8th	F. Cortese
	Enna G.P.	1st	F. Cortese
	Silverstone Production car race	1st	T. A. D. Crook
	British Empire Trophy	1st	S. Moss
	Targa Florio	1st	F. Cortese
	Tourist Trophy—Dundrod	3rd	F. R. Gerard
1951	Shelsley Walsh (Sports)	1st	T. A. D. Crook
	Class E record 200 miles		T. A. D. Crook
1952	Sebring 12 Hours	1st	L. Kulok/ H. Grey
	Prix de Monaco	3rd	T. A. D. Crook
	Jersey Road Race	2nd	K. Wharton
	Boreham Airfield races	1st	K. Wharton
	Goodwood 9 Hours	4th	F. R. Gerard/ D. Clarke
1953	Reims 12 Hours	7th	D. Clarke/ P. Scott-Russell
	British Empire Trophy	2nd	K. Wharton
	Shelsley Walsh (Sports)	1st	K. Wharton
	Tourist Trophy—Dundrod	7th	F. R. Gerard/ D. Clarke
	Goodwood 9 Hours	6th	F. R. Gerard/ D. Clarke
	Goodwood B.A.R.C. races	2nd	K. Wharton
		3rd	C. A. S. Brooks

EQUIPMENT: 12-volt electrical system. 5 in. diameter speedometer and tachometer, oil pressure gauge, oil and water temperature gauges. 'One shot' chassis lubrication.

BODYWORK: Light alloy two-seater body mounted on steel tube frame which is integral with the chassis. Full-width fold-flat windscreen, two aero-screens. Optional fabric tail cover or metal cover.

PERFORMANCE: 110 b.h.p. at 5,250 r.p.m. with 8·5 to 1 compression ratio, or 120 b.h.p. at 5,500 r.p.m. with 9·5 to 1 compression. 125·5 ft.lbs. torque, and 157 lb./sq. in. b.m.e.p. at 4,500 r.p.m. Maximum speed 120 m.p.h.

DIMENSIONS: Wheelbase, 8 ft. Track, 4 ft. Length, 11 ft. 9 in. Width, 3 ft. 9 in. Height, 3 ft. 1 in. Ground clearance, 7 in. Weight (dry) 13¼ cwt.

MAKERS: A.F.N. Ltd., Falcon Works, Isleworth, Middlesex.

The last of a long and successful line was the factory experimental Mark II, driven here by Ken Wharton. By this time the car was an out-an-out sports-racing car, with fibreglass body panels and the bare minimum of equipment, the spare wheel being mounted flat on the low tail. (Photo: Charles Dunn)

The Author and the Publishers gratefully acknowledge the assistance of Mr. W. H. Aldington in the preparation of this Profile.

The 1914 G.P. Vauxhall

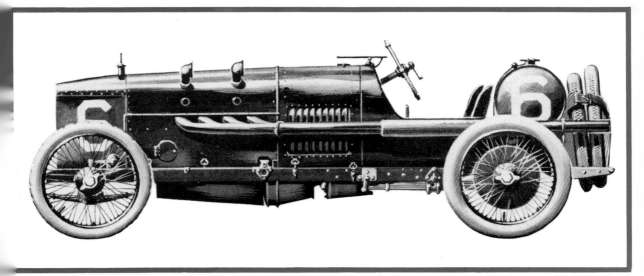

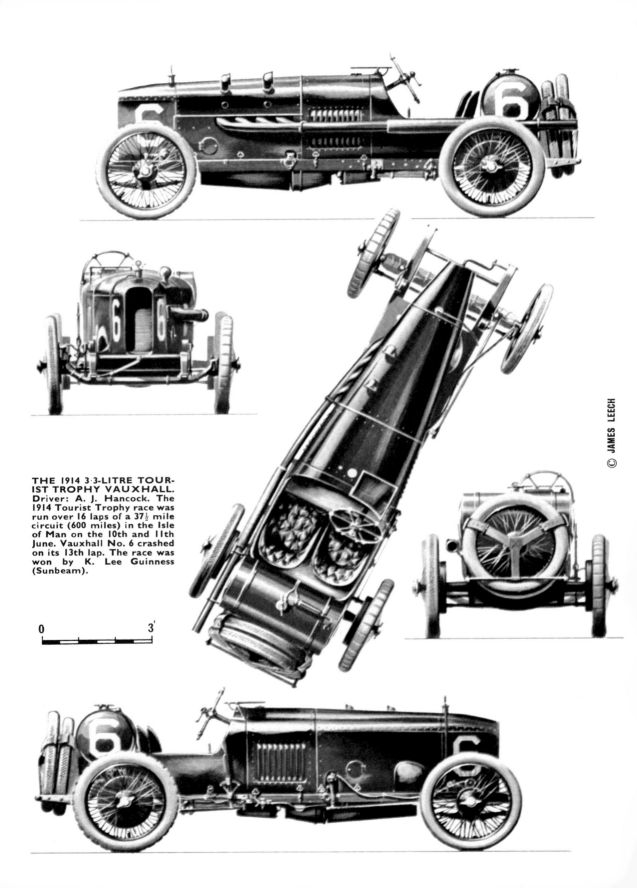

© JAMES LEECH

THE 1914 3·3-LITRE TOUR-IST TROPHY VAUXHALL. Driver: A. J. Hancock. The 1914 Tourist Trophy race was run over 16 laps of a 37½ mile circuit (600 miles) in the Isle of Man on the 10th and 11th June. Vauxhall No. 6 crashed on its 13th lap. The race was won by K. Lee Guinness (Sunbeam).

0   3'

The 1914 G. P. Vauxhall
by Laurence Pomeroy

1914 French Grand Prix at Lyons: A. J. Hancock's 4½-litre Vauxhall which broke down on its second lap.

At 8.01 hrs. on the cloudy morning of 21st September 1913, Guyot's Zenia left the line for the *Coupe de l'Auto* race to be run over 12 laps and 388 miles of a circuit on the outskirts of Boulogne. As was then the custom the remaining 18 cars, having drawn their position by ballot, followed at half minute intervals.

At 14.16.40.8 hrs. Georges Boillot crossed the line a winner at 63·1 m.p.h. despite having stopped at his pit on the 4th lap to take a drink and enquire how the rest of the race was getting on.

After an interval of 8 minutes he was followed by his Peugeot team mate, Jules Goux, who had experienced mechanical trouble and subsequently broken the lap record at 66 m.p.h. K. Lee Guinness on a Sunbeam finished third, 11 minutes behind the winner, and Hancock's Vauxhall took fourth place over 50 mins. after Boillot had crossed the line. When he had done so, Vauxhall's Chief Designer, L. H. Pomeroy, turned to the *Patron* of the Sunbeam team, Louis Coatalen, and made what most people must have thought was a very cryptic remark. This was: 'Well Louis, I fancy you and I will be going back to the office, looking up certain old drawings and pulling some old engines off the shelf.'

Only 12 months earlier the side-valve 3-litre Sunbeams and Vauxhalls had shown almost equal speed in the *Coupe de l'Auto* Race run in conjunction with the French G.P. at Dieppe. Both were considerably faster and more reliable than the double o.h.c. 4-valve-per-cylinder Peugeot that ran against them in the same class. Yet all three companies had just been running virtually the same cars with a very different result; indeed, it was plain that the game was up for the simple side-valve engine closely resembling a production type. But why 'old drawings'?

The explanation is that in 1910 Vauxhalls had built an experimental o.h.c. engine intended for competition in the Prince Henry trials that performed so poorly that tuned side-valve engines were actually used. In 1911 Louis Coatalen had produced an o.h.c. 4-valve-per-cylinder engine which successfully broke records at Brooklands.

Neither company persisted with these designs,

either at the track or in their road racing cars because they thought competition should closely resemble production models so that lessons learned could immediately be applied for the benefit of those that bought them. The racing car of to-day should be the production model at the next Olympia Motor Show. This was a theme to which the Continental constructors had never subscribed, and Pomeroy's reference to 'old drawings' was thus a call for a new approach to British racing car design.

In the Autumn of 1913, the R.A.C. announced that it would stage a two-day race for the Tourist Trophy on the 10th and 11th June 1914 for cars fitted with engines not exceeding 3·31 litres. The Automobile Club de France, after much discussion, said that the French G.P. would be held on the 5th July on a circuit outside Lyons for cars with unsupercharged engines not exceeding 4·5 litre capacity.

Vauxhalls decided to enter a team of three cars for both races. One set of engines would have a piston diameter of 93 mm. to race in the Isle of Man, and another set 101·4 mm. diameter for competition at Lyons with piston strokes of 130 mm. and 140 mm. respectively. After this, and with little more than seven months to go, L. H. Pomeroy and his Chief Draughtsman retired to Bevans Hotel at Lynmouth where in a few weeks they designed a completely new motor-car.

THE 1914 G.P. VAUXHALL CHASSIS DESIGN

Curious as it may seem it was generally supposed that the 1913 Peugeot success at Boulogne was more by reason of their light weight than the 90 b.h.p. of their advanced 78 × 156 mm. double o.h.c., 4-valve-per-cylinder, roller-bearing crankshaft engines. As both the 1914 races were to be run over twisty courses with many gradients (indeed a mountain in the Isle of Man), L. H. P. decided to put all he knew into weight reduction for his forthcoming racers. For this reason, together with an inbred audacity not yet tempered by long experience (he had designed his first and dramatically successful car at the age of 24 in 1907 and in 1910 had seen a derivative of it become the first 3-litre to exceed 100 m.p.h.) he discarded all but a few minor components of existing design.

The result was a genuinely novel car from stem to stern.

For the first time semi-elliptic front springs passed through opened-up rectangular spaces in the front axle beam, with a consequent stress reduction which was probably regarded as a means to reduce weight, but which would also have been valuable (as Bugatti proved ten years later) if in subsequent development brakes had been added to the front wheels.

The stern was even more heterodox. Cantilever springs were employed for the first time on a G.P. car, with the double motive of reducing unsprung weight (consisting only of that part of the spring behind the middle pivot point) and also lowering all-up weight by having an unstressed frame, for behind the pivot points it had only to support the weight of the bolster fuel tank, the fuel it contained, and the two spare wheels mounted across the back of it.

The rear suspension of the car was self evidently strange; the transmission, only to be observed with the car on a hoist, even stranger. Ruthlessly pursuing weight reduction, L. H. P. decided to substitute a torque tube with a spherical joint on its nose for the radius rods and trunnion rear axle used on his 1912/13 *Coupe de l'Auto* racers and, having the torque tube, in effect to enlarge its front end to contain the gears. He thus saved much of the weight of a normal gearbox, but as the rear axle rose and fell the gearbox would move through a small arc on the nose of the torque tube. With the gear lever positively fixed to the

L. H. Pomeroy, 1883–1941: a portrait of the Vauxhall Chief Designer taken in 1919.

frame, it was necessary to have some sophisticated connections between the moving selector rods and gear lever to accommodate this. As if this was not sufficient, provision was also made for a supplementary gear lever joined to a 2-speed unit so that the driver could choose between eight speeds in all by moving the levers in sequence. However, this was found to be too difficult to be used in either of the 1914 events or in subsequent racing appearances.

A second and most difficult problem posed by the transmission was how to accommodate the conventional transmission brake. Before the days of four-wheel braking systems (used by only four manufacturers in 1914 and none before) a hand lever expanded shoes in the rear brake drums, and the pedal was connected to a brake on the propellor shaft. This punished the transmission system and normal braking was on the rear wheels.

In view of this Pomeroy thought that thermal problems in the transmission brake could be ignored, and decided boldly to enclose it inside the torque tube, which was of course made from a plurality of castings bolted together.

In view of the car's subsequent history, it is impossible to judge whether this arrangement was as bad as it looks, but it must be remembered that the narrow-section tyres of the times limited the braking which could be used anywhere, and that soon after a race had started the road surface approaching any corner became so cut up and stony that it is very doubtful if rear braked cars could be slowed at more than 0·3 g, of which 0·1 g would be contributed by the engine. In other words, up till 1914, road racing cars were stopped from 100 m.p.h. and over at a rate which can be equalled to-day using an umbrella-type handbrake in rather poor order!

The transmission line was connected to the engine through a cone-type clutch with friction material riveted to the flywheel with the cone fabricated from boiler plate.

Although daring, and doubtless justified from the viewpoint of low weight, many of the novelties in the chassis design were what the French would call '*discutable*'. In particular the high roll centre and poor sideways location of the rear axle characteristic of cantilever rear springs gave a strong oversteer which, compounded by the torque tube drive, resulted in poor road holding, which stood strongly in contrast with the excellent reputation Vauxhalls had with their 'Prince Henry', and recently introduced 30/98, sporting models.

The frame was 63 lb. lighter than the 1912/13 *Coupe de l'Auto* racers but seems desperately shallow, and was without the central stout tubular cross member extended to carry the spare wheels which had torsionally stiffened the 3-litre racing cars.

It had five small diameter and two channel cross-members, and the rear tank was also a stressed stiffener, but one can see why Matt Park, remembering his drives at Brooklands in 1921, referred to 'those devils'.

THE 1914 G.P. VAUXHALL ENGINE

In a stormy debate with Fred Lanchester before the Institution of Automobile Engineers in 1910, Pomeroy had proved that piston speed was not (repeat not) a limiting factor in engine design and performance from the viewpoint of stress and mechanical failure. The reason was that stress would only become excessive,

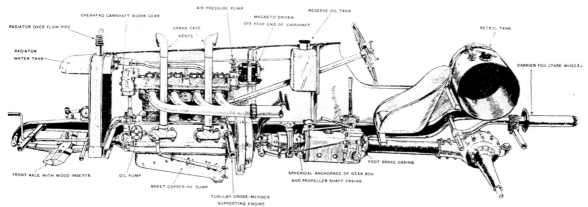

A Gordon Crosby drawing showing the general arrangement of the main units of the 1914 G.P. Vauxhall.   (*Autocar* copyright)

and failure follow, if engines with a bore and stroke of 126 mm. × 152 mm. exceeded 4,400 r.p.m., a crankshaft speed far beyond that possible at this time even with much smaller engines.

If crankshaft speeds were not limited by piston speeds in these times, by what then?

Partly crude cam design imposing critical loads on the steels then available for valve springs; partly exhaust valve steels unable to support the thermal loading of very high r.p.m. so that head and stem parted company; partly because sparking plugs over heated; and most importantly because the engine bearings were subject to increasing pressures which rose as the square of the crankshaft speed in addition to velocities varying directly therewith. So stepping up crankshaft speed by say 30 per cent, raised the PV factor by 90 per cent and should oil temperatures exceed 120°F. the white metal bearings of the time were dangerously near melting-point.

Pomeroy made a three-pronged attack on this basic problem. The aluminium crankcase casting ended on the centre line of the crankshaft, and bolted to it was a very deep sump made from a copper pressing to give good thermal conductivity and keep down oil temperature. The main bearings had fins formed on the lower half of the shells to increase stiffness and aid heat dissipation, and two marine-type cowls kept a constant flow of cooling air through the crankcase.

The loads on the main bearings were substantially reduced by the employment, for the first time on a racing car engine, of counter balance weights, that reduced the load on the centre main bearing of a four cylinder engine by as much as two-thirds and entirely eliminated the horizontal loads normally resisted on the dividing line of a split bearing.

As can be seen from the illustration on page 11, Vauxhalls avoided the complications of integrally forged balanced weights, and the cost of machining a shaft of this type from the solid, by having a separate weight on each crank with attachment by rivets so placed that they were outside the shaft diameter and thus did not weaken it.

The cylinder block and integral heads was a single casting, water jacketed over its top half, with the separated individual bores joined by a continuous flange where they were bolted to the crankcase. A feature of the design was first-class water circulation around the valves, which were closed by exposed springs and opened by rockers placed above cam

shafts which ran in tunnels cast-in with the block immediately above the inlet and exhaust ports. By this means manufacture was simplified, clearances could be closely controlled and the added depth of the main casting increased stiffness. More importantly (with an eye on possible fallibility of valve springs at the unprecedented high speed envisaged) lifting separate lids at the top of each camshaft tunnel also removed the rockers and their bearings so that a broken spring could quickly be removed; mechanical

Cross-section of the engine.   (*Autocar* copyright)

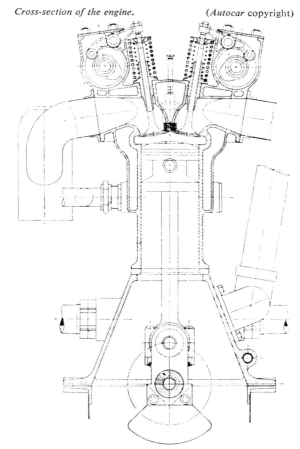

Inlet side of the Grand Prix Vauxhall engine.

Exhaust side of the Grand Prix Vauxhall engine.
(Photo: *Motor*)

disaster being avoided by the presence of an inner supplementary spring.

All the valves were made from a tungsten alloy steel, and the cam shafts were driven by a unique combination of a bevel gear driving a vertical shaft at engine speed, and a worm gear at the top of the shaft engaging with worm wheels at the end of each camshaft. With this arrangement expansion effects could be absorbed by the upper gears moving in relation to the worm and, by having unequal numbers of holes on the cam shaft flange and the main driving wheels, valve timing could be varied down to 1 degree.

A single magneto was driven off the end of the inlet camshaft with a small piston-type pump to maintain air pressure in the tank from the back of the exhaust camshaft. At the front, a skew gear low down on the vertical drive mated with a cross shaft connecting to a gear-type oil pump mounted well above the level of the sump on the left-hand side of the engine and a water pump opposite discharging into the inlet side of the cylinder block.

In its 3·3-litre form for the T.T. races, the Vauxhall engine gave 90 b.h.p. at 3,600 r.p.m. and was designed for 4,500 r.p.m. capability, both far above anything hitherto suggested. The 3·6 : 1 top gear ratio gave 3,850 r.p.m. at the 100 m.p.h. which might have been attained (given time for development), and 3,750 r.p.m. at 95 m.p.h. which, with the 90 h.p. actually realised on the test bed at the slightly lower crank-

shaft speed of 3,600 r.p.m., was well within the car's compass.

THE R.A.C. TOURIST TROPHY

Vauxhalls had only a tenth of the workmen available to their great rivals Sunbeam, and their racing cars had to be put through the machine shops in parallel with production models at a time when the limited resources of a small plant employing 350 persons was stretched to a limit of making seven cars a week.

In consequence, the first T.T. car was completed only 14 days before the race was due to start on 10th June, and did not arrive in the Isle of Man until 1st June.

Hancock immediately had engine trouble and Watson's time of 43 minutes 27 seconds, and Higginson's 63 minutes 38 seconds did not approach the Sunbeam times of 37/38 minutes.

On Thursday, 4th June, Higginson's engine cast aside a balance weight, and his two team mates, Watson and Hancock, had to add half a hundred-weight of ballast to bring their cars up to the required minimum of 21 cwt. 56 lb. This was easy; far more difficult was the fact that after Higginson's engine had been rebuilt, and as it was being run up in the garage, a connecting rod came out of the crankcase only 24 hours before the race was due to start.

All night work brought all three cars to the line, although it seemed at 6 a.m. that the race would have to be postponed for, as my mother wrote me on a post-card showing Hancock's car:
'The rain is simply pouring and the mist on the mountains prevents the drivers from seeing for 10 miles'.

However, at 9 a.m. the rain had stopped and the Vauxhalls set out well knowing that their cars were the worst prepared in the event.

Watson broke his crankshaft only 4 miles from the start, and during the first lap the wretched Higginson lost all the oil from the crankcase due to a stripped thread on an oil pipe over tightened by one of the weary men who had been working so hard on his car only a few hours before.

Hancock staggered on through the first of the two days racing and finished 12th (the last but one) 1 hour 48 minutes behind the leading Sunbeam after 300 miles of racing.

1914 Tourist Trophy race: Vauxhall No. 6 (A. J. Hancock) on the weighbridge. There was a minimum weight limit of 21 cwt. 56 lb.
(Photo: Radio Times Hulton Picture Library)

1914 Tourist Trophy race: Vauxhall No. 17 was driven by W. Watson, the holder of the Trophy from his victory on the Hutton in 1908. In the race, Watson retired on his first lap with a broken crankshaft, just beyond Union Mills four miles from the start.

On the second morning Vauxhalls spent 54 minutes on the car, so that at the end of the first lap of Thursday's racing he was last, and over 3 hours behind the leader. On the next lap he changed a magneto in an ineffective endeavour to cure misfiring, and three laps later when, with weakening dampers, the car had developed an exaggerated rock and roll, it left the road while travelling over the mountain and turned over three times with Hancock largely unscathed but his mechanic Gibbs seriously hurt.

*   *   *

By Sunday, 15th June, the cars were back at the Works at Kimpton Road, Luton, for the installation of the 4½-litre crankshafts, pistons, and cylinder blocks. At the same time it was obvious that three major problems were present in addition to the mysterious misfiring which, it might be hoped, could be solved by normal diagnosis. The location of the balance weights on the crankshaft had to be checked; some means found of preventing crankshafts breaking; the connecting rods obviously needed strengthening. There were three working weeks in which to make

these modifications, drive the cars 600 miles to Lyons and start in the French G.P. on Saturday, 4th July.

All that could be done about the balance weights was carefully to check the soundness of the fixing. Crankshaft breakage was caused by a too sharp fillet between the crankweb and pin, and L. H. P. daringly decided actually to cut back into the web so as to increase the radius at this point as it was impossible to machine new shafts in time.

The connecting rods were a key problem. The finest steel of the day came from B.N.D. whose works were at Liège, and immediately after returning home L. H. P. went to see the local manager of the London County, Westminster, and Parrs Bank, and left for Liège carrying with him a bag of gold (in sovereigns) together with blueprints showing revised contours in red. Crossing the channel in a colleague's motor yacht and travelling in an age without passports, he went straight to B. N. D. who hand-forged some sixteen rods in three days, and were paid in sovereigns. L. H. P. then returned by yacht to England, and after day and night work the G.P. cars left

The Vauxhall Team during practice for the T.T. Left to right: Hancock's car, Higginson's car and Watson's car. Higginson retired on the first lap.
(Photo: Radio Times Hulton Picture Library)

Hancock's car during practice. The spare wheels have been removed.

Oversteer: Hancock's 3·3-litre T.T. car on the first day—note the splash board rigged on the driver's side of the car.

Luton for Lyons on Wednesday, 1st July. They were driven straight to the scrutineering and weighing-in, arriving a little after the official closing time of 5 p.m. on 3rd July.

THE FRENCH GRAND PRIX

On the way down they ran superbly, and showed such acceleration that L. H. P. was quite confident that they would be faster over the first 200 yards from the line than their rivals, the start being in pairs at 30-second intervals, and the couplings, Hancock carrying number 4, against Nagant number 3; de Palma number 18, with a second Nagant, and Watson number 31 against Rigal's Peugeot.

Far from out accelerating their rivals the Vauxhalls departed from the line in a series of pops and bangs, and the fastest of them, driven by de Palma, took 26 minutes 29 seconds on the first lap which put him in twenty-sixth place with only eleven cars slower than he. Amongst them, Hancock, who took 2 hours 25 minutes 29 seconds for his first lap, and Watson 2 hours 46 minutes 29 seconds.

Hancock broke down on the second lap. Watson, having several times dismantled his ignition and carburation systems, went into the fourth lap before suffering mechanical failure, but later claimed that when he had got the car to run well he had been able comfortably to keep pace for some miles with one of the winning Mercedes team.

De Palma survived until the seventh lap when he was running last but one, with the best time 25 minutes 31 seconds, which compares with the 20 minutes 06 seconds of Sailer (Mercedes), which was the fastest of the day.

The Press was rightly critical of these poor performances of cars which had promised so well, made by a Company which had honourably represented England on the Continent, and in the breaking of World Records during the preceding three years.

* * *

Within a month all this was forgotten, but despite World War I, tests went on over the Bedfordshire roads and the cars continued to go very badly although they had been most carefully checked over. Months passed before one of the mechanics, Ernest Swain, brought into L. H. P.'s office one of the carburettor float needles and pointed out that it had an exceptionally fine taper. These were instruments of a new type specially designed for the cars and it was not until this moment that L. H. P. remembered that the Zenith representative had recommended on the night before the race that the air pressure in the rear fuel tank should be let down from 8 p.s.i. to 2½ p.s.i. to guard against cracking of the tank and flooding of the float chamber. Far from flooding, the float chambers had never been filling, and restoration of 8 p.s.i. immediately brought back full power.

During 1915, and in the expectation that the War would soon be over, the camshaft drive was revised to give a bevel unit at the top in place of the worm wheels which were thought to be somewhat power absorbing, and the suspension was redesigned at the back to accept semi-elliptic springs in place of cantilever. The cars were then stored for the duration.

Early in 1919 L. H. P. resigned his technical directorship of Vauxhalls and took up an appointment in the U.S.A.

This might well have been the end of the story so far as the unfortunate G.P. cars were concerned. However, in 1921 the Works decided to run two of them at Brooklands and in hill climbs and this made it possible for them to redeem their reputation seven years after they had been manufactured.

Left: Vauxhall I rounding Kirkmichael corner about 14 miles from the start. (Photo: Radio Times Hulton Picture Library). Facing Page: At Sulby Glen Hotel; and making smoke later in the race. (Latter photo: Radio Times Hulton Picture Library)

POST-WAR VICTORIES

Ernest Swain and Matt Park, both mechanics in the 1914 racing teams, were chosen as drivers, and at Brooklands on Whit Monday 1921 Park was second in the Short Handicap over 5¾ miles, that is to say two laps plus the length of the Finishing Straight. Off the same mark he beat the 10-litre Fiat (placed third) which was of the same type that had won the 1911 G.P. de France, and possibly the same car. Again starting from the same mark, he was beaten into second place by this car in the third lap 2nd Lightning Long Handicap.

At the Summer meeting of the B.A.R.C. in June, Park was joined by Swain who won the 10th Lightning Short Handicap at 92·25 m.p.h., and was second in the 24th 100 m.p.h. Long Handicap, and also in the 10th Lightning Long Handicap. Swain continued with success in the August Monday Meeting in which he was first in the 25th 100 m.p.h. Long Handicap at 99 m.p.h., and second in the 26th 100 m.p.h. Handicap after giving a 1912 15-litre G.P. Lorraine Dietrich a start of 4 seconds. During the day Park was third in the 11th Lightning Short Handicap and won the 11th Lightning Long at an average of 96·85 m.p.h., with Swain (who had to give him 9 seconds) second.

In the last meeting of the year, held in late

Hancock entering Ramsey hairpin.

September, Swain was 3rd in the 27th 100 m.p.h. Short Handicap. Some idea of his performance can be obtained from the fact that he was asked to give 16 seconds in 5¾ miles from standing start to H. W. Cook's stripped two-seater 30/98 Vauxhall, and no less than 34 seconds to the Works-entered 3-litre Bentley. In the 12th Lightning Long Handicap Swain came home first at an average speed of 101·34 m.p.h. after a lap at 108·74 m.p.h.

To sum up: during 1921 the 7-year-old Vauxhalls had given Swain three firsts, four seconds, and one third, and Park one first and a third, with two seconds.

They were overwhelmingly the most successful cars running during the Brooklands season, and with the exception of the 4·9-litre, 6-cylinder Indianapolis Sunbeam (fitted by the Works with a single-seater body), and excluding the aero-engined monsters, they were the fastest also. Only Count Louis Zborowski had more personal success than Swain, and although most of his wins were on the immortal Zeppelin-engined Chitty-Chitty-Bang-Bang, he also drove the 1914 Mercedes with which Lautenschlager had won at Lyons, and which had been surveyed by Rolls-Royce during the War when they were developing their aviation engines which used a similar system of cylinder construction. However, the fastest winning speed for the Mercedes was 97·7 m.p.h. with a best

Finis: on his 13th lap Hancock took a left-hander too fast, went through a stone wall and rolled over three times. The car finished on its side in the heather.

lap of 104·19 m.p.h.—in both cases 4 m.p.h. slower than Swain.

The Vauxhalls also competed in the two major hill climbs of the year. In July Swain drove the G.P. car faster up Aston Clinton than had Hancock when he set the record in 1913 with one of the 1912 *Coupe de l'Auto* cars into which the second 30/98 engine had been fitted. In 1921 Swain's 48·6 seconds was 1·8 seconds faster than the next best which was a 30/98 2-seater.

At Shelsley Walsh in September, Swain was extremely anxious to break the record of 55·4 seconds set up by Higginson in 1913 on the first 30/98 of all. After tuning his car to its peak he had the misfortune to experience mechanical trouble when driving to the Hill, and although Park (a slightly slower, if safer, driver) on the not-quite-so-sharply-tuned sister car, took only 55·4 seconds, Sir Charles Bird, driving the 6-cylinder, 4·9-litre Indianapolis Sunbeam, beat him with 52·2 seconds.

Shelsley Walsh thus confirmed that this was the only normally-engined car in Britain at that time which could claim to be faster than the Vauxhall, the Sunbeam's best winning speed at Brooklands being 104·76 m.p.h. with a lap of 111·17 m.p.h.

In June 1922, Vauxhalls ran three entirely new 3-litre cars, designed by C. E. King with engines by H. R. Ricardo, in the R.A.C. Tourist Trophy race and subsequently in hill climbs and at Brooklands. They sold the 1914 cars after comparative trials which showed the top speed of both to be equal, and the acceleration of the 4½-litre models, which were slightly the lighter of the two, to be somewhat superior.

1914 4½-LITRE G.P. VAUXHALL SPECIFICATION

Designer: L. H. Pomeroy, Wh. Ex.

Engine: 4 cylinders 101·5 × 140 mm. (SB ratio 1·39 : 1) giving 130 b.h.p. at 3,300 r.p.m. and 114 p.s.i. at 3,020 r.p.m. Double overhead camshafts driven by bevel and worm gears operating 4 O.H. valves at an included angle of 24 degrees through rockers, with central plug positions. Steel pistons and connecting rods with five bearing counterbalanced crankshaft and full pressure lubrication to all bearings. Vertical Zenith carburettor attached to water-heated inlet manifold on the right-hand side of the car with exhaust systems on the left side. H.T. magneto driven from back end of inlet camshaft with cross shaft at front, driving oil and water pumps.

Cast-iron cylinder block with integral head mounted on aluminium crankcase split on line of plain main bearings with white metal big end bearings. Wet sump made from copper pressing.

Transmission: Cone clutch to 4-speed and reverse gearbox contained in aluminium casting bolted to torque tube and oscillating on spherical joint. Aluminium rear axle containing straight bevel gears giving approx. 33 m.p.h. 1,000 r.p.m. Top gear 3 : 1.

Front Axle: Beam section with springs passing through it and off-set hubs to give positive trail.

Front Suspension: Semi-elliptic with vane-type hydraulic dampers.

Rear Suspension: Cantilever with vane-type hydraulic dampers. Cars raced in 1921 with semi-elliptic rear springs.

Brakes: Internal expanding to rear wheels linked to hand brake; internal expanding foot brake enclosed in transmission casing.

Steering: Worm and wheel, with cast aluminium six-spoke steering wheel.

Fuel System: Rear tank containing approximately 30 gallons with air pressure to carburettor.

Wheels: Rudge-Whitworth detachable with knock-on ears.

Tyres: Front 875 × 105; rear 880 × 120.

Wheelbase: 9 ft. 3 in. (111 in.).

Track, Front: 4 ft. 6 in. (54 in.).

Track, Rear: 4 ft. 6 in. (54 in.).

Frontal Area: 13 sq. ft.

Unladen Weight (at Lyons): 20·6 cwt. (2,300 lb.).

Max. Speed: 115/120 m.p.h.

No. of Cars Built: 3.

Years Raced: 1914 and 1921 by Works.

Drivers: *R.A.C. Tourist Trophy 1914.*
    A. J. Hancock (No. 6).
    W. Watson (No. 17).
    J. Higginson (No. 22).
    French G.P. 1914.
    A. J. Hancock (No. 4).
    R. de Palma (No. 18).
    W. Watson (No. 31).
    Brooklands 1921.
    E. Swain; M. C. Park.

From 1923 onwards a well-known Northern amateur, H. F. Clay, ran one of the G.P. cars in hill climbs, and as late as 1938/39 a survivor was driven by Mr. Baynes in minor club sprints, running with one of the 3·3-litre T.T. engines which Vauxhall presented to the owner. This was a spare that had never before run on the road, but unfortunately this car was in a dismantled state when its owner was killed in a road accident, and the parts were dispersed, so that nothing physical now remains of this bold engineering exercise. But this may not be important.

1914 French Grand Prix at Lyons: Ralph de Palma on his 4½-litre G.P. Vauxhall, which survived until the seventh lap.

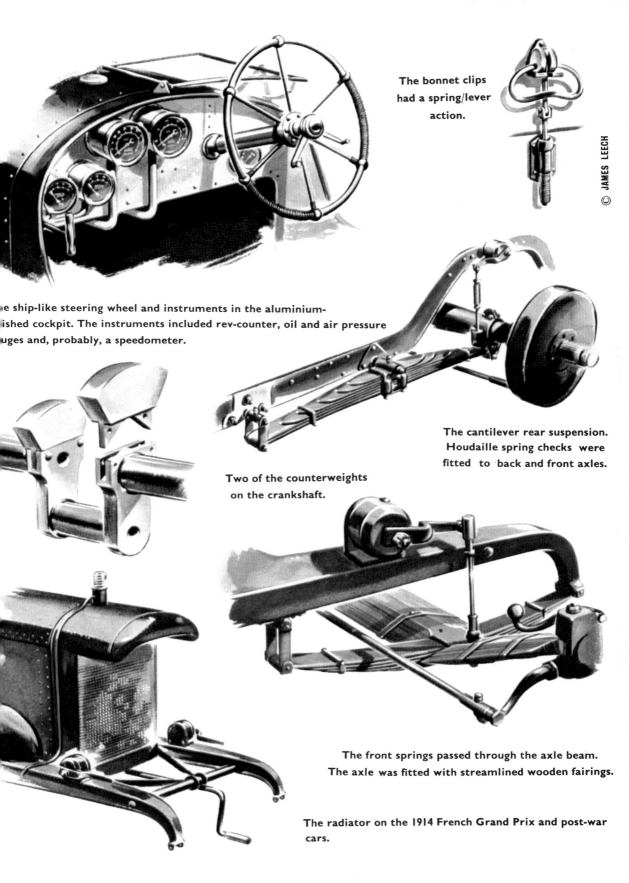

The bonnet clips had a spring/lever action.

…e ship-like steering wheel and instruments in the aluminium-
…ished cockpit. The instruments included rev-counter, oil and air pressure
…uges and, probably, a speedometer.

The cantilever rear suspension. Houdaille spring checks were fitted to back and front axles.

Two of the counterweights on the crankshaft.

The front springs passed through the axle beam. The axle was fitted with streamlined wooden fairings.

The radiator on the 1914 French Grand Prix and post-war cars.

Victorious Days: E. Swain and M. C. Park (Photo: Motor), with the slightly modified 1914 G.P. cars, at Brooklands in 1921. Between them, they scored 4 first, 6 second and 2 third places during the season.

CONCLUSION

L. H. Pomeroy, who had a mastery of words which equalled his skill with a slide rule, once said, 'When I am dead I shall not know it; if I know it I am not dead.'

If he 'knows it' he may think that the total failure of his 1914 cars in the races for which they were designed is more than counterbalanced by the universal acceptance today of the principles which he pioneered. And that, sad though it be that none of them have survived, Horace was right when he wrote:

A monument I've achieved more strong than brass,
Soaring kings' pyramids to overpass;
Which not corroding raindrip shall devour,
Or winds that from the north sweep down in power,
Or years unnumbered as the ages flee!
I shall not wholly die.

© *The Trustees of the late L. E. Pomeroy, 1966*

112

The 6½ Litre Bentley

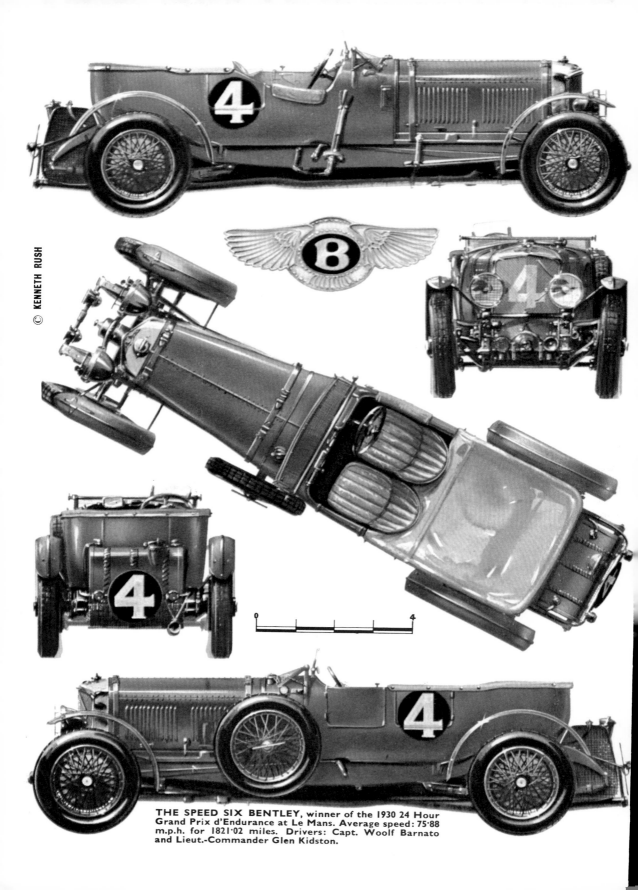

THE SPEED SIX BENTLEY, winner of the 1930 24 Hour Grand Prix d'Endurance at Le Mans. Average speed: 75·88 m.p.h. for 1821·02 miles. Drivers: Capt. Woolf Barnato and Lieut.-Commander Glen Kidston.

The 6½-Litre Bentley

by Darell Berthon

1929 Le Mans Twenty-four Hours Race. Barnato in the Speed Six passing the pits.

(Photo: Fox Photos)

In order to understand why the Speed Six came into being it is necessary to know something of the background which brought it about and to trace its development from the first six cylinder car which Bentley Motors made. The Standard Model 6½ Litre, or Big Six Bentley, as it was sometimes called, was in production long before the 4½ Litre appeared on the scenes and when the Three Litre was still only four years old. The smaller car, designed as an open rugged sports car for the enthusiast then looking for something to replace the excitements of the first World War, was rapidly becoming known to the public following its successes in sprints, hill-climbs, the Tourist Trophy of 1922 and Le Mans 24 hours races of 1923 and 1924. It was almost inevitable that all kinds of people with money and a taste for the latest novelty wanted a Bentley—but one with body-work a little more civilised than the open sports car. This led to totally unsuitable and heavy closed coach-work being fitted to the chassis in an endeavour to turn the car into a town carriage. To try to cope with this situation the firm introduced a long chassis version, the Standard or Long Wheelbase model Three Litre. History merely repeated itself, and the size and weight of coachwork was increased accordingly, killing all semblance of performance.

The time had come for a much more powerful engine and a stronger chassis, specially designed to carry spacious bodies under town and country conditions. It was in 1924 that W. O. Bentley started work on a chassis which would produce high speed touring in comfort with all types of closed coachwork. A six cylinder engine was an obvious starting point. Although there were several big engined cars on the market, they tended to be huge, unwieldy machines, comfortable enough, but their performance and road holding left much to be desired.

THE PROTOTYPE

The new engine followed closely the design of the Three Litre and was in fact much the same engine with two more cylinders added and the stroke shortened by 9 mm. Thus the engine had six cylinders of 80 mm. $\times$ 40 mm. with a capacity of 4,224 c.c. or 4¼-litres. The camshaft was driven by coupling rods from the rear instead of by a vertical shaft from the front as in the Three Litre. The steering, gear box, rear axle and frame were redesigned to give additional strength. Unfortunately figures for the b.h.p. of the engine are not known but they must have been around the hundred mark. The new car, disguised under the name of the 'Sun', an ugly angular radiator and an equally ugly Weymann saloon body with a huge trunk overhanging the rear, was taken over to France and driven by 'W. O.' for long distance testing which included a visit to the 1924 French G.P. It was on this trip that there occurred a chance encounter with the new prototype Rolls-Royce Phantom I which had a momentous influence on the future design and career of the Big Bentley.

'W. O.', who was driving at the time, gives a dramatic description in his Autobiography of seeing a long trail of dust raised by a car travelling very fast towards a Y junction for which he himself was making. Neither car gave way and they arrived together at the junction and continued, side by side, along the Route Nationale. 'W. O.' recognised his 'opponent' as the new Rolls-Royce Phantom I prototype, of which there had been rumours, and he in turn was recognised by the driver of the Rolls-Royce. As this was an opportunity not to be missed, both cars, still side by side, travelled flat out for mile after mile along the straight, deserted French road. The encounter ended abruptly when the Rolls-Royce driver's hat blew off

The prototype six cylinder engine (80 $\times$ 140 mm. 4¼ litres) disguised under the name of the 'Sun'. W. O. Bentley stands besides his latest creation in 1924.

The prototype 6½ litre Bentley engine (100 × 140 mm.), 1925. Note the rubber pads under the engine bearer arm. Believed to be the first time an engine was rubber mounted.

and he stopped to retrieve it, much to 'W. O.'s' relief as he was on his last set of tyres.

As the engine had proved deficient of power low down, and would probably not, even when developed, have a sufficient margin of speed over the Phantom I, 'W. O.' decided to increase the cylinder bore from 80 mm. to 100 mm. and the cubic capacity to 6½-litres. The new engine produced 140 b.h.p. on the bench and in practice gave greatly increased acceleration over all ranges and a higher maximum speed.

After months of experimental work and road testing, a polished Standard 6½ Litre engine and chassis were exhibited at the 1925 Motor Show where it attracted a great deal of interest.

THE CHASSIS AND ENGINE

All models of the 6½ Litre chassis and engine followed the same general design and differed only in modifications to strengthen components by use of newer materials or by increases in the section of certain parts; in the development of power and reliability and in variations of wheelbase, gear box and rear axle ratios to suit particular types of coachwork. The descriptions which follow, therefore, cover the Standard, Speed and 'Le Mans' models. More detailed variations will be found in the tables of specifications (see pages 10 and 12).

The frame is made of high grade steel and the side members are of exceptionally deep section. The

four press steel and three tubular cross members make the bracing of the frame complete in itself.

Front axle is of 'H' section 40-ton tensile steel which was progressively thickened as more powerful braking was evolved.

Rear axle is of semi-floating type with a four bevel pinion differential and spiral bevel final drive.

Gear box (all types) is mounted by three-point suspension and has four forward and reverse gears operated by a right-hand change.

Universal joints are of the internal ring type enclosed in oil-tight casings filled with oil. The fore-and-aft movement of the propeller shaft is taken on a splined coupling on the front joint.

Brakes are of the internal expanding type operating on four large steel drums. The braking on all four wheels is compensated by means of a balance beam differential. The operation of the front brakes is of a Bentley-Perrot design. The foot brakes are assisted by a Dewandre vacuum servo motor. The hand brake operates on the rear wheels only through a separate set of shoes.

Steering is by worm and sector adjustable for wear, the thrust being taken by ball bearings.

Lubrication, except for one grease cup on the water pump, is provided by Tecalemit connections which can be loaded with oil from a gun.

The engine. The six cylinders are cast in one block with non-detachable head. Each cylinder has two inlet and two exhaust valves operated by a totally enclosed overhead camshaft and valve rockers. The camshaft is carried in seven bearings and is driven from the rear end of the crankshaft, which ran in eight bearings.

Ignition is by twin synchronised magnetos (later one magneto and one coil unit were fitted) firing twelve plugs. The firing order is 1 4 2 6 3 5.

Lubrication is by pressure to the mains and big ends and through the hollow camshaft to the cams and rockers.

Overhead valve gear. The valves, each with two concentric coil springs, are grouped in sets of four, two inlet and two exhaust per cylinder. The inlet valves are operated by one forked duralumin rocker arm and the exhaust valves by two single rockers each having a steel roller at one end and an adjustable ball-ended tappet screw at the other. The set for each cylinder is contained in its own aluminium box.

Camshaft drive consists of a helical gear-driven three-throw crankshaft at the rear end of the engine

Left: *The production Standard 6½ litre engine with the Smith-Bentley 5-Jet carburettor.* Right: *The 1929 two-port block Speed Six engine with box form inlet manifold and twin S.U. carburettors.*
(Photos: Chas. K. Bowers)

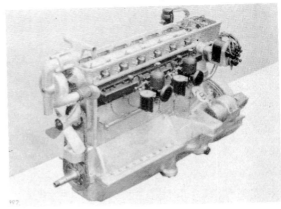

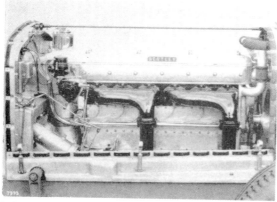

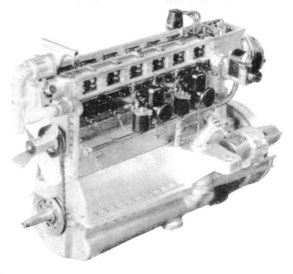

Left: *Exhaust side of the 1929 Speed Six.* Right: *Inlet side of 1929 and 1930 single port block Speed Six. Note the flat induction manifold and five gallon Elektron sump.*
(Photos: Chas. K. Bowers)

crankshaft to which are coupled three connecting rods which in turn are connected to a similar crankshaft direct driven by the camshaft. The upper big end bearings of these rods are fitted with an expansion device to compensate for changes in crankshaft centres due to temperature variations.

Dynamo and water pump are driven off the rear and front ends respectively of the camshaft and the two together damp out any irregularities set up by the action of the valves.

Cooling system. This is unusual in that it has two distinct water circuits controlled by a thermostat whereby the radiator is by-passed in a cold engine. As the engine warms up the circuit to the radiator is opened.

PRODUCTION MODIFICATIONS,
1926–1928

By March 1926, production models were in the hands of the public and by the end of the year 58 cars were on the roads. In the interval long range M.L. Type

ER 6 magnetos were fitted to give increased flexibility; a spring loaded clutch pressure plate replaced the cork insert plate to prevent clutch judder; and to save the batteries and make starting easier Ki-Gass injectors were fitted to the engine. All these modifications made the car much more pleasant to drive under town running conditions.

For the 1927 Motor Show big changes took place which were to be incorporated in the 1928 models. The more important of these changes were:—the half-engine speed dynamo driven by the camshaft was replaced by a new 5-brush dynamo placed between the dumb irons in front of the radiator and driven from the front end of the crankshaft through a flexible coupling, the dynamo casing being bolted to to the front cross member; the radiator tapered inwards towards the bottom and was redesigned to fit the dynamo and at the same time was given a fuller profile and a deeper, 100 mm. matrix which improved the frontal aspect of the car and made it even more imposing looking. For a time the camshaft had no

The Road Test Shop. 6½ Litre chassis being checked after their first road test.   (Photo: Chas. K. Bowers)

1929 Le Mans. Tim Birkin in 'Old No. 1' finishing 1st and Glen Kidston second in No. 9, the first of the racing 4½ Litres.
(Photo: *Autocar*)

1929 Double Twelve Hour Race. No. 2 is the first racing Speed Six known as 'Old No. 1'. (Photo: Montagu Motor Museum)

damping at the rear but after four months a torsional damper was fitted to a taper on the end of the camshaft to restore the damping effect exerted by the dynamo before its removal.

A Delco Remy coil ignition set replaced the off-side magneto and a Hardy Spicer propeller shaft took the place of the plunging (pot) joint type which needed frequent replacement of the blocks and slippers. To make braking lighter, a Dewandre Servo motor was coupled to the braking system. A third wheelbase chassis length, 12 ft. 7¼ in., was added to the range. By the end of 1927 the total of six cylinder chassis made had risen to 185.

In mid-1928 two further modifications were introduced. One was the change over to single pole wiring and the other the provision of an 'oil bath' in the base of the cam case. By this means the rocker rollers were sufficiently lubricated to prevent pick up and the additional lubrication helped to minimise the occasional squeak from the tappet ball-ends.

Towards the end of 1928 there were persistent rumours of the possibility of a 'Speed Model' version of the 6½ Litre. In fact a great deal of testing had been going on, in secret, in the Firm's Experimental Department for some months, and at the end of October the first Speed Six was available for demonstrations.

The total number of Standard 6½ Litres made by the end of 1928 was 284.

THE SPEED SIX

1929. The Speed Model 6½ Litre was conceived as a stage in the 'improvement of the breed' with an eye to long distance touring, and the design of the new car followed generally that of the Standard model but with certain important differences. The immediate outward differences between the two models were the new shape of the radiator, which had parallel sides, and the green background to the radiator and fuel tank badges to distinguish it from the Standard model which had a blue background.

Throughout all his designs W. O. Bentley insisted on reliability as the first consideration. When he wanted more power he built a bigger engine ('There is no substitute for horsepower'). When it became apparent that a larger car was needed to back up the hard-pressed 4½ Litre, it was natural that a Works' racing version of the new Speed Six should be developed.

Early in 1929 Speed Six chassis were being delivered to the public, though very slowly. On the 10th of May 1929 Woolf Barnato took delivery of the first of the 'Le Mans' racing models, destined to be known as 'Old No. 1'.

A 1965 rebuild of Douglas Simmond's modified Standard 6½ Litre.
(Photo: Red Daniells)

The standard model continued in production and by the end of the year 66 of them had been made, while 69 Speed Models had been completed. The total for the Standard model had risen to 350.

1930. The Speed Six for 1930 incorporated many of the items tried out in the 1929 'Le Mans' car, such as the single port block and induction manifold; the strengthened connecting rods; the 5 gallon Elektron sump; racing type rockers without the third rivet hole; Bosch magneto and a compression ratio of 5·3 : 1 giving 180 b.h.p.

Two new 'Le Mans' Speed Sixes were built for the 1930 season and 'Old No. 1' was brought up to date. The only major change was the introduction of the heavier front axle with integral jacking pads which were incorporated in the late 1930 models.

Production of the Standard model had almost ceased except for special orders and only 18 more were made, making the total up to 368. 108 Speed Sixes were made during the year bringing their total to 177, after which no more were made.

THE SPEED SIX IN COMPETITION

1929 DOUBLE TWELVE, BROOKLANDS

This was the Speed Six's first race and was driven by Barnato and Benjafield. The car was far and away the fastest on the circuit and led for the first four hours at a speed of 92 m.p.h. Just after its first pit stop it came in again with a broken dynamo drive. Driver and mechanic removed the radiator and dynamo but as it was impossible to repair the coupling on the spot, the car was forced to retire.

This was the only occasion on which a Speed Six retired from a race because of mechanical failure.

1929 LE MANS

Five Bentleys, including the Speed Six, were entered by the Works in opposition to three Stutz, two Chryslers, a du Pont and fourteen smaller cars. Birkin took the first spell and completed his first lap with not another car in sight. Then three Bentley's two Stutz and the fifth Bentley came round in a bunch. The last Bentley, which the week before had taken the Class 'C' Twenty-Four Hours record driven by the Hon. Mrs. Victor Bruce, retired early. Birkin set the lap record for the year on the slightly shortened circuit at 82·98 m.p.h. During the night the four Bentleys increased their lead in spite of faulty head-lamps which flickered on and off. In the early hours of the morning two Stutz and the du Pont dropped out. The ballast of Clement's car shifted and broke a brake rod which was repaired and by 10 a.m. the

1929 Six Hours Race, Brooklands. Barnato driving 'Old No. 1' through the chicane followed by a 7-litre supercharged Mercedes. (Photo: Montagu Motor Museum)

1929 Six Hours Race. Jack Dunfee and Wally Hassan (later of Jaguars and Coventry Climax) win in 'Old No. 1' applauded by co-driver Barnato while Stan Ivermee (later of Lagondas) looks on. (Photo: Fox Photos)

Bentleys were back in their places again. So great was their lead, the Speed Six was slowed down to a fast tour for the last twelve hours of the race and the 4½-litres were likewise slowed down for the last two hours.

At the finish four Bentleys crossed in line ahead, led by the Speed Six, to take the first four places. The winner's speed was 73·62 m.p.h. This was Bentley's third successive win at Le Mans and in addition they were first and second in the Index of Performance, the first time any car had won both awards.

1929 SIX HOURS, BROOKLANDS

Five Bentleys were entered, the Speed Six (Barnato

1929 Irish Grand Prix, Dublin. Glen Kidston, passing Field's burning Bugatti, in 'Old No. 1'.

1929 Tourist Trophy Race, Ards. Glen Kidston's crashed 'Old No. 1'. The trouble originated in a slide at the far corner.
(Photo: *Autocar*)

1930 Double Twelve Hour Race, Brooklands. Barnato and Wally Hassan take over 'Old No. 1' in the wet. Note the front apron scarred by heavy rain. The car won at 86.68 m.p.h.
(Photo: *Fox Photos*)

and C. Dunfee), a Le Mans 4½ (Cook and Callingham) by the Works, two 4½s entered privately and Birkin's prototype supercharged 4½ Litre.

The supercharged car was fast but it soon had engine trouble and retired. The Speed Six, lapping at 74 m.p.h., was leading on distance but was way back on handicap. After four hours' running it was in third place and had increased its lap speed to 75 m.p.h. One of the privately entered 4½s dropped out as did two Mercedes. At the fifth hour, having made up its handicap, the Speed Six took the lead and an hour later won the race at 75.88 m.p.h. An Alfa was second and the remaining two Bentleys third and eighth respectively.

Mercedes put in the fastest lap of the race with 81.19 m.p.h. but failed to finish.

1929 IRISH GRAND PRIX, DUBLIN

This was a two-day event, the winner being the car with the best performance on handicap on either day. Ivanovski's Alfa won the first day's race for cars under 1,500 c.c. at 75.02 m.p.h. The second day, for cars over 1,500 c.c., attracted Kidston's Speed Six, three 4½ Litres, two of the Birkin supercharged cars, a 7-litre supercharged Mercedes, three 1750 Alfas and eight other cars.

For 27 laps the Mercedes led Birkin, the two cars never far apart. Then the inevitable happened and the the Mercedes blew a gasket and retired. Meanwhile the three Alfas retained their lead on handicap but after two and a half hours one of them ran out of road and retired. Birkin's car was overheating and Kidston's Speed Six passed him to take fourth place on handicap.

Kidston again increased speed in an effort to catch the Alfas but slid on the melting tarmac and buckled a wheel. The wheel was changed at the pits in record time but it cost them the race nevertheless. In a most exciting finish Ivanovski's Alfa won by a bare fourteen seconds at 76.4 m.p.h.; the Speed Six was second at 79.8 and Birkin third at 79.0. All six Bentleys finished. Mercedes again made fastest lap (83.8 m.p.h.) but failed to stay the course.

1929 TOURIST TROPHY, BELFAST

This was again a handicap race over 30 laps of the 13.66 mile tortuous circuit with 65 starters taking part. Bentleys entered Kidston in the Speed Six; Birkin his 3 Blower cars ('W. O.' rode as Birkin's mechanic); and Hayes his private 4½. On scratch with the Bentleys were 2 official Mercedes and 2 private ones; 3 official and 4 private Alfas which received two credit laps. There were 49 other cars of various sizes including Austin Sevens with up to five credit laps handicaps.

The small cars held the lead for most of the race because of their handicaps. Rubin overturned his car. Then it rained, slowing all cars except Caracciola's Mercedes. At half distance Kidston got into a series of slides lasting about a quarter of a mile and crashed. Caracciola was steadily passing car after car but with half an hour to go the Austins were leading with the Alfas close behind. First Campari's Alfa, then Caracciola, passed the Austins. Heavy rain fell again but Caracciola, undeterred, went on to win at 72.82 m.p.h. The Alfa came in second at 67.54 m.p.h. and Birkin, with 'W. O.', finished 11th, having averaged

1929 500 Mile Race, Brooklands. Clive Dunfee finished 2nd with co-driver Sammy Davis at 109.4 m.p.h. in 'Old No. 1' with the long tailed body.
(Photo: *Fox Photos*)

69·01 m.p.h. Harcourt-Wood's supercharged car had retired and Hayes, still running, was flagged off at the end of the race.

Caracciola's Mercedes made fastest lap at 77·81 m.p.h. *in the wet.*

1929 500 MILES, BROOKLANDS

The Firm entered the Speed Six (Davis and C. Dunfee), fitted with a stubby two-seater body, one of the Le Mans 4½ Litres (Clement and Barclay), now with a long tailed body, and two other 4½ Litres. Birkin entered his prototype single-seater supercharged Bentley and Kaye Don two 4-litre and one 2-litre Sunbeams. There were five classes each with a time handicap, and all cars ran in stripped form.

Birkin lapping at 121 m.p.h. developed an oil leak and dropped back; Jack Barclay had two narrow escapes with monumental slides, but in turn with Clement continued to lap at around 110 m.p.h. The Speed Six lapped at 125 but had continual tyre trouble. Birkin's car caught fire and retired at the same time as one of the 4-litre Sunbeams and the 2-litre. Clement and Barclay went on to win at 107·32 m.p.h.

The Speed Six, having made the fastest lap of the day at 126·09 m.p.h., and being ordered to slow down, finished second at 109·4 m.p.h. Third place went to the remaining Sunbeam which had broken its frame.

1930 DOUBLE TWELVE HOUR, BROOKLANDS

The Works entered two brand new Speed Sixes, Dorothy Paget three Birkin supercharged 4½ Litres and Durand a privately owned 4½. 59 cars started including teams of Talbots and M.G.s in their first race.

On the first day, Kidston, in one of the supercharged Bentleys, led the two Speed Sixes for a time, then slowed and later retired with a broken valve. Birkin retired with a broken frame and Durand's 4½ caught fire and later retired with a broken back axle. The third supercharged 4½ caught fire at the pits but continued. Clement led in the Speed Six with Davis in the other Speed Six in second place. The latter broke a valve spring which was replaced without the car losing its place. Two of the Talbots were involved in a serious accident and the third car of the team was withdrawn.

On the second day the Speed Sixes led comfortably. Marinoni's Alfa, well ahead of its handicap, retired and Benjafield refitted a new back axle to the remaining supercharged Bentley but retired shortly afterwards. Davis' Speed Six broke another valve spring and later an oil pipe, both of which were remedied without losing second place.

In the afternoon it rained heavily but at last the race was over and the two Speed Sixes finished 1st and 2nd at 86·68 and 85·68 m.p.h. respectively. M.G.s won the team prize.

The dress rehearsal for Le Mans had proved very successful.

1930 LE MANS

Seventeen starters came to the line, among which were three Works' Speed Sixes, two of Dorothy Paget's supercharged 4½ Litres and Caracciola's 7-litre Mercedes.

Caracciola led off, pursued by Birkin, who had passed Kidston in 'Old No. 1'. Birkin passed the Mercedes, lost a rear tread, broke the lap record at 89·69 m.p.h. and continued for another lap before coming slowly into the pits. Davis in No. 3 Speed Six increased speed, on orders, to make the Mercedes keep using its supercharger. Dunfee took over Davis'

Le Mans 1930: Frank Clement in No. 2 Speed Six about to rejoin the race after a pit stop, closely watched by Stan Ivermee on the pit counter. Dick Watney carries the oil drip tray.
(Photo: Fox Photos Ltd)

Le Mans 1930: Woolf Barnato driving the winning car ('Old No. 1') past the pits in the closing stages of the race.
(Photo: Fox Photos Ltd)

Le Mans 1930. Dick Watney in one of the new 1930 'Le Mans' Speed Sixes at Mulsanne corner. (Photo: *Motor*)

Le Mans 1930: Bentleys first and second. Frank Clement and Dick Watney stand talking between the two cars while Barnato sits in his car. (Photo: Fox Photos Ltd)

car and crashed it. Barnato and Kidston in turns began to reduce the Mercedes' lead and finally passed it. On the next lap the Mercedes, using its supercharger continuously, passed the Bentley only to be re-passed again. Thereafter the Speed Six gradually drew away until on the 83rd lap the Mercedes retired, defeated by the 'World's Finest Sporting Car'.

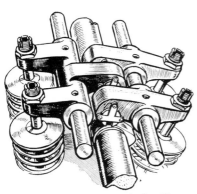

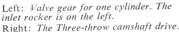

Left: *Valve gear for one cylinder. The inlet rocker is on the left.*
Right: *The Three-throw camshaft drive.*

to win Le Mans for the fourth successive time at a speed of 75·88 m.p.h. Close behind, Clement and Watney brought their Speed Six into second place at 73·73 m.p.h. These two cars also finished first and second in the Index of Performance.

*　　　*　　　*

An interesting sidelight on Bentley's racing is that 'W. O.' never allowed his cars to show more speed than was necessary to win; in consequence no one knew what their potential really was. Daimler-Benz completely underestimated the Speed Six. How much faster the Speed Six could have gone has never been disclosed but from strip reports after the race, it was stated both cars could have continued for another eighteen hours untouched.

Both Speed Sixes were ordered to reduce speed to a fast tour and hold first and second places. Both the Birkin cars continued during the night in third and fourth places. Four hours before the end, Birkin's car broke a connecting rod and an hour later Benjafield's similar car retired with a broken piston. At 4 p.m. the Barnato/Kidston Speed Six crossed the line

Shortly after Le Mans, Bentley Motors announced their retirement from racing for the time being, so as to incorporate the lessons they had learned in their production models.

At the Motor Show of 1930 the magnificent 8 Litre made its appearance but the clouds of the 'great depression', spreading from the West, were already looming up on the horizon.

© *Darell Berthon, 1966.*

RECORD OF SPEED SIXES IN RACES

EVENT	RACE NO.	DRIVERS	RESULTS
1929			
Double Twelve Hour, Brooklands	2	Barnato and Benjafield	Retired
Le Mans	1	Barnato and Birkin	1st 73·62 m.p.h.
Six Hours, Brooklands	3	Barnato and J. Dunfee	1st 75·88 m.p.h.
Irish G.P. Dublin	4	Kidston	2nd 79·8 m.p.h.
Tourist Trophy, Ards	73	Kidston	Crashed
500 Mile, Brooklands	35	Davis and C. Dunfee	2nd 109·4 m.p.h.
1930			
Double Twelve Hour, Brooklands	2	Barnato and Clement	1st 86·88 m.p.h.
	3	Davis and C. Dunfee	2nd 85·68 m.p.h.
Le Mans	4	Barnato and Kidston	1st 75·88 m.p.h.
	2	Clement and Watney	2nd 73·33 m.p.h.
	3	Davis and C. Dunfee	Crashed
1931 (after the liquidation of the Old Company			
500 Mile Race, Brooklands	46	J. Dunfee and C. Paul	1st 118·39 m.p.h.
(A private entry by Barnato)			

*　　　*　　　*

Acknowledgement is made for the assistance received from:—*The Autobiography of W. O. Bentley*, the records of the Bentley Drivers Club, The *Autocar* race reports, *Motor Sport* and W. Boddy's *History of Brooklands Motor Course*.

SPECIFICATIONS OF 6½ LITRE BENTLEYS

	All Types	6½ Litre Standard	Speed Six	'Le Mans' Speed Six
ENGINE Cylinder bore & stroke	100 mm. × 140 mm.			
Cylinder block		Two port	Two port (1930 some single port)	Single port
Cubic capacity	6,597 c.c.			
Valves (valve springs)	24 (48)	Tulip	Tulip	Flat head
Camshaft	Overhead, seven bearings. Three-throw coupling rod drive	BM. 5091　　BM. 6159	BM. 7032　BM 6159　BM. 7055	BM. 7032
Tappet clearances: Inlet Exhaust		·004″ ·006″ 　 ·004″ ·006″	·019″ ·004″ ·006″ ·019″ ·006″ ·006″	·019″ ·019″

continued

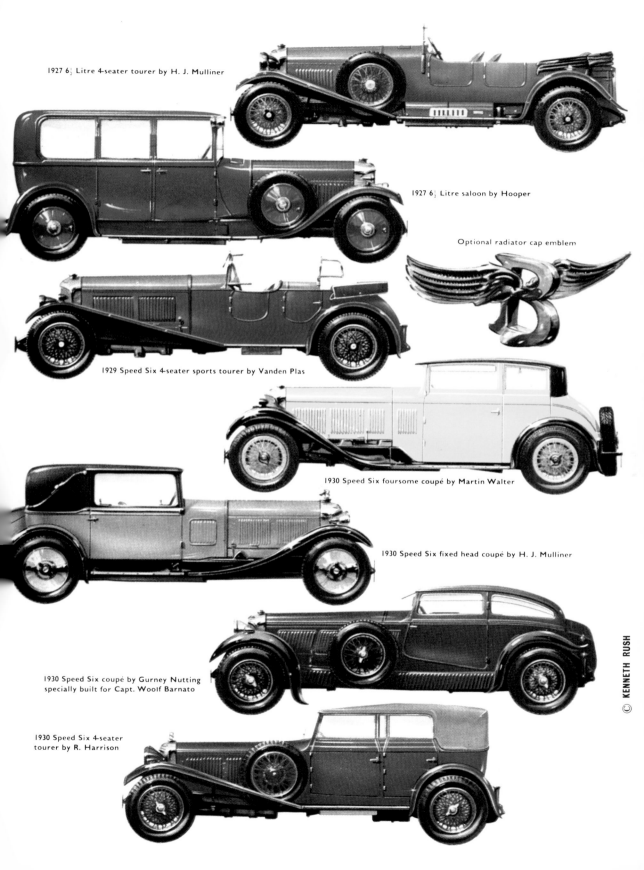

1927 6½ Litre 4-seater tourer by H. J. Mulliner

1927 6½ Litre saloon by Hooper

Optional radiator cap emblem

1929 Speed Six 4-seater sports tourer by Vanden Plas

1930 Speed Six foursome coupé by Martin Walter

1930 Speed Six fixed head coupé by H. J. Mulliner

1930 Speed Six coupé by Gurney Nutting specially built for Capt. Woolf Barnato

1930 Speed Six 4-seater tourer by R. Harrison

© KENNETH RUSH

	All Types	6½-Litre Standard	Speed Six	'Le Mans' Speed Six
Pistons		B.H.B. split skirt	B.H.B. split skirt	Hour-glass racing type
Compression ratio		4·4 : 1	5·1 : 1 and 5·3 : 1	6·1 : 1
B.H.P.		147	160 180 with single port block	200
R.P.M.		3,500	3,500	3,500 normal; 3,750 emergency
Connecting rods		Two bolt direct metal. BM. 5208. BM. 5262	Two bolt direct metal. $\frac{5}{16}$" increase in radius. BM. 6589	Two bolt Shell type. BM. 6821
Ignition		Two magnetos. ML.GR6. or ER6; or one magneto, one Delco-Remy coil	One magneto ML.ER6 and coil; 1930 Bosch magneto FU6B and Delco coil	One Bosch magneto FU6B and Delco coil
Firing order	1 4 2 6 3 5			
Plugs		K.L.G., K1 or J1	Champion	Champion
Carburettor(s)		Smith Bentley 5-jet BVS 50	Two vertical S.U. Type HVG 5	Two vertical S.U. Type HVG 5
Fuel feed		Autovac	Autovac	Pressurised
Fuel tank capacity		19 gallons. Later 25 gallons	25 gallons	39 gallons road racing 43 gallons track racing
Sump capacity		3 gallons	3 gallons. 1930: 5 gallons	5 gallons filled to 5½ gallons
Starter motor		Smith Type 4LSA	Smith Type 4LSA. 1930: some Bosch BNE 2/12 RS2	Smith Type 4LSA
Dynamo	Smith 5 brush Type 2 DAC 5			
Batteries	Two 6V	Peto & Radford. Young	Young	Young
CHASSIS				
Wheelbase		11' 12' 1¼" 12' 7¼"	11' 8½" 12' 8½"	11'
Length overall		15' 1" 16' 1" 16' 7"	15' 7" 16' 7"	15' 1" approx.
Width overall	5' 8½"			
Track	4' 8"			
Frame	Deep section high grade steel. Thickness increased to 4·5 mm. after 1928			
Brakes	Foot: F.W.B. Hand: rear only. Front brake operation of Bentley-Perrot design	1930: self-wrapping type	Self-wrapping type	Self-wrapping. Linings $\frac{7}{16}$" Ferodo
Front axle	"H"-section 40-ton tensile steel	1930: heavy-type axle bed	Heavy-type axle bed. Late 1930: with jacking lugs	Heavy-type axle bed with jacking lugs
Rear axle	Underslung—semi floating. 4-bevel pinion differential	Ratios, spiral bevel 12/50, 13/50	Ratios, spiral bevel 13/46, 13/50	Straight cut 15/50, 15/47, 15/42 (for track racing), all with special differential plate
Springs	Semi-elliptic. Types according to body			
Gearbox	Right-hand change. Three point suspension	'B.S.' (high 3rd gear) 'C'-Type	'C' Type. Some with 'D' Type	'D' Type straight tooth. 5 or 7 D.P.
Propeller shaft		Plunging joint, later Hardy Spicer	Hardy Spicer	Hardy Spicer
Clutch	Single dry plate			
Wheels	Rudge Whitworth centre lock			Dual spoke
Tyres	Dunlop	33" × 6·75" 21" × 6·75"	21" × 6·00" 21" × 6·75"	21" × 6·75" racing
Instruments	White figures on black face	Smith and Jaeger. Some early models had 'A.T.'	Smith and Jaeger	Smith and Jaeger
Electrical equipment	Smith's		Lucas P100DB lamps	Lucas P100DB lamps
Weight, complete car: open closed		42 to 45 cwt. 45 to 48 cwt.	42 cwt. 45 cwt.	Not known
Guarantee	5 years			
Speeds (approx.)		85 m.p.h. with 12/50 axle ratio	92 m.p.h. with 13/46 axle ratio	106 m.p.h. with 15/50. 112-120 m.p.h. with 15/47. 134 m.p.h. with 15/42. (track)
Prices		£1,975 to £2,780	£2,230 to £2,500	

The Fiat Tipo 508S

THE 1935 FIAT TIPO 508S BALILLA SPORTS TWO-SEATER. Owner: The Hon. Lady Montagu of Beaulieu.

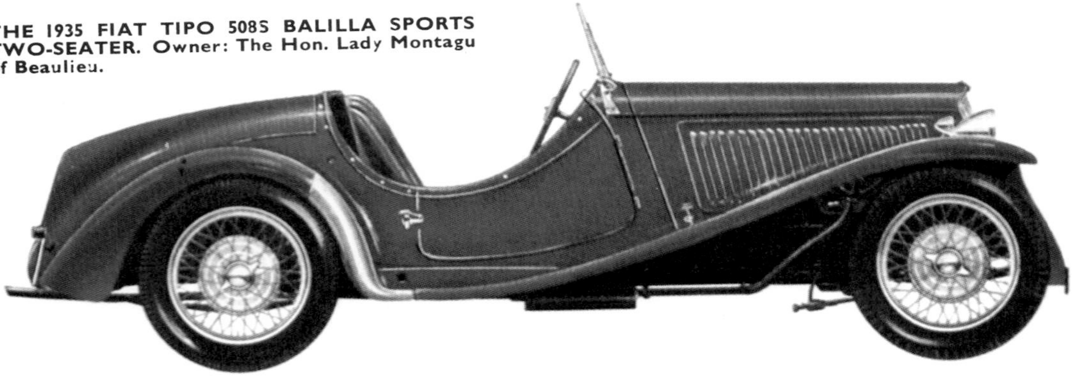

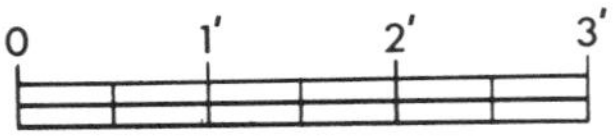

© GORDON DAVIES

0   1'   2'   3'

Fiat

BCR 336

BCR 336

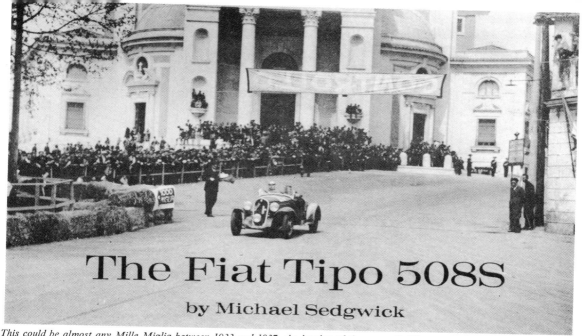

The Fiat Tipo 508S

by Michael Sedgwick

This could be almost any Mille Miglia between 1933 and 1937, the heyday of the sports Balillas. Only the crowd-discipline of the Mussolini era is apparent from this shot taken in the Rome control.
(Photo: Wide World Photos)

The FIAT Balilla was launched in the Spring of 1932—hardly an auspicious time for a new model. FIAT, it is true, had the dual advantages over their rivals of a firm foothold in other realms of transport, and a virtual monopoly of the Italian family-car market; but equally as makers of 90 per cent of Italy's private cars they could not afford a bad mistake. Nor was Italy the healthiest of home markets: in 1929, only 172,000 cars overall had been in use, and a high rate of production depended upon substantial exports. Their last light car, the 1·4-litre Tipo 514, had been somewhat of a lemon; uninspired in appearance and performance alike, it was too big and thirsty for the lean years, while an attempt to save the day with an 'austerity' version, Tipo 515, had been rewarded by derisory sales. The 995 c.c. Balilla was to prove a worthier successor to the 509 of similar capacity made between 1925 and 1929.

The period phrase 'Family Ten' conjures up visions of side-valve engines with two-bearing crankshafts of dubious strength, mated to wide-ratio three-speed gearboxes. In the chassis department one might expect conventional semi-elliptic springs, and cable-operated brakes that were unpredictable in a forward direction, and only too predictable in reverse. The influence of Detroit was reflected in ribbon-type radiator shells, wire wheels painted to match the body colour, and instruments arranged in the interests of symmetry rather than legibility. The fashionable chromium-plated hub caps were best removed with the aid of a blunt kitchen knife. On the credit side, it should be remembered that many of these soulless vehicles had their lives forcibly prolonged by the second World War, during which they rendered yeoman service despite a lack of spares and service alike.

THE BALILLA

On looks alone, FIAT's 1932 offering differed little from its competitors, having inherited its Chrysler styling from the Tipo 514 and the companion 2½-litre Tipo 522; but its specification was advanced by comparison with other small saloons of the period, such as the 201C Peugeot from France, the 1·2-litre Opel from Germany, and such British contributions as Hillman's Minx, Standard's Little Nine, and Austin's Ten, all new for 1932, and all fighting hard for sales in a constricted market. Side valves were almost universal in this stratum of automobile design, and FIAT were not alone in adopting a three-bearing crankshaft, also used by Hillman, Austin, and Opel. Where they differed was in their espousal of nearly 'square' engine dimensions of 65×75 mm., all their rivals opting for piston strokes in excess of 85 mm. As yet this configuration's value in lowering piston speeds and thus prolonging engine life was not fully understood and FIAT's advertising made much of the point. Maximum power (a modest 22 b.h.p.) was developed at 3,400 r.p.m., and the little 508 had an excellent reputation for durability. Synchromesh on small cars was virtually unknown in 1932, and three forward speeds were as yet deemed adequate, only Austin offering a four-speed gearbox. However, the Balilla's 5·2:1 top gear was respectably high by the standards of the times, and this allied with the short-stroke power unit enabled the little car to hold 50–55 m.p.h. all day. The Peugeot, by contrast, had a top gear ratio of 6·25:1, in which respect it was by no means unique! The gravity feed from dash-mounted tank to Zenith carburettor was a trifle archaic—all the competing cars save the Peugeot had their tanks at the rear, and Hillman, Austin, and Opel made use of mechanical pumps—but it had the merit of simplicity and was to be retained by FIAT on their famous 'Topolino' until the late 1940s. 6-volt electrics were deemed sufficient for all save FIAT and Peugeot, and FIAT's pedal-operated starter, which first set the pinion in mesh with a toothed ring on the flywheel, and then switched on the current, was quiet in operation. The ignition distributor was

127

Trasformazione Ghia, 1932, or how an Italian specialist coach-builder anticipated the front-end treatment of the four-speed cars made from 1934 onwards. A resemblance to the style of contemporary coupé Alfa Romeos can be seen.
(Photo: Montagu Motor Museum)

mounted on top of the engine, a location which made it flood-proof.

As for the chassis, FIAT were well ahead of all their rivals. True, they did not as yet, like Peugeot, aspire to independently-sprung front wheels, but their new car was equipped with hydraulic brakes of proven efficiency. The company had been using them since the end of 1930, when they were first applied to the 3·7-litre Tipo 525. These were supplemented by the traditional FIAT transmission handbrake, a device retained until the 1960s. It was strictly a sudden-death affair, and reserved for parking. By contrast, the other cars in our group had mechanical brakes, Standard and Hillman favouring the Bendix type. With a wheelbase of 7 ft. 4½ in., the Balilla was 1½ in. shorter than any of its rivals, while the taxi-like steering lock was reflected in a turning circle of 29 ft. 6 in. In other respects the chassis was conventional, with spiral bevel final drive. The fabric couplings on the propeller shaft had a relatively short life, but were quick and inexpensive to replace. A

stop light was standard equipment, and FIATs, then as now, came equipped with a hand throttle. A free wheel mounted behind the gearbox was an optional extra, control being by a knob on the dashboard.

Maximum speed of early 508s as tested was 58 m.p.h., and fuel consumption at 35 m.p.g. represented a great improvement on the cumbersome 514. In less lean times it is possible that the FIAT at £198 might have furnished serious competition even in England for the Standard at £155 or the Hillman at £159. Unfortunately, the horse-power tax then in force favoured the long-stroke engine, and British buyers expected more car than Turin offered in an 'Eleven'.

The name 'Balilla', incidentally, is best translated as 'plucky little one', and was derived from a Fascist youth movement corresponding roughly to the Boy Scouts. The correct designation of the 995 c.c. engine was 'Tipo 108', this being in accordance with FIAT's inter-War practice of assigning prefixes in the '500' series to chassis, and in the '100' series to power units.

THE 508S 'SPYDER SPORT'

Production did not get under way until July, 1932, but immediate success is reflected in the sale of 12,424 units in the first half-year. Four body styles were standardised—the basic two-door saloon, a roadster with dickey seat, a four-door open tourer, and a light delivery van. In January, 1933, the higher of the two available compression ratios (6·3:1) was standardised, while at the same time the range was augmented by the introduction of a 'Spyder Sport' model designated Tipo 508S. Chassis changes were relatively few: output was boosted to 30 b.h.p., the axle ratio was raised substantially to 4·3:1 in the interests of fast cruising, and fuel was fed by mechanical pump from a twelve-gallon tank at the rear. Friction-type shock absorbers replaced the 508's hydraulics. The bodywork, however, represented a complete breakaway from the American idiom, and owed a good deal to the Zagato-bodied Alfa Romeos of the period. Rakish lines were accentuated by long flared wings, and the circular dials on the fascia were

American influences are clearly visible in this 1933 three-speed 508 torpedo with its slightly-raked windscreen, belt moulding, and side-mounted spare wheel.
(Photo: FIAT (England) Ltd.)

Externally the side-valve 508S cars were identical to the later and better known o.h.v. machines, but the simpler windscreen is the most obvious difference between the stock Italian body and the English versions. At the wheel of this car is veteran works driver Carlo Salamano.
(Photo: FIAT (England) Ltd.)

laid out in a line, Alfa-fashion. A handsome raked radiator grille was doubtless inspired by some of the *trasformazioni* effected on this chassis by Italian specialist coachbuilders (see page 2). The high gearing gave these side-valve sporting versions a top speed in the region of 70 m.p.h.

A standard Balilla took eighth place in general classification in the 1933 Monte Carlo Rally, and that year's Mille Miglia was to see the *début* of two of the outstanding sports cars of the 1930s. One of these was, of course, M.G.'s K3 Magnette. Its principal opposition in the 1,100 c.c. class came from Maserati, but also in the lists were four sports Balillas. Not that

A semi-custom style was this four-seater cabriolet by Garavini, which cost £258 on the four-speed chassis in England in 1935. This one has acquired a later style of front bumper.
(Photo: G. N. Georgano)

Most of the four-speed saloons sold in England had four doors, but a two-door style using the same pressings was also made. A factory picture of the 1935 version.
(Photo: FIAT (England) Ltd.)

these were exactly representative of the Spyder Sport as sold by the factory: Count 'Johnny' Lurani, who was driving for M.G. on this occasion, has described them as 'very non-standard indeed'. They had o.h.v. heads by SIATA, which firm also furnished the four-speed gearboxes. Even with this 'tweaking', however, output was still a modest 35–40 b.h.p. to the M.G.'s 100 plus, and they were running unblown. M.G. won their class deservedly, Eyston and Lurani on the leading car putting up an average of 56·89 m.p.h. By contrast, the fastest FIAT, driven by Ambrosini and Menchetti, turned in 54·67 m.p.h. over the thousand miles. The difference in speed would doubtless have been greater had the cars from Abingdon not been dogged by plug trouble, but the lesson was there to see. The catalogue price of a K3 was over £600, while the cost of a Balilla complete with all modifications could not have exceeded £350; photographs suggest that standard Spyder Sport bodies were used. In the touring category, FIAT's record was even more impressive, for these entries really were standard—apart from raised compressions and higher gearing—yet the class-winner averaged nearly 54 m.p.h. and was followed home by twelve similar machines 'at intervals of four minutes'.

Otherwise the 508's competition record in 1933

E. Kozma and I. Martinek with their Balilla which won the light-car class of the Monte Carlo Rally in 1936. The extra horns and lamps furnish a clue to their success in the Concours de Confort with what was, after all, a fairly austere family saloon.
(Photo: *Autocar*)

There was plenty of room for the 995 c.c. o.h.v. engine under the bonnet of the 1935 508S, and everything is accessible, even if the mounting of the distributor was not quite flood-proof.
(Photo: Montagu Motor Museum)

L.C.C. Relay Race, Brooklands, 1936. Best of the three FIAT teams entered this year was Miss D. Chaff's all-feminine équipe. One of the cars is here seen at the pits.
(Photo: William Boddy Collection)

Despite their high gearing, the Balillas did quite well in trials in England. Here Major C. J. S. Montague-Johnstone is seen on Darracott in an M.C.C. event. The registration number—London, mid-1935—indicates one of the first o.h.v. cars with r.h.d. to come to England.
(Photo: W. J. Brunell)

Blackpool Rally, June, 1936. Stanley Tett with the o.h.v. 508S on which he won the event outright. (Photo: W. J. Brunell)

THE 1933–34 MODELS

At the 1933 London Show, the company exhibited a four-door pillarless saloon on the standard side-valve chassis. This type of body, used by FIAT until 1952, offered easy access to all four seats. The short-stroke principle was also extended to a brace of big fours (Tipo 518) powered by 1·7-litre (78×92 mm.) and 2-litre (82×92 mm.) engines. As yet the three-speed gearbox was still fitted to the Balilla, but by the time deliveries of the new saloon model were under way, the side-valve design had been finalised into a form that would prevail until the end of production in 1937.

At the Milan Show in 1934, a four-door saloon with four forward speeds had been displayed, and by June production was concentrated on the new type. This featured a sloping grille similar to the 518's, while a four-speed box, with synchromesh on the top two ratios, was now standardised. Top and third were fairly close, at 5·1 and 7·5 to 1, but there was the usual long gap between third and second. The wheelbase was lengthened by two inches, and the tourers as well as the saloons had integral luggage boots. Weight of the saloon went up to 15 cwt., but with a 6·6:1 compression ratio 24 b.h.p. was now available, and road test figures show no appreciable difference in performance. Wire wheels remained an option, and a single central dial was now used for the instruments. English prices were drastically reduced, the saloon costing £210 in 1935 as against £270 in 1934, but the high horsepower tax and prevailing antipathy to all things Italian conspired to keep the Balilla a rarity on this side of the Channel.

Elsewhere, however, sales were booming. The peak year was 1934, with 27,774 cars delivered, but this figure was nearly equalled in 1935 despite Italian preoccupation with the war in Abyssinia, and overall sales of all types between 1932 and 1937 exceeded 113,000. Cars were also built under licence in Germany by N.S.U. and in France by Simca. Apart from minor differences of styling, these French and German FIATs were identical to the Torinese article. Body styles listed in the last three seasons of manufacture were two- and four-door saloons, both with integral trunks, a tourer, a roadster, and a delivery van, though some pretty four-seater cabriolets were turned out on a semi-series basis by Garavini.

After the advent of the o.h.v. 508S in 1934, the basic Balilla took a back seat in competition, but in 1935 C. E. Stothert won his class in the Welsh Rally, and a far more important success was Kozma's eleventh place in the 1936 Monte Carlo Rally. He also won the light-car class and took second place in the appropriate section of the *Concours de Confort*.

was unspectacular. Prince Narischkine fielded a team of three cars in the International Alpine Trial, but these were trounced by the M.G. and Singer opposition, while in the 1,100 c.c. class of the Coppa Acerbo Cecchini on the fastest of the Balillas had to trail behind Whitney Straight's K3 Magnette and three Maseratis. The 508's day was yet to come.

Black Diamonds. A. C. Westwood's team of 508S cars seen during the North-West London Motor Club's Team Trial in 1936. Drivers are (l. to r.) Westwood, R. M. Sanford and S. G. E. Tett, and the FIATs still wear the standard flared wings.

(Photo: A. C. Westwood)

(One wonders what he did to the FIAT's usually rather austere interior appointments!)

THE O.H.V. 508S

Meanwhile yet another 508 variant had shared the honours of the 1934 Milan Show with the four-speed Balilla saloon—the wholly delightful o.h.v. 508S. This was one of these limited-production cars that FIAT brings out from time to time. The 'full' sports Balilla followed logically on the efforts of the amateur tuners and of firms like SIATA. By the end of 1933 Ambrosini had achieved considerable success in sprints and hill-climbs with a single-seater based on the Spyder Sport, but with o.h.v. head, a chain-driven Roots-type blower, and Cozette carburettor. On a 4:1 axle ratio this had clocked 96 m.p.h.—not surprising when one considers that the little unit was now delivering 48 b.h.p. at 4,000 r.p.m., and the whole outfit weighed 10 cwt. as against 13½ cwt. for

A 1935 shot of the berlinetta aerodinamica. *The disc wheels are unusual on an o.h.v. sports model, while the streamlined nose of what is probably a* trasformazione *by SIATA anticipates later FIAT touring-car styling by a good twelvemonth.*

(Photo: *Autocar*)

Stripped for action, Westwood's and Sanford's Balillas are seen as they appeared in the Light Car Club's 1936 Relay Race at Brooklands.

(Photo: A. C. Westwood)

the contemporary two-door saloon, and 12½ cwt. for the sports model in road trim.

FIAT's own sports version was externally identical to the 1933 Spyder Sport, and there were no chassis changes. Nor, for all their pioneering work in Grand Prix racing, did they have recourse to a supercharger. The 1934 synchromesh box was used, with respectably close ratios, and the higher overall gearing of its s.v. predecessors. This 4·3:1 ratio made for higher cruising speeds than were comfortably attained with the FIAT's English counterparts—the Le Mans Singer and the PB-type M.G.—which had top gears of 5·57 and 5·75 to 1 respectively, and developed their maximum power at over 5,000 r.p.m., a state of affairs which was hard on the Singer's two-bearing crankshaft. *The Autocar* commented with pleased surprise on the fact that on the 508S 60 m.p.h. in third was the equivalent of a mere 4,500 r.p.m.—neither M.G. nor Singer could attain this speed on this ratio. A manual ignition control was provided on the sports FIATs.

Cylinder capacity was unchanged at 995 c.c. which suggests that the car was regarded as a development model rather than a serious contender in the 1,100 c.c. category, but an entirely new cast-iron head with pushrod operated o.h.v. was provided, boosting output to 36 b.h.p. on a 7·1:1 compression ratio, sufficient to propel the 508S at over 70 m.p.h. This, incidentally, was the first use of pushrods on a touring FIAT engine since the demise of the big 4¾-litre Tipo 519 in 1928, though the company had been racing cars with full overhead valves as early as 1905. The 108S engine was destined to point the way to a gradual switch from the L-head principle, completed in 1948 with the introduction of the 500B version of the 'Topolino'.

Testers were unanimous over the car's handling and stopping powers, though the headlamps were deemed inadequate for the sports model's performance and the hood was unsatisfactory. *The Light Car* slated the exhaust note as 'nice, but decidedly naughty'. It was more than a match for either M.G. or Singer, the British cars excelling only in standing-start acceleration as a consequence of their lower gearing. The FIAT's steering was delightfully responsive, but this model is not recommended to drivers with large feet, thanks to the location of the brake pedal in uncomfortable proximity to the steering-column.

Mille Miglia, 1937. Of the two 508S cars visible, the one in the foreground carries lightweight two-seater bodywork, while behind the elderly Maserati can be seen a stock berlinetta aerodinamica. Just visible in the right background is a 500 Topolino—the shape of things to come. (Photo: *Autocar*)

By 1937 the T.T. had moved from the Ards Circuit to Donington, and the 995 c.c. Balillas were fading out of the limelight. Mrs. Dobson's English entry was unplaced, though still running at the end. (Photo: Louis Klemantaski)

Strained relations with Mussolini's Italy might restrict sales of touring FIATs in Britain, but there was no mistaking the enthusiasm with which the Sports Balilla was greeted when it went on show at Olympia in October, 1934. FIAT made a determined attempt to recover their once-strong position in the British market by subjecting the l.h.d. demonstrator (BHX 91) to a tough test at Brooklands. Driven by J. Wren and Dudley Froy, it covered a thousand miles over the Mountain Circuit in two days running, encountering, as its makers proudly asserted, 1,700 corners in the process. In spite of poor weather conditions, the mean average speed was 55·11 m.p.h., petrol consumption worked out at 21 m.p.g., and oil was consumed at the rate of a pint every 200 miles. The English price of £299 was a trifle high at a time when an M.G. Midget could be bought for £222; but this was later reduced to a competitive £238.

Cars sold in England were bodied over here, and are recognisable by the more pronounced tail fin. The two-seater was the only version of the o.h.v. model regularly available, though the last six chassis imported were fitted with four-seater bodywork, and one of these was shown at Olympia in 1936. The Italian buyer had, however, a wider choice. In addition to the *spyder normale*, there was the *spyder corsa*, or Coppa d'Oro variant. Contrary to the generally expressed view, this had an identical mechanical specification, the extra m.p.h. being gained by the use of a lighter and starker body shell and cycle-type wings. This was joined in April, 1935, by the Mille Miglia type, or *berlinetta aerodinamica*, a fastback coupé with recessed rear number plate and attractive flowing wings. Fuel tank capacity was increased from ten to fourteen gallons, which made it into a delightful little G.T. with 30–35 m.p.g. on tap. Finally there was an engaging Q-car in the shape of a standard 'Balilla saloon powered by a 34 b.h.p. version of the o.h.v. Tipo 108S engine'. About 1,000 of these were produced. It is difficult to trace the number of overhead-valve cars made in all, as chassis serials ran concurrent with the touring versions, but I doubt if more than 2,000 left the works. Some were also made by Simca and N.S.U., Amédée Gordini winning his spurs on the former, while Brendel achieved quite a few successes on the Heilbronn-built sports cars.

RACING, 1935–37

1935 and 1936 were the peak years of the Balilla's competition career, Singer being their strongest opponents. M.G. were out of racing by mid-1935; Adler and Riley concerned themselves mainly with bigger cars, and B.M.W.'s 'works' participation really began with the advent of the Type 328 2-litre in 1936. Surviving Salmsons and Amilcars, though still capable of giving a good account of themselves,

Doughtiest of the British-owned 508S cars was V. H. Tuson's DPH 968, here seen on the Campbell Circuit at Brooklands in its last season with its original owner in 1937. The tail fin is clearly apparent. (Photo: William Boddy Collection)

Balilla Airborne. One of A. C. Westwood's 508S cars as it appeared in an Autocross in the middle 1950s, a time when the machines were not as yet collectors' pieces.
(Photo: A. C. Westwood & Richmond Pike)

were pretty long in the tooth. On occasions, however, they could still turn the tables on the cars from Turin, as happened in the 1935 Alpilles Hill Climb.

The FIAT factory, of course, dropped out of International competition in 1927, never to return, and the great protagonist of the Balilla was a young and still unknown Italian domiciled in France, Amédée Gordini. He had started his career on the pedestrian Tipo 514, and during 1935 he was making himself felt with a car that looked like a standard 508S, but was in fact largely *Le Sorcier's* own work. With an alloy block of his own conception, he was extracting 48 b.h.p. from an unblown unit, sufficient to propel a road-equipped car at 90 m.p.h. His score in 1935 was impressive: an outright win in the Bol d'Or 24-Hour Race, and class victories in the Circuit of Orleans, the Grand Prix de Lorraine, and the Grand Prix de la Marne.

FIAT also recorded class wins in the Eifelrennen, the Czechoslovak 1,000-Mile Stock Car Race, the Circuit des Vosges (a sort of miniature Alpine Trial) and in numerous hill-climbs, including the Gross-glockner, the Stelvio, the Feldberg, and a couple of forgotten Hungarian contests at Rakosfalva and Mount Gugger. Alas! they shone neither at Le Mans nor in the T.T. In the former, the 1,100 c.c. class went to Jacques Savoye's Singer, while in the latter three FIATs found themselves ranged against three Adlers and four Singers. The German cars were nowhere, but a terrific battle ensued between ffrench-Davis's Balilla and the Singers of Langley, Norman Black, and S. C. H. Davis, with the FIAT generally in the lead. On the eleventh lap 'Sammy' Davis at last built up a good lead for Singer, but the three works cars from Coventry were eliminated spectacularly by steering-arm failure, while ffrench-Davis retired with mechanical trouble towards the end of the race. Sole survivor of the whole class was Dobson's FIAT, dismissed as 'still running at the end'.

The four dozen cars sold in England were also making an impression, notably the 'hot' versions conducted by Tuson (DPH 968) and Metcalfe (CMG 99).

Tuson's car proved astonishingly reliable, running through three seasons with only minimal replacements. He found that the car's weight distribution was unsatisfactory for trials, but it never failed to win its class in any speed event for which it was entered, while it would turn in 92 m.p.h. on the Outer Circuit at Brooklands. It ran on a compression ratio of 9:1. Metcalfe's car, with 8·2:1 compression, copperised and polished cylinder head, enlarged ports, 36 mm. Stromberg carburettor, Tuson manifold, and a ten-pint sump replacing the standard five-pint type, was good for 42 b.h.p., giving 105 m.p.h. stripped, and 88 m.p.h. in road trim. When fifteen years old, it could still lap the Goodwood circuit at 68·7 m.p.h.

Gordini's Balillas ran as Simcas in 1936, and appeared with narrow bodies and raked radiators reminiscent of the 1933 G. P. Maserati. Gordini himself won his class at Miramas in the Coupe de Provence, despite a mistral, and the cars followed this victory up with a hat-trick in the sports-car class of the Bol d'Or, *Le Sorcier* leading Zanardi and Martin home. He also collected a class win in the Belgian 24-Hour Race at Spa. This year there was no Le Mans, though the French ran their Grand Prix as a sports-car event. This policy prevented a German victory, but it also excluded the Simcas from the awards list, since the smallest class embraced everything up to 2 litres. Brendel, Soergel, and Zinn took the first three places in the 1,100 c.c. category at the Eifelrennen. The T.T., last of the series to be staged on the Ards Circuit, was again an inauspicious occasion—though Sullivan won his class, he was placed thirteenth out of fifteen finishers.

In Britain, the Balillas were at their zenith. In its report of the Dancer's End Hill Climb that Autumn *Motor Sport* referred to the 1,100 c.c. sports class as 'the domain of the FIATs', and in the minor events they were ubiquitous. The Light Car Club's Relay Race at Brooklands saw no fewer than three teams of sports Balillas in circulation—Tuson's, an all-feminine team captained by Miss Chaff, and A. C. Westwood's 'Black Diamonds', regular competitors

133

Coupe de la Commission Sportive, Montlhéry, 1937, showing Gordini's and Camerano's Simca-FIATs challenging Arthur Dobson in 1½-litre Riley No. 66 at the start. The British car's extra half-litre told in the end. (Photo: *Autocar*)

in rallies. The ladies finished in fourth place at an average speed of 75·12 m.p.h. Stanley Tett won the Blackpool Rally outright in June, and Stothert's Balilla won a first-class award in the M.C.C. Torquay Rally in July.

By 1937, however, the cars were past their heyday, even if Vernet and Largeot at last annexed the 1,100 c.c. class at Le Mans. N.S.U.-FIATs were beaten by an M.G. in the Eifelrennen. The T.T., now transferred to Donington Park, was a triumph for Singer, Barnes's and Black's Nines, in fourth and sixth places, being the highest-placed British cars. Gordini was tenth and last after running out of petrol, and Mrs. Dobson's English-entered Balilla was flagged off at the finish.

SWAN SONG

Further, the new look was moving in on Turin. The last of the long-stroke models, the 72 × 103 mm. six-cylinder 527, had been discontinued at the end of the 1936 season, and already the 518 had been replaced in July, 1935, by the six-cylinder 1500, with coil-spring independent suspension, backbone frame, and aerodynamic pillarless saloon bodywork. It shared the Balilla's cylinder dimensions of 65 × 75 mm.,

How to Get Into The Saloon-Car Class, A. C. Westwood's CVX 204 with home-made hardtop, as it competed in the 1938 R.A.C. Rally. (Photo: *Keystone Press Agency Ltd.*)

and the valves were overhead. Hot on its heels in 1936 came the immortal 'Topolino' or 500, with 570 c.c. side-valve engine, which sold for £120 in England, and represented an entirely new concept of baby car. The Balilla looked very old-fashioned in this company, and sales slumped to just over 8,000 in 1937. A replacement was clearly indicated.

It came that Autumn in the shape of the original Millecento (Tipo 508C). This was a 508 in name only, for it looked like a scaled-down 1500 or scaled-up 500. The front wheels were independently sprung, and the o.h.v. engine had its bore enlarged to 68 mm. to bring it close up to the 1,100 c.c. limit. The cylinder head was now of aluminium alloy, and it was a remarkable little performer, being very nearly as fast as the 508S two-seaters on only 32 b.h.p. Though the 508C and its derivatives are often erroneously called Balillas, they are a breed in their own right.

Mrs. Wisdom's 1936 T.T. 508S (DPL 998) was tried by FIAT (England) Ltd. in 1937 with a prototype '1100" engine. This car featured in an interesting experiment conducted by the FIAT Register at Goodwood in September, 1964, when George Liston Young and Ian Smith sought to repeat the exploit of Wren and Froy in 1934. The engine was sleeved back to the standard capacity of 995 c.c., to counterbalance the increased power conferred by the alloy head and twin S.U. carburettors, the car ran with wings and lamps in position, whereas BHX 91 had run stripped. In the absence of Brooklands, Goodwood was selected, as 421 laps of this circuit would produce the right number of corners. Despite pouring rain and forty-knot gusts of wind, the objective was attained, and the thirty-year-old FIAT covered its thousand miles at 55·52 m.p.h. Though both drivers were nearly afloat in the very open cockpit, a fastest lap was made at 65·5 m.p.h. Petrol consumption was much the same as in 1934, and only four pints of oil were used, as against five at Brooklands.

CONCLUSION

FIAT's Balilla remains a highly significant product of its era. The original design started the breakaway

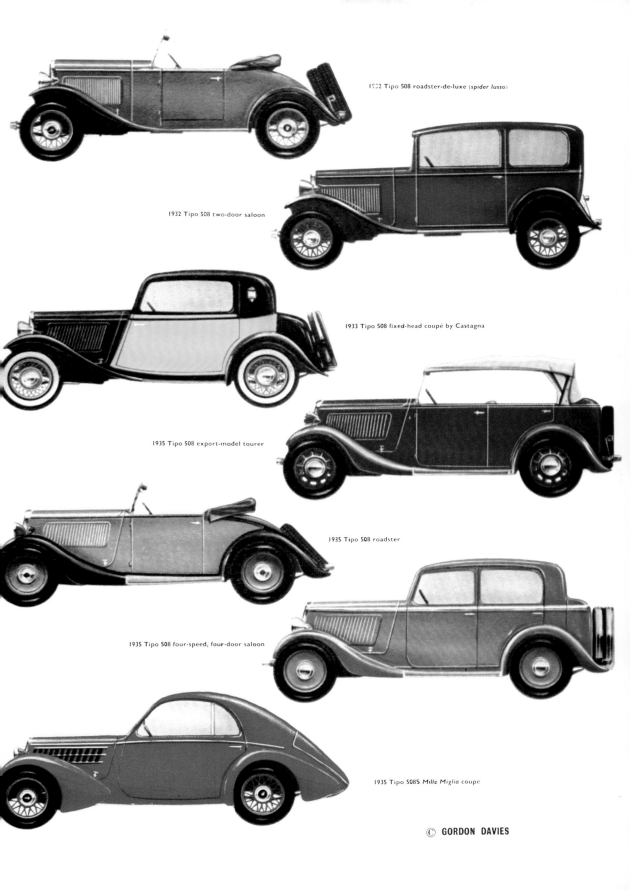

1932 Tipo 508 roadster-de-luxe (*spider lusso*)

1932 Tipo 508 two-door saloon

1933 Tipo 508 fixed-head coupé by Castagna

1935 Tipo 508 export-model tourer

1935 Tipo 508 roadster

1935 Tipo 508 four-speed, four-door saloon

1935 Tipo 508S *Mille Miglia* coupe

© GORDON DAVIES

The ex-Elsie Wisdom 508S DPL 998, Ian Smith astride, fights its way round Goodwood in wind and rain, September, 1964. Its thousand miles at over 55 m.p.h. was a vindication of a thirty-year-old design, if any vindication was needed!
(Photo: Montagu Motor Museum)

The rivals, Ulster T.T., 1935. ffrench-Davis's FIAT fights it out with the Singers of S. C. H. Davis and Barnes.
(Photo: *Autocar*)

from the tyranny of the long-stroke engine. It was some time before the lead was generally followed. While Adler, Opel and Peugeot were making short-stroke power units in the later 1930s, British manufacturers were still hemmed in by an archaic taxation formula, and even Renault's small saloon which appeared at the 1937 Shows had the conservative dimensions of 58 × 95 mm. The Balilla's hydraulic brakes were no novelty, even in the small-car class, for Triumph had offered them on their Super Seven in 1928; but this was hardly an international best-seller, and was little known outside the British Commonwealth. The historical significance of the 508 is not so much what it did, as what it foreshadowed. In it we can see the genesis of two of the outstanding light cars of the immediate pre-War period, the 500 and the 1100. These, along with the B.M.W., Lancia's Aprilia, and the front-wheel-drive Citroens, set a new standard of handling in their class.

Much of the company's know-how on short-stroke engines was learnt with the sporting 508S, though its reputation now hangs mainly on its 'vintage' driving characteristics. It would be untrue to say that it was unique in 1935. Cars of moderate cylinder capacity, faultless handling, and gear ratios suitable for objectives other than assaults on the perpendicular could be bought, but the FIAT's great virtue lay in its modest price. The 1½-litre Aston Martin cost £600, the Frazer Nash perhaps £75 less, and £335 was being asked for a sporting version of the 1½-litre Riley. For all its Vintage ways, the 508S, more than the M.G. Midget, was the true ancestor of the small sports car as we know it today.

© *Michael Sedgwick, 1966*

SPECIFICATIONS
Fiat Tipo 508 and 508S (Side Valve)

Engine: 4 cylinders, monobloc, side valves, detachable cast iron head, 4-point suspension, 3-bearing crankshaft. Bore 65 mm. Stroke 75 mm. Capacity 995 c.c. Nelson Bohnalite alloy pistons. Full pressure lubrication by submerged gear type pump. Thermo-syphon cooling with fan assistance.

Fuel feed: 3-speed 508, Gravity feed by 6-gallon dash tank to Solex 26FH or Zenith 26VF downdraught carburettor. 7-gallon tank on 4-speed 508 models. 508S has mechanical pump feed from 12-gallon rear tank to Zenith 30VEIZ downdraught carburettor.

Compression ratios: Optional 5·8 or 6·3:1 in 1932. 6·3:1 standard on later 3-speed 508, January 1933-1934. 6·6:1 on 4-speed cars. 7:1 on 508S.

Output: (3-speed 508) 22 b.h.p. at 3,400 r.p.m. (4-speed 24 b.h.p. at 3,600 r.p.m.: 508S, 30 b.h.p. at 4,000 r.p.m.

Gearbox: (3-speed 508) 3 speeds and reverse, central change. Ratios (saloons) 5·2, 9·5, and 14·9 to 1. Top gear ratio 4·89:1 on roadsters, 5·375:1 on light delivery vans. 508S has 4·3:1 top gear.

(4-speed gearbox) 4 speeds and reverse, central change, synchromesh on top and 3rd gears. Ratios (saloon and tourer), 5·1, 7·5, 11·4 and 18·9 to 1. Top gear ratio 4·875:1 on roadsters. 5·375:1 on light delivery vans. Free wheel optional extra on all versions except 508S.

Clutch: Single dry plate.

Transmission: Open propeller shaft, universally-jointed at each end. Spiral bevel final drive.

Ignition, Lighting and Starting: Marelli 12-volt coil and distributor, with belt-driven dynamo. 12-volt lighting and starting, five-lamp lighting set (3-lamp on standard 3-speed models of Tipo 508).

Chassis: Cruciform-braced with deep channel section side members.

Brakes: Foot, hydraulic internal-expanding on four wheels. Handbrake, transmission type on drum behind gearbox.

Steering: Worm and wheel.

Suspension: Semi-elliptic front and rear. Hydraulic shock absorbers on 508, friction type on 508S.

Wheels: FIAT bolt-on disc or wire detachable (wire only on 508S).

Tyres: Pirelli, 4·00 × 17.

Dimensions: Wheelbase (3-speed 508 and 508S) 7 ft. 4½ in. (4-speed 508) 7 ft. 6½ in. Track 3 ft. 10¾ in.

Weights: Standard two-seater, 3-speed, 13 cwt. Standard 2-door saloon, 3-speed 13¼ cwt. Standard 4-door saloon, 4-speed, 15¼ cwt.

Performance: (3-speed Tipo 508) maximum speeds, on top gear 58 m.p.h.; on second gear 28 m.p.h.; on 1st gear 14 m.p.h. (4-speed Tipo 508) maximum speeds, on top gear 58 m.p.h.; on 3rd gear, 50 m.p.h.; on 2nd gear, 34 m.p.h.; on 1st gear, 18 m.p.h. (3-speed Tipo 508S) maximum speeds, on top gear 68 m.p.h.; on 2nd gear, 43 m.p.h.; on 1st gear 23 m.p.h. Fuel consumption, all types, 35 m.p.g.

FIAT TIPO 508S (O.H.V.) 1934 to 1937

Engine: 4 cylinders, monobloc, pushrod-operated overhead valves. Detachable cast iron head, 3-bearing crankshaft. Bore 65 mm. Stroke 75 mm. Capacity 995 c.c. Nelson Bohnalite alloy pistons. Full pressure lubrication by submerged gear type pump. Thermo-syphon cooling with fan assistance. Mechanical pump feed from 10-gallon rear tank (14 galls. on *berlinetta aerodinamica*, 1935 on) to Zenith 30VEIZ or 30VIM downdraught carburettor.

Compression ratio 7·1:1. Output 36 b.h.p. at 4,400 r.p.m.

Gearbox: 4 speeds and reverse, central change. Synchromesh on 3rd and top gears. Ratios, 4·3, 5·7, 8·6 and 14·4 to 1.

Clutch: Single dry plate.

Transmission: Open propeller shaft, universally jointed front and rear. Spiral bevel final drive.

Ignition, Lighting and Starting: Marelli 12-volt coil, with belt-driven dynamo. 12-volt lighting and starting, 5 lamp lighting set.

Brakes: Foot, hydraulic internal expanding on four wheels. Handbrake working on drum behind gearbox.

Steering gear: Worm and wheel.

Wheels: FIAT bolt-on wire detachable.

Tyres: Pirelli, 4·00 × 17.

Dimensions: Wheelbase 7 ft. 6½ in. Track 3 ft. 10 in.

Weight: (Two-seater) 11½ cwt.

Performance: Speeds on gears: Top, 70 m.p.h., 3rd 60 m.p.h., 2nd 42 m.p.h., 1st 24 m.p.h. Acceleration through gears, 0–50 m.p.h., 18·6 secs.; 0–60 m.p.h., 30·4 secs. Fuel consumption approx. 30–35 m.p.g.

Note: This o.h.v. engine was also installed in a limited-production version of the Tipo 508 4-speed 4-door saloon.

The
Ford
Mustang

24

THE 1966 FORD MUS-TANG GT is identical with standard Mustang convertibles except for styling alterations. Additional pair of lights in grille, and exhaust tips protruding through rear panel mark this model.

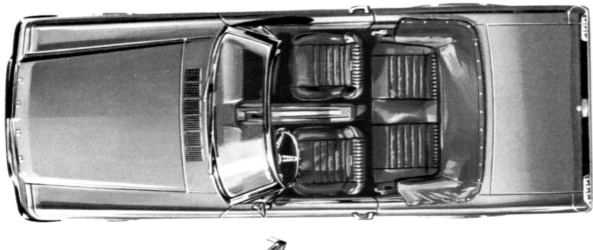

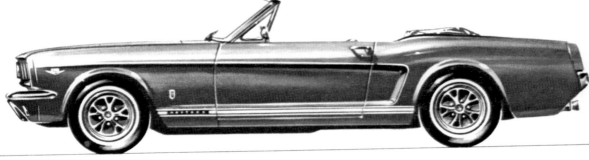

© JAMES LEECH

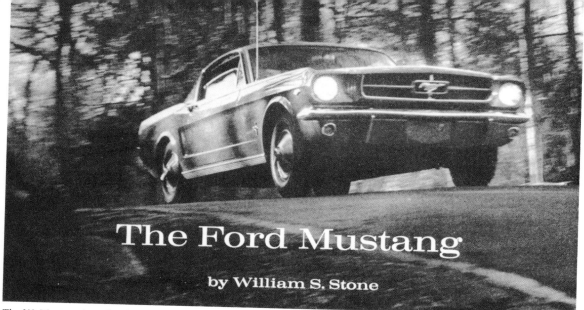

The Ford Mustang

by William S. Stone

The 2/2 Mustang, introduced in late 1964, was first of the current American crop of Fastbacks.   (Photo: Erika, New York)

The Ford Mustang, officially introduced in April of 1964, is the star of one of the most remarkable automobile success stories of modern times. Within five months of its introduction, it had become third most popular make in the U.S., ranking behind only the full-sized Chevrolet and Ford. Over 400,000 Mustangs were sold within a year of its introduction. 1964 sales totalled 248,916 Mustangs; 1965, 524,791.

Mechanically, the Mustang is not remarkable. With the exception of its body-styling, it is almost wholly a product of Ford components from their other compact and medium-size cars: Falcon, Fairlane and Mercury Comet. Nevertheless, it is an extremely effective blend of these components—offering excellent performance even in its milder forms, a suitably soft ride for American highways, and reasonably-good handling qualities. Unquestionably, it is the look and flavour of the Mustang which captures buyers' hearts, not its mechanical novelty or outstanding excellence.

BACKGROUND AND ANCESTRY

Behind the Mustang lies almost a decade of Ford experimentation with what Ford calls the 'personal car' concept. While this concept is somewhat vague, it can in general be taken to mean a car with somewhat more 'sporty' qualities than those of the workaday American family sedan.

Ford's first postwar effort in this direction produced the two-seater Thunderbird. This relatively small car

Two-seater Thunderbird—Ford's first post-war attempt at a 'personal car'. This is a 1957 model, last of the two-seat line.

was introduced in 1954 and ended its existence in 1958. In 1958, the Thunderbird name was attached to a four-seater of considerably larger dimensions, which has through the years become a popular luxury car. Some 53,000 of the two-seater Thunderbird were sold—not enough to justify its existence by the standards of American mass-production economics. The death of the two-seater Thunderbird left only one two-seater car on the American scene: the Chevrolet Corvette.

Early in 1961, Ford took the decision to re-investigate the 'personal car' field. Within a year, a number of experimental designs were created on paper, in clay or in model form. Among these was a prophetic design dubbed 'Median' by Ford. Prophetic, because it contained at least two of the Mustang's distinctive features: the long bonnet (hood) line, and the four-seater configuration.

Both of these features account for a great deal of the production Mustang's success. The long bonnet (hood) is aesthetically pleasing and quite unique in American styling . . . while the four-seat configuration makes the car practical for the average American family. (Wisely, Ford wasted little serious thought on the two-seat configuration. The Corvette and imported two-seaters seem to fill that market gap adequately.)

The first car to bear the Mustang name was designated Mustang I. Built as a show car to stimulate public interest, Mustang I was an extremely sophisticated vehicle; one which many enthusiasts hoped would be produced. That Ford really had no intention of producing Mustang I was evident in the car's tubular steel space frame and stressed aluminium body—a frame and body totally unsuited to mass-production techniques.

Mustang I was mid-engined, powered by a modified version of the 60° V-4 built by Ford of Germany for its Taunus 12M and 17M cars. In Mustang I, this engine displaced 1500 cc., had a bore and stroke of 90 mm. × 59 mm., and a compression ratio of 11·0 to 1. Specifications for two degrees of tune were published. A 1-barrel carburettor version was said to produce

Sketch of the 'Median' prototype. The long bonnet (hood), and four-seat configuration of the production Mustang, are evident here.

89 b.h.p. at 6,500 r.p.m.; a version with two two-barrel carburettors, 109 b.h.p. at 6,500 r.p.m.

A fully-synchronised 4-speed gearbox in unit with the rear axle (transaxle) lay behind the V-4. Rear-suspension was fully-independent with single cardan joints at the wheels and pot joints at the differential. Rear brakes were 9" drums, while at the front, $9\frac{1}{2}$" discs were fitted.

Mustang I was marked by several rather exotic features. Twin rear-mounted radiators were fitted, cooled either by natural air flow or electric fans. Since seat travel could not be adjusted, the pedal 'cluster' (accelerator, brake and clutch) could be adjusted fore-and-aft for a total travel of 4". A permanently-fixed roll bar was an integral part of the frame. Concealed headlamps—rather like those of the Lotus Elan—were fitted.

Mustang I was designed in Dearborn, Michigan, by Ford. It was built in California in the noted Los Angeles racing shop of Troutman and Barnes. Completed before the 1962 U.S. Grand Prix, the car was shipped to the Watkins Glen circuit in upstate New York and actually driven through a few demonstration laps by the American driver Dan Gurney before the Grand Prix.

While Mustang I was throwing dust in the eyes of enthusiasts, work on the real Mustang was going on apace. At least twenty prototypes were finished in varying degrees as Ford continued to explore its true goal: a four-seater Mustang. Most significant of these prototypes was Mustang II. This one, too, made its debut at Watkins Glen—a year later at the 1963 U.S. Grand Prix. Mustang II was a rather exact preview of the production Mustang. Wheelbase and track of the two cars are identical, so is the powerplant: the 289 cubic inch, 271 b.h.p. OHV V-8.

Guiding the Mustang's development through the labyrinth that leads to the introduction of an American production car was Lee Iacocca, then General Manager of Ford Division, now head of Ford's Car and Truck Group. Although trained as an engineer, Iacocca is no Porsche or Issigonis. Thoroughly sales-oriented, Iacocca played an important role in the success of the Falcon, Ford's massively-successful compact car. His generalship is evident in the Mustang. This is not a car of unusual design, but rather one of unusual public appeal.

MUSTANG BODIES

Mustangs are produced in three basic body styles: a hard-top coupé (really a 2-door sedan with no pillar between front and rear windows), a convertible and a true 2+2 fastback coupé. The dimensions and weights of all three body styles are virtually identical. Less than 200 pounds separates the heaviest of the cars from the lightest.

All 1965 models have individual front 'bucket' seats as standard equipment, although a bench seat became optional in April, 1965. Three passengers can be squeezed into the rear seat of the hardtop, but only two will fit the rear seat of the convertible, since the side wells for the hood (top) encroach on rear seat width in this model. The 2+2 fastback has two small occasional rear seats, suitable for short distances only.

All three Mustang body styles are built on the same steel platform chassis. Square-section front and rear side rails are tied in to boxed-in side members (box-section rocker panels). Heavy cross members beneath the floor pan provide a ladder of support for the side members. A full-length drive-shaft tunnel gives the chassis a rigid backbone. Side panels of the engine compartment are welded to the front side-rails at the bottom, and to the bulkhead (firewall) at the rear. These side panels are joined at the front by a panel with a deep channel section at the top. Body panels are of sheet steel and, with one exception, are welded to the chassis. The exception is the front wings (fenders). These are bolted on, for easy replacement in case of collision damage.

ENGINES

Since their introduction, Mustangs have been available with either six-cylinder OHV in-line engines or OHV V-8 engines. It is safe to say that both the six-cylinder and V-8 engines used in 1966 production are two of the finest and most reliable of American production engines. The 289 cubic inch V-8 was in fact the one selected for use in the Ford Cobra, prior to the installation of the 427 cubic inch Ford engine.

The 289 cubic inch engine may be tuned to produce as much as 385 b.h.p. with the use of Weber carburettors and other equipment.

Six-cylinder engines. The Six used in the earliest Mustangs was a 170 cubic inch cast-iron in-line

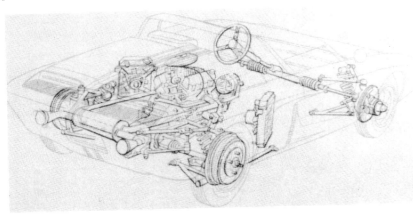

Under the skin of 'Mustang I' Note fully-independent four-wheel suspension, twin radiators, midship V-4 engine.

'Mustang I'—a sophisticated prototype two-seater that was actually built. No hint of the production car was given here.

OHV engine with four main bearings. It started life in Ford's compact Falcon of 1960 in a 144 cu. inch version. The 144 was enlarged to 170 by increasing the stroke. Later in 1965, the 170 cu. inch Six was replaced with a 200 cubic inch cast-iron Six. Both bore and stroke were increased to reach 200 cubic inches. Intake and exhaust valves of the 200 are larger than those of the 170, and a slightly 'hotter' cam profile is used. But most important, the 200's crankshaft runs in seven main bearings, rather than in four as in the 144 and 170. The 200 cubic inch engine used in 1966 production develops 120 b.h.p. (SAE).

Eight-cylinder engines. Early Mustangs were offered with either a 260 cubic inch V-8 or a 289 cubic inch V-8. In late 1965, the 260 V-8 was dropped, and only 289 V-8s are currently offered. Both the 260 and 289 cubic inch engines are developments of a 221 cubic inch Ford V-8 first offered in the 1962 Ford Fairlane. The stroke has remained unchanged (2·87″) as the displacement has been increased.

Three different variations of the 289 are offered in 1966. The least potent of these versions develops 200 b.h.p. (SAE), uses a two-barrel carburettor, and has a compression ratio of 9·3 to 1. With compression raised to 10·1 to 1, and a four-barrel carburettor, this engine develops 225 b.h.p. (SAE), but requires premium fuel. Both of these V-8s use the same cam profile, and employ hydraulic tappets (valve lifters).

The third and final version of the 289 is the high-performance version developing 271 b.h.p. (SAE). It differs from the less potent V-8s in many important respects. Solid tappets (valve lifters) permit higher

r.p.m., and more precise valve opening and closing. Valve-lift and duration are increased, as is valve spring pressure. Beefed-up exhaust valves, connecting rods, and camshaft bearings are fitted. Compression is raised to 10.5 to 1, and of course premium fuel is required. A dual exhaust system is connected to individual free-flow exhaust headers.

All Mustangs have 12-volt electrical systems, charged by an alternator. Engine instrumentation in 1965 Mustangs was sparse, consisting of only a water temperature gauge, with warning lights for low oil pressure and charge indicator. In 1966 models, instrumentation is more complete, with gauges replacing the oil pressure and charge indicator lights. No tachometer is fitted as standard equipment, but one is available at extra cost as part of a two-dial accessory cluster fixed to the steering column. This cluster, dubbed the 'Rally Pac' by Ford, consists of electric clock and 6,000 r.p.m. tachometer. (On Mustangs equipped with the 271 b.h.p. V-8, the tach reads to 8,000 r.p.m.)

TRANSMISSIONS

A wide variety of transmissions—both manual and automatic— may be fitted to the Mustang. Three-speed or four-speed manual transmission may be ordered with all engines, with the exception of the

'Mustang II', a rather exact preview of the final car, was powered by 289 V-8. It was unveiled in the fall of 1963.

289 cubic inch High Performance V-8. No three-speed manual is fitted to this engine. All Mustangs, including those powered by the High Performance V-8, may be ordered with automatic transmission.

Three-speed manual transmissions. A three-speed manual transmission with unsynchronised first gear is standard equipment on 6-cylinder Mustangs. When the size of the six-cylinder engine was increased from 170 cubic inches to 200, the first and second gear ratios in this transmission were lowered, while the rear axle ratio was raised.

On V-8 Mustangs (again excepting the High Performance engine), a more rugged 3-speed manual transmission is standard. It is unusual among American 3-speeds in that all three forward gears are synchronised—a feature which greatly increases the gearbox's usefulness to the driver ignorant of double-declutching techniques (surely a majority of American drivers).

Four-speed manual transmissions. 4-speed manual transmissions differ with engine choice. With the six-cylinder engine, a fully-synchronised four-speed is fitted. This transmission is borrowed almost intact from the English Ford line where it is fitted to the 6-cyl. Zephyr and Zodiac cars. It is in fact referred to in Mustang workshop manuals as the 'Dagenham Four-Speed'. With the V-8s, a fully-synchronised 4-speed of American design is supplied. This transmission is equipped with one set of ratios if it is fitted to the High Performance V-8, a second set if fitted to one of the lesser V-8s. Overdrives are not fitted to any of the Mustangs.

Automatic transmissions. All Mustangs may be had with automatic transmission . . . even those equipped with the High Performance V-8. (When the Mustang was introduced, the High Performance V-8 could be coupled only with a four-speed manual. But for 1966, the automatic was also made available with this engine.)

The Ford automatic transmission is remarkable in that it is a three-speed automatic, offering a considerable degree of driver control. (Many American automatic transmissions are of the two-speed variety. At middle road-speed ranges, these tend to offer the driver only the Hobson's choice of either over-revving or lugging.)

Ford's 3-speed automatic (called the 'Cruise-O-Matic') is of the torque-converter type with planetary gears. In the Mustang, the control lever is floor-mounted, and provided with six positions. These are

Lee Iacocca, head of Ford Division when the Mustang was introduced, was largely responsible for the car's design.

(P) Park, (R) Reverse, (N) Neutral, (D2) Drive II, (D1) Drive I, and (L) Low.

When the lever is in the Drive I position, the car makes two upshifts from rest: low to second, second to high. Drive I is the normal driving position. Placing the lever in Drive II locks out first gear, and the car makes but a single up-shift: from second to high. While this obviously reduces the car's performance, it is useful for starts on ice, snow or other slippery surfaces. Forced downshifts to second gear may be made at speeds below 70 m.p.h. in either drive position by flooring the accelerator pedal. With the lever in the Drive I or three-speed position, forced downshifts may also be made into first at speeds below 25 m.p.h.

CLUTCH, DRIVELINE, DIFFERENTIAL, REAR SUSPENSION

Clutches used with all manual-transmission Mustangs are of the single-disc dry plate type. With the 4-speed 'Dagenham' transmission, a non-centrifugal clutch is used. All others are semi-centrifugal. Clutch linings are of woven asbestos, varying in diameter from 8·5″ to 10·4″; in total lining area from 68·1 sq. in. to 103·5 sq. in. All clutch release bearings are ball thrust, pre-packed with lubricant and sealed.

An exposed propeller-shaft, fitted with two universal joints and a splined slip-yoke, carries power from transmission to differential. Universal joints are of the cross-type, and are fitted with needle roller bearings.

Two types of differential are employed in the Mustang. On 6-cylinder cars, the differential is of the

Two tiny rear seats of 2 + 2 Fastback (left) can be converted to broad luggage space (right) for two-place touring.

overhung pinion type, and the differential carrier is integral with the axle housing. On 8-cylinder cars, the differential is fitted with a straddle-mounted pinion. On these differentials, the differential is bolted to the axle housing and may be removed from the housing for service. 'Limited slip' differentials are available as an extra-cost option on both V-8 and 6-cylinder cars.

Few cars are without their weak points, and the rear suspension of the Mustang is certainly not of the most sophisticated modern design. The live rear axle, located solely by the semi-elliptical leaf springs, leaves a good deal to be desired insofar as road-holding is concerned. On rough or slippery surfaces the car's rear end is decidedly skittish. Sudden applications of power will break the rear wheels loose with somewhat unnerving ease. Proprietary torque arms such as 'Traction Masters' can help alleviate the latter condition.

Constant rumours about the development of independent rear suspension for the Mustang have been met with equally constant denials by Ford. The need for some improved form of rear suspension is immediately obvious to the experienced driver. It is significant that on the Ford GT 350, Carroll Shelby's race-worthy derivation of the Mustang, much attention is lavished on rear suspension modifications. These include the installation of heavy torque reaction arms between axle and chassis, plus adjustable Koni shock absorbers.

FRONT SUSPENSION

Front wheel suspension of the Mustang is by unequal length arms: a short triangular arm above and a single, longer arm below. A coil spring between upper arm and chassis provides springing, and encloses a tubular double-acting shock absorber. The upper arm pivots on a bushing and shaft assembly which is bolted to the underbody bracket. The spindle assembly, which joins the two arms and carries the wheel, is attached to the arms by ball joints. These joints are 'permanently' lubricated—and need lubrication only every 3 years or 36,000 miles. A link-type stabiliser bar is used in the front: ·69″ in diameter on all Mustangs except those equipped with the High Performance V-8; ·84″ on the H.P. cars.

The cast-iron Ford Six is typical American production unit. Breathing is limited by single downdraught carburettor.

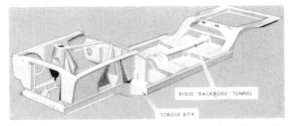

Backbone of the Mustang is this welded steel platform. The car has no separate frame rails, but is remarkably rigid.

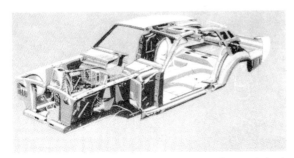

The body of the car is welded to the platform frame. Only the front wings (fenders), missing here, are bolted to the body.

STEERING GEAR

Steering gear on all Mustangs is of the worm and recirculating ball and nut type. Since the car is rather nose-heavy, power steering is a popular option. Power steering is made by Bendix and is of the proportional type which retains rather good 'road feel'. With the power assistance, steering ratio is set at 22:1. This

289 cubic inch V-8. The High Performance version lacks hydraulic tappets (lifters) shown here, and has clearance adjustment on the rocker arms.

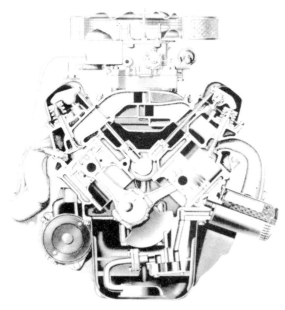

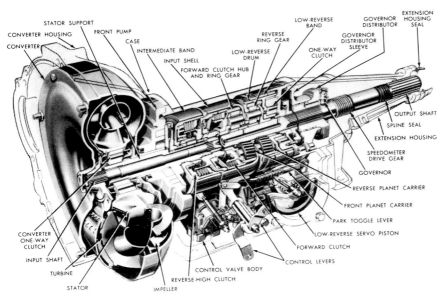

STATOR SUPPORT
CONVERTER HOUSING
CONVERTER
FRONT PUMP
CASE
INTERMEDIATE BAND
INPUT SHELL
FORWARD CLUTCH HUB
AND RING GEAR
LOW-REVERSE
DRUM
REVERSE
RING GEAR
LOW-REVERSE
BAND
ONE-WAY
CLUTCH
GOVERNOR
DISTRIBUTOR
GOVERNOR
DISTRIBUTOR
SLEEVE
EXTENSION
HOUSING
SEAL
OUTPUT SHAFT
SPLINE SEAL
EXTENSION HOUSING
SPEEDOMETER
DRIVE GEAR
GOVERNOR
REVERSE PLANET CARRIER
FRONT PLANET CARRIER
PARK TOGGLE LEVER
LOW-REVERSE SERVO PISTON
FORWARD CLUTCH
CONTROL LEVERS
CONTROL VALVE BODY
REVERSE-HIGH CLUTCH
IMPELLER
STATOR
TURBINE
INPUT SHAFT
CONVERTER
ONE-WAY
CLUTCH

The complexity of the three-speed Cruise-O-Matic transmission is evident, but the unit is one of the most reliable in production

ratio is also available with manual steering in a special heavy-duty handling package. It makes steering rather heavy for all but the most muscular drivers—particularly when parking. The normal steering ratio supplied with non-power assisted steering is 27:1—very slow, but reasonably light.

BRAKES

Drum brakes are standard on Mustangs, with front discs an extra-cost (about $60) option. Six-cylinder cars carry 9″ drums front and rear, V-8s carry 10″ drums. Both front and rear drum brakes have a single wheel cylinder and, like the brakes on all American Ford products, are self-adjusting. As linings wear, the self-adjusting feature compensates for the increased lining/drum clearance. It keeps the brake pedal high and eliminates the need for manual adjustments. Linings are of moulded asbestos, riveted rather than bonded to the brake shoes.

American brakes have come under a good deal of criticism in recent years and, considering the weight of American cars and the speeds common on American roads, perhaps rightly so. Certainly, hard driving on mountain roads will severely tax the Mustang's drum brakes. It is not surprising, therefore, that Ford was quick to offer front disc brakes on this car.

Mustang disc brakes are 11·375″ in diameter, ventilated by some forty internal radial fins, and constructed of cast-iron. Each pad is approximately 4·8″ × 1·8″, with an approximate thickness of ·400″. Like the drum brakes, they are self-adjusting. Unlike the drums, however, they are practically free from fade.

A diaphragm-type brake booster is available on drum-braked Mustangs. It employs engine manifold vacuum to assist in the braking operation.

WHEELS AND TYRES

Stamped steel disc wheels are standard on all Mustangs. All 1965 cars carried 13″ tyres, with the single exception of those equipped with the High Perform-

Body roll with stock suspension is alarming, but can be corrected with the heavy-duty handling package.

A standard, three-speed Mustang 260 (except for Koni shock absorbers and racing tyres), in a tricky corner at Bridgehampton Race Course, Long Island, New York. The Mustang lapped the course in 2 : 16·8. (Photo by courtesy of Holley-Thomas, Inc.)

Mustangs placed 1st and 2nd in 1964 Tour de France touring car class.

ance V-8, which had 14″ tyres. For 1966, 14″ tyres were made standard equipment on all cars. 6·95″ × 14″ rayon tyres are standard except on 271 b.h.p. cars, which carry nylon high-performance (120 m.p.h.) tyres. 15″ wheels and tyres may also be fitted.

SPECIAL-HANDLING PACKAGE

With even the 6-cylinder Mustang capable of speeds close to 100 m.p.h., and all 8-cylinder Mustangs capable of speeds in excess of 100 m.p.h., the car is clearly in need of something more effective than its rather soft stock suspension and slow stock steering if it is to be driven safely at such speeds. Such improvements in handling can be attained with the accessories which Ford calls its 'special handling package'. This package, factory-installed for less than $100, consists of heavier front and rear springs, larger and stiffer front and rear shock absorbers, a front stabiliser bar of increased diameter, and the 22:1 steering ratio mentioned earlier. Coupled with the optional disc brakes, this package improves the road manners of the Mustang to a noticeable degree.

THE 'TAILORED' CAR

The Mustang is an almost impossible car to categorise. There are no fewer than eleven combinations of engine and transmission possible. And a vast range

A one-off Bertone-bodied Mustang, commissioned by the American magazine Automobile Quarterly *for 1965 New York Auto Show. It is now property of Greek shipping owner.* (Photo by courtesy of *Automobile Quarterly*)

Level ride: Sir Gawaine Baillie's Mustang in a Production Car Race at Silverstone, 1965.

of both performance options (disc brakes, 'handling package', tachometer, etc.) and convenience options (air-conditioning, power convertible top, stereophonic tape recorder) are available. So it can be tailored to be anything from a gentle in-town ladies car to an impressive 130 m.p.h. highway performer. Undoubtedly, its almost infinitely variable personality is one of the car's chief attractions. While no particular favourite with the enthusiast, it has found favour with a broad segment of the American public, and seems destined to continue its remarkable sales record for at least several years to come.

© William S. Stone, 1966

MUSTANG PERFORMANCE (TYPICAL)

Type	0–60 m.p.h. Accel.	Standing quarter mile	Top speed
170 cu. in. 6-cyl. with auto. trans.	13 secs.	20 secs.	95 m.p.h.
260 cu. in. V-8 with auto. trans.	11·5 secs.	19 secs.	105 m.p.h.
289 cu. in. V-8 (210 b.h.p.) with 4-speed manual	8·5 secs.	16.5 secs.	110 m.p.h.
289 cu. in. V-8 (271 b.h.p.) with 4-speed manual	8 secs.	16 secs.	120 m.p.h.

All illustrations not acknowledged are reproduced by courtesy of the Ford Motor Company Inc.

The GT 350—Shelby-American's derivation of the Mustang. The competition version shown here on a Texas course boasts 350 b.h.p., and a fibreglass bonnet (hood). The body is lightened; the 289 cu. in. engine employs Cobra components, and free-flow exhaust.
(Photo: Shelby-American, Inc.)

cubic inch V-8 fender badge. This engine, the smallest V-8 red in the Mustang range, was dropped in the fall of 1964.

High Performance 289 cubic inch V-8 fender badge. Less powerful V-8 289 engines carry only 289 badge, no checkered flag design.

1965 Fastback version of the Mustang. Interior is true 2 + 2, with small rear seats that fold down to allow more cargo space.

1966 Hardtop. 1966 cars are distinguished from earlier cars by grille emblem, rear fender ornament, and chrome strip beneath door.

Shelby American GT 350 boasts modified High Performance 289 V-8, and improved suspension. Only Fastbacks are available.

rome petrol filler cap is typical
f car's elaborate detailing.

GT fender badge. GT is Ford styling option; reflects no mechanical changes.

Mustang fender badge remained unchanged from 1965 to 1966 models.

*Street version of the GT 350—Shelby-American's deriva-
tion of the Mustang. Obvious exterior changes are
bonnet air scoop, functional rear-wheel air scoops, and
rear quarter windows instead of ventilators.*

*In the Mustang GT 350, the street version 289 cu. in.
V-8 pumps out 306 b.h.p. The tubular brace across the
engine compartment is to reduce body vibration.*
(Photo: Dave Friedman, Shelby-American Inc.)

1966 MUSTANG SPECIFICATIONS

Dimensions	Hardtop	2+2 Fastback	Convertible
Overall length	181·6″	181·6″	181·6″
Width	68·2″	68·2″	68·2″
Height	51·5″	51·6″	51·4″
Wheelbase	108″	108″	108″
Front track	8-cyl. 56·0″; 6-cyl. 55·4″		
Rear track	56·0″	56·0″	56·0″
Curb Wgt., 6-cyl.	2606 lb.	2636 lb.	2768 lb.
Wgt. dist., 6-cyl.	54/46	53/47	53/47
Curb Wgt., Hi. perf. V-8	2924 lb.	2955 lb.	3086 lb.
Wgt. Dist. Hi. Perf. V-8	55/45	55/45	55/45
Fuel capacity	16 gals. (US)	16 gals. (US)	16 gals. (US)
Luggage capacity	9·0 cu. ft.	7·2 cu. ft.	5·0 cu. ft.

MUSTANG ENGINES

Displ.	Type	Bore	Stroke	B.h.p. (SAE).	Torque	Comp.	Carbur.	Model yr.
170 cu. in. (2781 cc.)	In-line 6, OHV	3·50″	2·94″	101@4400	156@2400	8·7	1–1Bbl.	Early '65
200 cu. in. (3273 cc.)	In-line 6, OHV	3·68″	3·13″	120@4400	185@2400†	9·2	1–1Bbl.	Late '65, '66
260 cu. in. (4260 cc.)	90°V-8 OHV	3·80″	2·87″	164@4400	258@2200	8·8	1–2Bbl.	Early '65
289 cu. in. (4728 cc.)	90°V-8 OHV	4·00″	2·87″	210@4400	300@2400	9·0	1–4Bbl.	Early '65
289 cu. in.	90°V-8 OHV	4·00″	2·87″	195@4400 *	282@2400	9·3	1–2Bbl.	Late '65, '66
289 cu. in.	90°V-8 OHV	4·00″	2·87″	220@4800 *	295@3000‡	10·1§	1–4Bbl.	Late '65, '66
289 cu. in.	90°V-8 OHV	4·00″	2·87″	271@6000	312@3400	10·5	1–4Bbl.	'65, '66

* 5 b.h.p. added for '66   † 5 ft. lbs. added for '66   ‡ 10 ft. lbs. added for '66   § 10·0 for '66.